WOMEN ON THE HILL

WOMEN
ON THE HILL

Challenging the Culture
of Congress

CLARA BINGHAM

TIMES 𝕿 BOOKS

RANDOM HOUSE

To DAVID

Library of Congress Cataloging-in-Publication Data

Bingham, Clara.
Women on the Hill : challenging the culture of
Congress / Clara Bingham.—1st ed.
p.   cm.
ISBN 0-8129-6351-2
1. United States. Congress (103rd, 1st session : 1993) 2.
United States. Congress (103rd, 2nd session : 1994) 3.
Women legislators—United States. 4. United States—Politics
and government—1993– 5. United States—Social policy—
1993– I. Title.
JK1059 103rd.B55   1997
328.73'073'082—dc20   96-27801

Random House website address:
http://www.randomhouse.com/
Printed in the United States of America on acid-free paper
24689753
First Edition
Book design by Mina Greenstein

CONTENTS

v

WOMEN ON THE HILL

Introduction

In a single October week in 1991, Anita Hill changed the course of modern gender politics. Her televised testimony before the all-male, all-white Senate Judiciary Committee graphically exposed the fact that women and their interests were being trivialized and ignored in Congress.

A little over a year later, fifty-five women were swept into power on Hill's coattails. They came to Washington with a mandate, invading one of America's last remaining professional men's clubs. They were determined to show that the phrase used to describe 1992—the Year of the Woman—was more than empty rhetoric. With their numbers almost doubled, the women on the Hill set forth to reframe the public debate and challenge the culture of Congress.

This is a chronicle of four women: one senator and three members of the House of Representatives—Patty Murray, Pat Schroeder, Cynthia McKinney, and Louise Slaughter. It is a tale of their idealism and ambition, their failures and achievements. It is a story about how in their attempts to change the system, they were transformed. Hailing from the Pacific Northwest, the West, the South, and the Northeast, each woman had a different political style and different priorities. They were all Democrats, but they stood for something much larger than themselves: They represented the electorate's wish to bring women's voices into the tradition-bound halls of Congress.

Although this book touches on the views of some Republican women, it focuses primarily on those women who were at the forefront of change in the 103rd Congress. Of the twenty-four newly elected congresswomen in the House, only three were Republican; in the Senate, only one of the five freshwomen senators was a Republican. With Democrats in the majority in both the House and the Senate, and Bill Clinton controlling the White House, Democratic women were in a stronger position than their Republican counterparts to drive the agenda in the 103rd Congress—an agenda supported by Republican women in much larger numbers than Republican men.

Of course, all this would change after the 1994 election. The liberal politics of these four women would go out of fashion. The Republican agenda would prove openly antagonistic toward feminism and women's-rights issues, especially abortion. But some of the changes made by women in the 103rd Congress would survive. The new Republican leadership, sensitive to women's growing clout on the Hill, promoted women to politically powerful positions on committees and in the party hierarchy. And on September 7, 1995, Senator Bob Packwood announced his resignation, forced out by his female colleagues, chiefly California Democrat Barbara Boxer. Packwood departed in disgrace, proving that sexual harassment would no longer be tolerated by the nation's highest deliberative body.

Through the points of view of Murray, Schroeder, McKinney, and Slaughter, this book will document the real and Pyrrhic victories of the women on the Hill during the 103rd Congress. Their emphasis on issues that affect women's rights—sexual harassment, abortion, women's health, and family leave—led to the creation of a largely bipartisan women's political culture that for the first time gained mainstream recognition on the Hill. They and their female colleagues sparked a dramatic series of gender wars on the House and Senate floors, in committee hearing rooms, and in closed-door meetings, upsetting the time-honored, male-dominated Hill power structure.

Elected for the first time in 1992, Patty Murray, forty-three, and Cynthia McKinney, thirty-seven, embodied a new generation of women in Congress. Murray's upset election victory in Washington, her populist "mom in tennis shoes" campaign slogan, and her everywoman approach to governing in the Senate personified the ideals of the Year of the Woman. Cynthia McKinney's election in Georgia, like Murray's, was a long shot, due largely to the political phenomenon created by the Anita Hill hearings. McKinney, a black woman, divided her loyalties in Congress between the civil rights causes of African Americans and women's issues. She went to Washington a militantly liberal Georgia state legislator, determined to wield the levers of power in Washington.

Pat Schroeder, fifty-two, first elected in 1972, when McKinney and Murray were still schoolgirls, was the longest-sitting woman in Congress. Her strong commitment to women's rights had been shaped by the severe discrimination she had faced in her early years in the House. The influx of new congresswomen in 1992 presented a dilemma for Schroeder: while it added political legitimacy and votes to her women's-issues agenda, it also created competition for publicity and recognition.

Louise Slaughter's penchant for playing the inside game would contrast and sometimes conflict with Pat Schroeder's uncompromising style. Slaughter, a sixty-three-year-old former housewife from Rochester, New York, went to Congress in 1986 from the New York State Assembly. She was elected in a decade when women were more readily accepted by Congress, and by dedicating herself both to women's issues and achieving political power through compromise and connections, she rose quickly to a position of power within the Democratic caucus.

All four women and the members of their staffs agreed to provide this writer with regular interviews throughout the course of the 103rd Congress. This is not, however, an authorized group profile. None of the women had permission to change the content of the book before its publication. In researching this book, I chose to focus my exploration specifically on how these four congresswomen set about doing their jobs differently from their male colleagues. They shared many characteristics with their fellow congressmen—oversized egos, a competitive drive, and the hunger for reelection. Rather than belaboring the universal traits that characterize almost every person who enters the rough-and-tumble world of the electoral arena, I chose to focus instead on what made these women different—what obstacles they faced as *women,* and how their political priorities were affected by the fact of their gender.

High office, it turned out, would change these women. They were politicians, after all. In 1991, outraged by the

Hill-Thomas hearings, Patty Murray ran for the U.S. Senate, asking, "Who's speaking for me out there?" True to her word, she took to the Senate floor as a voice for women and the middle class. A little more than a year into her first term, however, Murray found herself sharing an elevator late at night with a fellow United States senator who made her the object of a sexual overture. Shocked and embarrassed, Murray would nevertheless conceal the potentially inflammatory incident in order to preserve both her own privacy and the political gains she had made.

This book is not about partisan politics; it is about the politics of gender. The issues I chose to explore—sexual harassment, abortion, women's health, and family leave—received bipartisan support from female members of Congress because they were primarily women's-*rights* issues: issues that addressed sexual discrimination, not just budget line items. Sixty-six bills benefiting women and families were passed in the 103rd Congress, more than in any other congress, making 1993 and 1994 a brief but significant moment for women in American political history.

The women of the 103rd Congress were not trailblazers. They were settlers. Their courage to defy the rules and challenge the system came from a long line of women preceding them. They followed in the footsteps of pioneers like Jeannette Rankin, Margaret Chase Smith, Martha Griffiths, and Shirley Chisholm.

These early women in Congress are perhaps best remembered for their political courage. They were free to perform uncommon acts of conscience because they were on the edge of power, not at its center. They neither wrote the rules nor enforced them. They were mavericks in an institution that preferred to keep women, without apology, on the sidelines.

Before April 6, 1917, no woman had ever voted in Congress or in the national legislature of any Western democracy. Jeannette Rankin would be the first, elected to the House of Representatives in 1916. In elegant clothing and broad-brimmed hats of her own making, Rankin looked out of place in a masculine institution where shiny brass spittoons and Cuban cigars were still customary. Rankin's presence on the floor of the U.S. House of Representatives seemed all the more incongruous in light of the fact that it was still against the law in most states for women to vote.

Rankin was a settlement-house social worker and an activist in the suffrage movement. As the field secretary of the National American Women's Suffrage Association, she traveled across the nation organizing state-by-state suffrage referendum campaigns. She launched a crusade to gain the vote for women in Montana, which succeeded in 1914. The first time Jeannette Rankin voted, in 1916, she voted for herself.

Rankin was not only Congress's first woman, she was the institution's original feminist. She campaigned for her statewide seat promising to fight for universal women's suffrage, child welfare, Prohibition, and social justice. Rankin was a product of an altruistic tradition, characterized by the efforts of the nineteenth-century women's movement to end slavery, ban alcohol, humanize labor conditions, and gain the vote. Once women had the right to vote, the suffragists argued, America would be a better country. Female political participation would bring morality to political leadership. Women's differences from men, it was believed, would improve the political system. "Pure in spirit, selfless in motivation, and dedicated to the preservation of human life, women voters would remake society and turn government away from war and corruption," wrote historian William Chafe. As it turned out, however, women voters did not initially revolutionize the system. They gave their loyalty instead to their class, race, region, and husbands. Women's political apathy was demonstrated by the fact that they voted in fewer numbers than men until as late as 1968.

Rankin will always be remembered for the first vote she cast. At stake that night, April 6, 1917, was the resolution that would send American soldiers to fight in Europe's "war to end all wars." She sat silent on the floor of the House as her name was called in the roll.

"Miss Rankin?" repeated the clerk. Rankin gave no answer. The clerk went on to the next name, and the galleries began to buzz.

On the second roll call, Rankin's name was called again. Again she sat silent. All eyes turned to her. In silence, the chamber waited. She rose. Her voice cracking slightly, she violated a 140-year rule against speaking during a roll-call vote to say, "I want to stand by my country, but I cannot vote for war. I vote no." Applause broke out on the floor and in the galleries. Rankin was joined in her opposition to American involvement in the war by forty-nine other members of the House. Yet none of the other no votes was mentioned by name. The next day's *New York Times* announced: "One Hundred Speeches Were Made—Miss Rankin, Sobbing, Votes No."

Jeannette Rankin voted against the war because she saw it as her duty to oppose hostilities. If war could be stopped, then it would be women, Rankin believed, who would stop it. "I felt that the first time the first woman [in Congress]

9

had a chance to say no to war she should say it," Rankin explained years later. But women did not uniformly share her pacifist views. Some of Rankin's fellow suffragists feared that her unpopular vote would undermine the ability of women to be taken seriously as officeholders and thus damage the women's-suffrage cause.

Rankin was also taken to task for showing too much "womanly" emotion during the vote. Although newspapers reported that Rankin had "sobbed" while voting, she had not in truth broken down crying. The fact that several congressmen wept openly during the vote remained unnoticed.

(Fifty years later, Pat Schroeder would suffer a similar humiliation. During a campaign rally in September 1987, Schroeder announced her decision to drop out of the presidential race. As her supporters shouted, "No, no," and "Run, Pat, run," Schroeder wept on her husband's shoulder. For months afterward, she was the butt of jokes across the country. Schroeder's tearful moment as the stereotypical weeping girl—the cliché that women politicians after Jeannette Rankin had tried so hard to avoid— was declared a disaster for the future of women running for office. But as the 1988 campaign season continued, crying became such a common way for male candidates to show they were compassionate leaders that Schroeder began keeping a "tears file" of men who cried on the stump. Later in the campaign season, Democratic presidential candidate Gary Hart paid Schroeder a visit. He needed his fellow Coloradan's advice. What could he do, Hart asked Schroeder, to show more empathy on the campaign trail?)

In 1919, both the House and the Senate voted to approve women's suffrage. The following year, two-thirds of the states ratified the Nineteenth Amendment. Jeannette Rankin's antiwar vote, however, had damaged her political career. She ran for the Senate in 1918 and lost in the primary. She then proceeded to dedicate herself to the cause of pacifism, and in 1940, with America on the brink of entering the war in Europe, Rankin was again elected to represent Montana in Congress. This time she joined eight other women in the House.

On December 8, 1941, the day after the Japanese bombed Pearl Harbor, the House took up a resolution to enter World War II. When it came Rankin's turn to vote, she said "No," and again breaching protocol, she added, "As a woman I can't go to war, and I refuse to send anyone else."

The final vote on the war resolution was 388 to 1. Rankin stood alone. Shouted down by a chorus of hisses and boos, she took refuge in a Capitol Hill anteroom. A mob of onlookers crowded the phone booth where Rankin had barricaded herself to telephone her office. Capitol Hill police escorted her out of the building for her own safety.

Rankin's lonely protest again cost her reelection, but she lived up to her reputation as a woman who voted her conscience, and as such gained eventual public respect As Fiorello LaGuardia, her former House colleague from New York, once said of Rankin, "This woman has more courage and packs a harder punch than a regiment of regular-line politicians." Seventeen years after Rankin voted against joining World War II, John F. Kennedy included her in his *McCall's* magazine article entitled "Three Women of Courage," in which he wrote, "Few members of Congress since its founding in 1789 have ever stood more alone, more completely in defiance of popular opinion than former Representative Jeannette Rankin of Montana." In 1968, women protesting America's involvement in Vietnam formed the Jeannette Rankin Brigade, marching from Union Station to the Capitol. Several thousand women marched, led by the eighty-eight-year-old Jeannette Rankin.

Before World War II, women in Congress were perceived more as oddities than as serious politicians. Over two-thirds of the women who served in Congress during that period were widows of congressmen or appointed to temporary seats by their governors. Hattie Caraway went to the Senate when her husband, Arkansas Democrat Senator Thaddeus Caraway, died, in 1931. One year later, with the help of Senator Huey Long, she won reelection, becoming the first woman elected to the U.S. Senate. "Silent Hattie" gave only fifteen speeches on the Senate floor during her thirteen years in office. She explained, "I haven't the heart to take a minute away from the men. The poor dears love it so."

Because these women were not elected on their own merits, they were seldom seen by the men around Congress as anything but faintly amusing incompetents. As one writer said of Hattie Caraway, intending to pay her a compliment, "While talking to her—as nice a way to pass an hour as could be imagined—one expects her to start shelling peas."

Ruth Hanna McCormick, one of the few accomplished female politicians of her generation, was elected to the House of Representatives from Illinois in 1929 for one term. A reporter asked her if she had run for office as a woman. She spoke for almost all women in politics at the time when she angrily replied that she hadn't. But she had run as the daughter of Mark Hanna, the powerful Ohio senator, and as the wife of Medill McCormick, an Illinois senator and a member of the *Chicago Tribune* publishing family. In her own words, she had therefore come equipped for office "by heredity and training."

For 150 years, the federal government had systematically kept women out of government jobs. But after the onset of World War II, the expanding bureaucracy and manpower shortage forced a break in the taboo against employing women. In the 1940s, female secretaries and clerks, called "government girls," flooded the capital city. While "government girls" gained approval by working for "patriotic goals," women with ambition were not as readily accepted. They were accused of having "a reputation" and were discredited for their unladylike ambition.

Clare Boothe Luce served in the House for two sessions, in 1942 and 1944. Not only ambitious, she was also notorious. A former magazine editor and Broadway playwright, she was ridiculed as the "little lady from Broadway" and held under suspicion for her marriage to Time-Life founder Henry Luce. When she asked to sit on the Foreign Affairs Committee, for which she was better qualified than most of the committee members because of her war reporting for *Life* in Europe, Luce was considered "insufferably arrogant" for having overstepped tacit boundaries. In the end, Clare Boothe Luce could only gain power by marrying power. "She wanted to do all the things men did, but if she didn't need a man under the bed, she needed one behind the throne," wrote her friend Wilfrid Sheed, characterizing her as a "bridge figure between a courtesan and the career girl."

The war had changed America but it had not changed Congress. In 1947, Congressman Charles Gifford of Massachusetts, a senior and respected member of the House, summed up the typical attitude toward his female colleagues: "The lady members we have today are extremely satisfactory to us. But they, like all women, can talk to us with their eyes and their lips, and when they present to us an apple it is most difficult to refuse. Even old Adam could not resist . . . these ladies are so attractive. They are dangerous in that they may influence us too much. Suppose we had fifty of them?"

From 1949 to 1973, Margaret Chase Smith was the only elected female member of the Senate. Known as the "Lady from Maine," she began her career in the old-fashioned manner, filling her husband Clyde H. Smith's seat in the House in 1940 after he died of a heart attack. Margaret had served as her husband's executive secretary, and she soon proved to be a skillful politician in her own right. Unlike Clare Boothe Luce, though, Smith learned to work within her boundaries and was therefore taken seriously by her male colleagues. Smith ran for the Senate in 1948 against the advice of the Maine Republican party and won in a landslide. She become the first woman to be elected to both the House and the Senate, as well as the first woman ever to enter the Senate without first being appointed. For more than twenty years, she was the senator-at-large for American women.

A little more than a year into her service in the Senate, Smith took a huge risk. The date was June 1, 1950. Four months earlier, Joe McCarthy, the junior senator from Wisconsin, had held up a piece of paper for the ladies of the Wheeling, West Virginia, Republican Women's Club to see. McCarthy claimed to have in his hand a list of 205 names, all of them Communists, all supposedly working at high-level jobs in the State Department. Within days of the speech, when he promised to unveil another 81 cases of "Red infiltration," the news media and Congress flung themselves at McCarthy's feet. No one in the Senate and no one in the Truman administration dared to call McCarthy's bluff. No one asked for evidence, and no one had the courage to defend the accused as McCarthy went right on naming names.

Margaret Chase Smith decided that "somebody had to do it." She addressed the Senate, promising to speak "as briefly as possible because too much harm has already been done with irresponsible words of bitterness and selfish political opportunism." It was a powerful speech—a "Declaration of Conscience," she called it. And though Smith never mentioned McCarthy's name, the Senator from Wisconsin turned white as a sheet as he listened to Smith declare that the American people were "sick and tired of seeing innocent people smeared and guilty people whitewashed." She then added, "I don't want to see the Republican party ride a political victory on the four horsemen of calumny—fear, ignorance, bigotry, and smear." When Smith finished, McCarthy hurried from the Senate chamber. He responded, as usual, with names, calling Smith and the six Republican senators who co-signed her Declaration of Conscience "Snow White and the Six Dwarfs."

The next day, the national press celebrated Smith's courage. "Not in a long time, in either house of Congress, has there been a finer or more pertinent address," the *Washington Star* commented. *Newsweek* ran a picture of the stately forty-eight-year-old Senator on its cover and floated Smith as a possible vice-presidential candidate (in 1964, Smith would seek the Republican party nomination for president). *Newsweek* reported that the speech had been a battle between the sexes, and emphasized that it had taken a woman to say "what many a bewildered citizen had waited to hear for a long time." The story implied that the weaker gender had put the strong men of the Senate to shame.

The fraternal order of the Senate rewarded Smith's honesty by dubbing her a "Girl Scout with a mission" and dropping her from two posts she had held in the Republican party leadership. Four more years passed before the Senate found the courage to censure McCarthy.

Before the 1960s, most bills that affected women were sponsored by male lawmakers. In the hands of congresswomen, ironically, women's issues instantly became political Kryptonite. The new conservative values of the 1950s—the decade's "cult of domesticity" and suburban exodus—had dealt a strong blow to the prospects of women in politics. But the civil rights movement and President Kennedy's Commission on the Status of Women helped to inspire the rebirth of the feminist movement. During the 1960s, no less than 884 bills of special concern to women were introduced in Congress. Only ten passed. Of those ten, two were especially important pieces of legislation.

The Equal Pay Act became law in 1963 with the support of congresswomen like Edith Green, Edna Kelly, and Martha Griffiths. For the first time, women in America would have the right to earn equally with men. The new bill, amending the Fair Labor Standards Act of 1938, prohibited sex discrimination in earnings and allowed for back pay where bias had taken place. By the mid-1970s, a total of $84 million in back pay had been awarded to 171,000 employees under the provisions of the Equal Pay Act.

Women also made civil rights advances in the debate over Title VII of the 1964 Civil Rights Act. Title VII barred discrimination in the workplace on the basis of race, creed, color, and national origin. Martha Griffiths, a Democrat, wrote an amendment to the statute that would also bar sex discrimination. Griffiths was first elected to Congress in 1954, when half the class's congresswomen were widows filling their husbands' seats, and developed a reputation as a serious legislator and a strong advocate for women. Having practiced law in the 1940s, serving in the Michigan state legislature and as a judge, she was one of the first women who came to Congress with a professional political career under their belt. She gained credibility among her male colleagues because of her intelligence and professional experience and became the first woman to sit on the powerful Ways and Means Committee.

Griffiths declared that without a sex clause, Title VII was blatantly unfair. White women, for instance, would not be protected by the law against job discrimination, but black women would have the right to claim discrimination because of their color. "I made up my mind that all women were going to take one giant step forward, so I prepared an amendment that added 'sex' to the bill," Griffiths later explained. But before Griffiths introduced her amendment, Howard Smith—the Virginian leader of the Southern conservative members of Congress and chairman of the Rules Committee—beat her to it. Smith, who opposed the civil rights bill, introduced the "sex" amendment in hopes that it would kill any chances Title VII had of passing. Griffiths held back and let Smith introduce the amendment, knowing that Smith could attract a hundred conservative votes that she, alone, could not. Griffiths later admitted that she "used Smith" to pass the amendment.

The debate over Smith's amendment was nothing short of burlesque. Smith, who was in his eighties, said that the purpose of the amendment was to set aright "the imbalance of spinsters." New York Democrat Emmanual Celler, the seventy-five-year-old chairman of the Judiciary Committee, who opposed the amendment, chanted in retaliation, "Vive la difference," and claimed that in his family, women were not considered a minority. The debate caused members on the House floor to break into peals of laughter.

Then Martha Griffiths took the stand. She began by saying, "I presume that if there had been any necessity to point out that women were a second-class sex, the laughter would have proved it." With this, the laughter stopped. Griffiths then gave some examples of how the law discriminated against women—for instance, the Supreme Court had as recently as 1938 upheld a Michigan statute prohibiting a woman from bartending unless her husband or father owned the establishment. She then made an appeal to conscience. "Your great-grandfathers were willing to be prisoners of their own prejudice to permit ex-slaves to vote, but not their own white wives. A vote against this amendment today by a white man is a vote against his wife, or his widow, or his daughter, or his sister." Griffiths' speech helped push the amendment to passage by a vote of 168 to 133.

During the first press conference after Title VII went into effect, the administrator responsible for enforcing the law joked about the ban on sex discrimination. "It will give men equal opportunity to be Playboy bunnies," he said. In light of the government's continuing resistance to take sex discrimination in the workplace seriously, Griffiths spent much of the remaining decade making sure that the Equal Employment Opportunity Commission, which was created by Title VII, enforced the new law. Her congressional office became the nerve center for women across the country who believed they had been victims of discrimination. As a result of the need for women to be represented in sex discrimination lawsuits, the first modern advocacy group for women, the National Organization for Women, was founded in 1966 by a group of women's-rights advocates. Betty Friedan, author of the 1963 bestseller *The Feminine Mystique,* was elected the organization's first president.

The 1970s brought a new breed of women to Congress, along with the Equal Rights Amendment. Ever since the ERA was first introduced in the House in 1923, women's rights activists had been deeply divided over the issue. Most women's groups in the pre–World War II period opposed the constitutional amendment because it threatened protective labor laws for women—laws they had worked hard to install. After World War II, supporters of the ERA in Congress were conservative, pro-business Republican women—Margaret Chase Smith and Edith Nourse Rogers, among others. Progressive Democratic congresswomen like Helen Gahagan Douglas and Chase

Going Woodhouse tried to obstruct consideration of the amendment. By the mid-1960s, protective labor legislation for women had been rendered obsolete by the Equal Pay Act and the Civil Rights Act. Both pieces of legislation called for equal treatment of the sexes in the workplace, rather than special protection for women. Women's groups and progressive Democratic congresswomen soon joined forces behind the ERA, and the breach that had long debilitated the feminist movement finally healed.

In August 1970, fifty years after women's suffrage, Martha Griffiths led a campaign to pass the ERA in the House. Griffiths felt that the constitutional amendment was necessary because the Supreme Court had refused to apply the equal-protection clause of the Fourteenth Amendment to women as it had to African Americans. For example, as Griffiths argued in a committee hearing, the Air Force required only female enlistees to be high school graduates and unmarried. Women were required to submit photographs with their applications; men were not. Many colleges expelled unwed mothers but did not discipline unwed fathers.

Although the ERA passed in the Senate in 1950 and 1953, the bill had been held hostage on the House side, in the Judiciary Committee, for almost fifty years. The chairman of the Judiciary Committee, Emmanual Celler, opposed the amendment and refused to hold hearings on the ERA during his twenty years as chairman. Celler called the Equal Rights Amendment a "blunderbuss amendment" and argued, "Ever since Adam gave up his rib to make a woman, throughout the ages we have learned that physical, emotional, psychological, and social differences exist and dare not be disregarded." Against Celler's will, Griffiths filed a "discharge petition." Discharge petitions are rarely used because they require going over the head of the powerful—and in this case feared—committee chairman. If 218 members (a majority of House members) sign a discharge petition, a bill can hopscotch over the committee of its jurisdiction and go directly onto the House floor for a vote. Griffiths defied Chairman Celler and personally persuaded each and every member to sign the petition. After considerable arm twisting, she even convinced the Republican minority leader, Gerald Ford, and the Democratic majority leader, Hale Boggs, to sign on. Ford would later call the ERA "a monument to Martha."

The second wave of the feminist movement arrived with the passage of the ERA in the House in 1971 and the Senate in 1972. For the first time since suffrage, politicians in Congress could not afford to ignore women or women's issues.

In 1968, Shirley Chisholm became the first black woman ever elected to Congress. She represented a mostly black and Puerto Rican section of Brooklyn, New York. Chisholm, a former teacher and state legislator, went to Congress in 1969 as one of only nine black and ten women members of the House. She had managed to beat her popular male opponent in the 1968 campaign by targeting female voters, something that had never been done before. In her district, female registered voters outnumbered male registered voters 2.5 to 1.

With a motto of "unbought and unbossed," Chisholm went to Congress knowing she did not want to play by the rules. When she was placed on the Agriculture Committee—an assignment so obviously irrelevant to a representative of the urban ghetto that it verged on insult—she broke the rules of seniority and tradition by asking Speaker John McCormack to take her off. McCormack refused, advising Chisholm to "be a good soldier." Chisholm had no intention of doing any such thing. When the Democratic caucus met to approve the new committee assignments, Chisholm forced herself onto a microphone to explain her problem and appeal to the leadership to put the few black members in the House on committees relevant to the problems of their constituents. Chisholm then proposed a resolution to remove herself from the Agriculture Committee. Her stunned colleagues voted with her. The resolution passed, and Chisholm was reassigned to the Veterans' Committee. "There are a lot more veterans in my district than there are trees," she said.

After Chisholm gave her speech to the Democratic caucus, a congressman told her that she had just committed political suicide. The leadership, he warned, would never forget her breach of etiquette. He would learn otherwise. "It is incomprehensible to me, the fear that can affect men in political offices," Chisholm later wrote. "It is shocking the way they submit to forces they know are wrong and fail to stand up for what they believe."

In 1972, Shirley Chisholm ran for president. At the Democratic convention, 40 percent of the delegates were women (up from 13 percent in 1968). The first female governors were elected—Ella Grasso in Connecticut in 1974 and Dixie Lee Ray in Washington in 1976. Female representation in federal, state, county, and local elective offices would increase from below 5 percent in the early seventies to 10 percent by 1980. More and more women ran for office, but the high reelection rate of incumbents made entry difficult. From 1973 to 1983, the number of women in Congress increased by only nine.

Though their numbers were few, many of the women elected to Congress in the late sixties and throughout the seventies were self-proclaimed feminists: Shirley Chisholm, Bella Abzug, Elizabeth Holtzman, Margaret Heckler, Pat Schroeder, and Lindy Boggs. As Congressman Don Reigle described it in a memoir, women like Bella Abzug and Shirley Chisholm brought "a new kind of female militancy to the House."

Congress would continue to hold these women at arm's length. Former Congressman James Symington remembers a House page of that uneasy era who would stand by the door of the Democratic cloakroom, waiting first for the former speaker of the House, John McCormack, and then for Representative Abzug, who was known for wearing wide-brimmed hats. "McCormack would hand the kid his huge, fat cigar and Bella would hand him this enormous pie-pan of a hat. The young man would stand perplexed, patiently holding the cigar as far away from his face as possible in one hand and Bella's huge hat in the other."

Bella Abzug's 1970 campaign slogan caught on nationally: "A woman's place is in the house—the House of Representatives." A lawyer and activist, Abzug was the first woman since Jeannette Rankin to run for Congress on a women's-rights platform. "The other women in Congress were running not *because* they were women, but because they *happened* to be women. I was running *because* I was a woman," Abzug said in a recent interview. Abzug fought passionately to end the war in Vietnam; she championed the Equal Rights Amendment and other feminist issues.

Abzug was a tough and able legislator, but she was also abrasive, self-righteous, and a consummate outsider. She had no fear of—or respect for—the congressional leadership.

Like Abzug and Chisholm, Pat Schroeder had no intention of playing by the rules. Elected in 1972 on an anti–Vietnam War platform, Patricia Scott Schroeder was the first woman Colorado ever sent to Congress. She was also the first female member of Congress with young children—her daughter, Jamie, was then two, her son, Scott, six. Schroeder's husband, Jim, a Denver lawyer, was her campaign manager, and after Schroeder won, the whole family uprooted itself and moved to Washington. Schroeder was the only member of Congress who carried diapers in her purse. She threw birthday parties for her children in the members' dining room.

Eleven months after being sworn in, Schroeder sealed her fate as an outsider. In November 1973, *Redbook* magazine put her on its cover, posed in front of the Capital dome, her near-black hair pulled into a loose ponytail. Schroeder resembled a nineteenth-century pioneer woman in her 1970s shirt with its long, pointy collar buttoned at the neck, but mostly she looked young, beautiful, and righteous. She believed that America should not be involved in the Vietnam War, and she fought her way onto the committee where the most discretionary money was being spent: the House Armed Services Committee. The committee chairman, F. Edward Hébert, told her that she was not "worthy" of the seat.

Hébert, a seventy-two-year-old Louisiana Democrat, didn't mind being called a "male chauvinist." When he summoned Schroeder to his office, he boasted of having both an "adult" and an "adultery" room. Then he told her the rules: "The Lord giveth, the Lord taketh away, and I am the Lord. You'll do just fine on this committee if you remember that." Getting down to business, Hébert declared that women had no place on his committee because women know nothing of combat. Schroeder studied the records of all of the current Armed Services Committee members. She learned an interesting fact: Several of the men on the committee had never served in the armed forces. The next day, as it happened, one of those men asked her, "How can you serve on this committee? You've never been in combat." Schroeder replied, "Then you and I have a lot in common."

Reluctantly, Hébert gave Schroeder a seat on the committee, if only as the lesser of two evils: Bella Abzug had tried and failed the year before to get on Armed Services. "I hope that you aren't going to be a skinny Bella Abzug," Hébert said to Schroeder. He punished Schroeder by making her share a seat with another new member Hébert didn't like, the black liberal Ron Dellums.

Unlike Abzug, Schroeder used humor and charm to disarm her opponents, even though the substance of her politics was the same. Schroeder took on Hébert. She voted against his weapons-procurement bills, condemned the bombings in Cambodia, and accused the committee of being the "Pentagon's lobby on the Hill." Hébert tried to discipline Schroeder by refusing to allow her to attend the SALT Disarmament Conference in Geneva. "I wouldn't send you to represent this committee in a dogfight," he told her. Schroeder went to Geneva only after Speaker Carl Albert waived the rule requiring the committee chairman's permission. Schroeder struck back against Hébert by telling all this and more to *Redbook*. In an act of insubordination unusual for the time, Schroeder told the magazine, "Hébert is a sexist. He doesn't believe that any-one with a uterus can make a decision on military affairs."

Hébert retaliated. During the Yom Kippur War in 1973, the Armed Services Committee flew to Egypt and Israel. The *Redbook* story had hit the newsstands only days earlier. When Schroeder climbed aboard the Air Force plane on the way to the Middle East, she saw her own face staring up from her seat—and from every seat on the plane. She knew at once that it was a cruel ploy. "When was the last time the Air Force bought *Redbook* for their in-flight mag-azine?" Schroeder remarked. For the rest of the trip, Schroeder was treated like a pariah. Nobody had ever taken on the chairman in public before, and no one on the committee wanted to be seen with someone who had. But Schroeder got the last word. In 1975, with the help of the post-Watergate class of '74, Schroeder spearheaded Hébert's ouster from the committee chairmanship.

With the rise of feminism came the fall of Margaret Chase Smith. "I never was a woman candidate," she once said. "I never was a woman member. . . . Had I been one, I wouldn't have been elected." Smith had long ignored the kind of sexism that inflamed feminists. Having achieved seniority and power on the Armed Services and Appropriations Committee, Smith had gained acceptance by her male colleagues in the Senate. Although Smith had been an early co-sponsor of the ERA, was instrumental in keeping the "sex" clause in the Senate version of Title VII, and had fought for regular status for women in the armed services, she rejected the feminist movement. Smith did not believe that gender should be relevant to a politician's identity. Moreover, the militancy of the feminist movement insulted Smith, who scorned political extremism. Smith's career goal had been to gain power within the patriarchal system of the Senate, and becoming a women's advocate, she believed, would have hindered her success.

By 1972, when Smith ran for her fifth term in the Senate, the political landscape had changed. The senator who had once been one of the few role models for women in politics had become the victim of the very cause that purported to elevate women into public life. The Maine chapter of the National Organization for Women actively and successfully worked to defeat her.

Twenty-two years later, in the Republican sweep of the 1994 elections, Pat Schroeder and her fellow Democratic feminists in Congress would suffer a similar setback as the political landscape made another shift, redefining yet again what it means to be a successful woman politician.

I

The Year of the Woman

From the moment it began—on October 11, 1991, with the televised Hill-Thomas hearings—the Year of the Woman offered a unique opportunity in contemporary politics. Women candidates had an automatic advantage (some pollsters said as many as 10 percentage points) over their male opponents by the mere fact of their gender. In an unusual reversal of fortune, the farther away a woman was from power, the better her position to attain it. No one that day could have been farther from the halls of power than Patty Murray, whose campaign for the U.S. Senate amounted to a textbook model of the Year of the Woman.

It was her forty-first birthday, but as she sat in her living room in Shoreline, Washington, staring at the television, she was in no mood to celebrate. For seven hours, she hadn't done anything but watch the hearings. Her daughter, Sara, and her son, Randy, came home from school. Her husband, Rob, a computer systems designer, came home from work in Seattle. Murray kept on watching.

As Murray watched Anita Hill describe how she had been sexually intimidated and embarrassed by Clarence Thomas, and noted the behavior of the members of the Senate Judiciary Committee—fourteen men on the attack—she kept saying to herself, *I can't believe this.* Then after a pause, *Yes I can.* She thought, *How dare these Senators denigrate this woman, making her look like a liar, a sex-crazed vixen?* Later that night, the Murrays went to a fundraiser for a school board member. The only talk was about Anita Hill.

Weeks passed, but Murray's anger didn't subside. Remembering the lineup of Senators, Murray asked herself, "Who's speaking for me out there?" Who, she wondered, on the Judiciary Committee, or in the Senate as a whole, represented her—her gender, her class, her priorities?

By Thanksgiving, after talking to her family, friends, and political confidants, Murray, a first-term state senator who had never considered running for national office before, decided that she would run for the United States Senate.

At a young age, Patty Johns, one of seven children, was told that if she wanted anything she would have to work for it. When she was ten, Patty and her identical twin sister, Peggy, went to work on a neighboring farm picking strawberries. Earning money and contributing to the family income gave Patty a strong sense of self-confidence.

Her family lived in Bothell, a town with a population of 1,200 located 20 miles north of Seattle, near the coast of Puget Sound. Bothell's largest industry was a lumber mill. Patty's father, David Johns, managed the five-and-dime store on Main Street. Every Friday night and Saturday, from the sixth through twelfth grade, Patty and Peggy worked at the store. Patty swept floors, counted inventory, and stocked shelves for fifty cents an hour. At sixteen, she worked the cash register. With the money she earned, she paid for her own clothes. David Johns ran a tight ship. "When you were at work, you were at work," Murray recalled. "You didn't mess around."

In an era when greasers were gods at Bothell High, Patty and Peggy were "too good," as Peggy remembers it. The sisters played in the marching band and were known as "the smart twins." They made straight As with only the occasional B. They did everything together, but Patty stood out as a natural leader. In the family, it seemed as if she was always in charge. Her older brother, Rob, ceded her the older-sibling role. "When Patty told us to do something, we would never question it. We would just do it," said Peggy, now an elementary school teacher. In the ninth grade, Patty ran for secretary of the girls' club against an opponent who was very tall. Her first campaign slogan won the election: "Good things come in small packages."

One Sunday morning when Patty was thirteen, as the family walked to Mass together, David Johns' knees buckled and he fell to the ground without warning. Two years later, he was diagnosed with multiple sclerosis. The Johnses were too proud to tell their neighbors; for the next two years, Patty and her siblings kept the secret. Four years later, David Johns could no longer report to work at the five-and-dime. Patty's mother had never graduated from college and she had no job skills, but she signed up for accounting courses, got a degree, and found a job. From then on, Beverly Johns supported the family.

In 1968, Patty enrolled at Washington State University in Pullman, Washington. She was eighteen and had never left the state. But here, in the far eastern corner of Washington, near the Idaho border, Patty had her first taste of leaving home. It was also her first exposure to the sixties. Antiwar marches, sit-ins, and bra burnings had come to Washington State. Patty Johns didn't join the movement. She was working too hard. She paid her way through college by working as a secretary—in the winter for the veterinary and physical education departments and in the summer for a glass company near Bothell.

Patty didn't have to go to consciousness-raising groups to get in touch with herself as an independent woman. The tragedy of her father's illness had forced her to start becoming self-reliant. Patty had always expected to work her whole life out of necessity. Her life experience had taught her that one couldn't always depend on a husband's financial support. She therefore assumed one of the basic tenets of feminism—that women should not have to choose between family and career, between private well-being and public rights.

In 1968, Murray staged her own small protest. The university had a rule requiring female students to wear dresses to dinner. Every evening, after class, Murray changed from pants into a dress and trudged her way through three-foot snowdrifts to the dining hall. Every evening, as the women arrived wet and cold, the men breezed into dinner dry and warm. Murray decided that the rule was unfair. She organized the women in her dormitory, and one night, every woman in Murray's dorm arrived at dinner wearing pants. The change in the rules, allowing female students to wear pants to dinner, stands today as a tribute to Murray's activism.

Three years later—two years before the Supreme Court legalized abortion—a college friend of Murray's went on a date and was raped. "There was no word for date rape at the time," recalled Murray. "She went out with some guy and came back devastated. Then she found out that she was pregnant. I remember her crying. She had lived through this horrible night, and then she was faced with being pregnant."

Murray had known students who had gotten pregnant, but they could afford to fly to Europe or Mexico for an abortion. Murray's friend had no money. She resorted to a back-alley abortion and came home sick and bleeding. Murray was scared, and angry that the abortion prohibition clearly punished poor women. A year later, Murray found out that her friend had had to have a hysterectomy because of complications from the abortion. "When she told me she could never have kids, I thought, Oh my God, what have we done?"

In 1972, the year Shirley Chisholm ran for president and Patricia Schroeder ran for Congress, Patty Johns graduated from college and married Rob Murray, a fellow Washington State University student whom she had met on a blind date. The Murrays lived in Seattle, where Patty tried to find a job in the field she had studied in college—recreational therapy, working with disabled children. The only openings were volunteer positions, so Murray had to take a job as an executive secretary. In 1976, when Patty became pregnant, her employer asked her to leave.

In 1980, Murray was thirty years old and the suburban mother of two children, ages one and four. Her husband, Rob, worked for Stevedoring Services of America. They lived in the tree-sheltered middle-class Seattle suburb of Shoreline. Silver Airstream campers and basketball hoops adorned the driveways on the narrow, winding streets of Shoreline. In small back yards, 200-foot fir trees loomed over modest two-story, cedar-shingled houses.

Every Monday, Wednesday, and Friday, Murray volunteered at the Shoreline Community Cooperative School, a parent-child education cooperative. Randy and Sara attended the preschool, and Murray and a group of parents ran the co-op program. Murray played the guitar and led sing-alongs with the children. She conducted arts-and-crafts classes. She taught parent education—discipline, nutrition, child development. She was good at her job, because she was pragmatic and organized and never lost her cool. Every day, she wore a sensible uniform: jeans and tennis shoes.

When the Washington state legislature planned to slash funding for parent-child preschool programs in 1980, Murray vowed to fight it. She loaded her children into the car and drove an hour and a half south to Olympia. With Randy and Sara in tow, Murray knocked on doors in the Capitol building, pleading with legislators not to cut funding. Halfway through her rounds, one of the many male state senators she approached made a fateful mistake. Exasperated by this woman's persistence, he blurted out, "You can't do anything; you're just a mom in tennis shoes."

Murray drove home in a huff. No one realized it then, but that simple remark would change Patty Murray's life. A close friend later observed that although the state senator believed he was putting a docile housewife in her place, he had actually "waved a red flag in front of a bull." Murray started working the phones.

In less than a week, a battalion of 12,000 parents from all over the state descended on Olympia to protest the co-op cuts. Phone lines were jammed, the hallways of the Capitol were clogged, thousands of letters piled up on lawmakers' desks. The state Capitol was under siege, and a "mom in tennis shoes" was commanding the rebellion. Cowed by the powerful grassroots response, the state senate spared the co-op funding.

Inspired by the triumph, Murray ran for the Shoreline school board in 1982. She lost. A year later, however, she was appointed to a vacant seat on the board. She served as school board president for two terms, during which she continued to pressure state government, advocating dropout prevention programs, smaller classes, and higher salaries for teachers. But after five years on the school board, she concluded that the only way she could make a difference was to be the person who "wrote the checks."

In 1988, Murray ran for the Washington state senate in the 1st District against a well-financed Republican incumbent named Bill Kiskaddon. Kiskaddon had a bad attendance record and he was indifferent to the issues Murray cared about—education, jobs, children, and family issues. On the campaign trail, Murray worked as doggedly as her volunteers, who dropped literature in the neighborhoods at 4:00 A.M. to beat the morning paper. Murray started ringing doorbells in January, and by Labor Day she had walked to every single household in the district— 17,000 all together. At each house, Murray talked to residents and took notes. After Labor Day, she returned to the households she had marked "persuadable" for one last pitch. Beth Sullivan, a political consultant who worked for the Washington Democratic party that year, was astounded by Murray's effort. "Many candidates work hard," said Sullivan. "But no one *ever* walks to all the households in their district and then goes back again." Murray's perseverance and footwork paid off. In a *Seattle Times* endorsement, she was called "an energetic community and school leader, [who] displays a greater sense of urgency on upgrading K–12 and higher education and finding solutions to transportation problems." On November 8, 1988, Murray won.

On December 4, 1991, Patty Murray, age forty-one, announced her candidacy for the U.S. Senate. There was no hoopla surrounding the news of her bid: Murray just picked up the phone and called a few political reporters, telling them that she would be the voice of middle-class families and women. There were only two women in the Senate, Nancy Kassebaum and Barbara Mikulski. But now, with the Hill-Thomas hearings imprinted on the public eye, it looked as if voters might be willing to consider sending more women to the Senate.

No one, however, thought Murray could win. The *Seattle Times* declared her bid "the longest of long shots." Washington State's idea of a U.S. senator had been formed during World War II and the years after by two politically powerful figures, Henry Jackson and Warren Magnuson, "Scoop and Maggie," who had represented the Evergreen State for a combined eighty-seven years.

The man Murray proposed to unseat was another Democrat—Brock Adams, first elected to the House of Representatives in 1965, a one-term senator, known for his support of women's issues. Murray herself voted for him in 1986. Now Adams felt betrayed by the upstart candidate and wasted no time saying so. His objections to Murray's candidacy sounded reasonable. On issues they both cared about—the environment, abortion, and social welfare—there appeared to be little difference between the two Democrats. "The fact that he's a man and she's a woman is irrelevant," said an Adams spokesman. But the Anita Hill hearings had proved that gender was more relevant than ever in the election. Men, even liberals like Paul Simon and Howard Metzenbaum, both of whom sat on the Senate Judiciary Committee, were tone-deaf when it came to understanding a woman's point of view on an issue like sexual harassment. They demonstrated that only women could truly represent women's interests.

Some women's groups, however, seemed to agree with Brock Adams' spokesman. In 1992, the price of a U.S. Senate race would start at $2 million. Powerful organizations like the Women's Campaign Fund, the National Abortion and Reproductive Rights Action League (NARAL), and EMILY's List (Early Money Is Like Yeast)—a donor network that supported pro-choice Democratic women—refused to endorse or support Murray. Adams was too close an ally of the women's movement. The state Democratic party offered no help either. Party leaders told Murray she didn't have enough experience to run for the Senate—Congress, maybe, but certainly not the U.S. Senate. Murray's populist motto, "Once you work in day care, you can work anywhere," infuriated self-important local politicians.

Still others predicted that she would be defeated because she was a woman. In December 1991, the Year of the Woman was still four months away. Murray didn't listen. "I look at the U.S. Senate," she said, "and I don't find anybody back there who's real. I'm real." Murray joined a historic slate of twenty-nine woman candidates vying to change the U.S. Senate. In the 203-year history of the U.S.

Senate, only six women had ever been elected in their own right.

Three months later, on March 1, the *Seattle Times* broke an astonishing story claiming that Brock Adams had sexually harassed and molested eight women. He denied the charges but announced that day that he would not seek reelection. Adams, who had been married for forty years, said the allegations were politically inspired; nearly all the accusers were Democrats, however, including one unnamed Democratic party activist who said that in the early 1970s Adams drugged her drink, raped her, and left $200 on her table. In addition, Adams' former congressional aide, Kari Tupper, had publicly accused Adams in 1988 of drugging her drink with pink liquid and sexually molesting her. Adams had denied Tupper's charges as well, but a pattern seemed to have been established when several of the women interviewed by the *Seattle Times* described Adams drugging their drinks with a "red sweet-tasting fluid" and then physically taking advantage of them.

Overnight, Murray had become the only Democrat in the race. The appearance of sexual impropriety by Adams gave Murray's candidacy a strong boost by localizing a national issue—sexual harassment. Simply by being a woman, Murray now had credibility. Best of all, with Adams out of the race, women's groups were free to support her.

Murray needed to raise a minimum of $500,000 before the September 15 primary. By April, she had collected only $39,239. Back in Washington, D.C., EMILY's List remained skeptical, because the Murray campaign couldn't afford to conduct a poll—a mandatory requirement for an EMILY's List endorsement. But Murray had assembled a team of professional consultants, received endorsements from teachers' unions, and developed a convincing campaign plan. EMILY's List's president, Ellen Malcolm, was willing to take a chance and "turn on the network" of donors for Murray.

In late April, Murray's campaign got two more breaks. EMILY's List officially recommended Murray's campaign to their donors; and Lynn Yeakel won a surprise victory in the Pennsylvania Democratic primary for the U.S. Senate. Yeakel, a fundraiser for women's charities, was the second candidate to prove that a woman could win a long-shot primary. A month earlier, Carol Moseley-Braun, an unknown Cook County recorder of deeds, had won an upset victory in the Democratic Senate primary, beating incumbent Senator Alan Dixon. Moseley-Braun's victory had been viewed as a fluke, but when Lynn Yeakel beat four men in her primary, Moseley-Braun looked as if she had started a trend. Both races were unofficial referendums on the Hill-Thomas hearings. Moseley-Braun's victory was provided by suburban women voters who were angry at Dixon for his vote to confirm Clarence Thomas to the Supreme Court. Yeakel entered the race specifically to unseat Arlen Specter, whose relentless grilling of Anita Hill personified male indifference to sexual harassment. The popularity of Yeakel and Moseley-Braun's campaign messages proved that Anita Hill was having a direct impact on the politics of 1992.

The Illinois and Pennsylvania primaries officially inaugurated the Year of the Woman. In late April, a Times-Mirror Center poll showed that 69 percent of the respondents (74 percent of women and 63 percent of men) thought the country would "be better off if more women served in Congress." In hindsight, the actual span of the Year of the Woman would begin with Anita Hill's testimony in October 1991 and end on election day in November 1992. But before Yeakel's primary victory, Anita Hill's impact on the political climate was difficult to predict.

Yeakel's Democratic primary victory and the EMILY's List endorsement pushed Murray's campaign from the political fringe to center stage. Two days after Yeakel's victory, Washington Governor Booth Gardner ended months of speculation and decided not to run for the Senate seat. Former Democratic Congressman Mike Lowry decided to run for Governor instead of Senator. That left Don Bonker, a lobbyist and former seven-term congressman.

Murray called Bonker on the phone. "I want to know if you're in or out," she asked him. "Can you give me an answer?" Without hesitation, Bonker replied that someone had to win the seat for the Democrats. He thought it was going to be Don Bonker.

That spring, in Walla Walla, in Cashmere, and in Concrete, Patty Murray had virtually no name recognition. In town after town, she lashed out at Congress, at "all the men in dark suits and red ties." She frequently referred to Anita Hill and the need to elect more women to the U.S. Senate. She told the audience her mom-in-tennis-shoes story, and the comparison was obvious. The Washington state legislator who told Murray that she was just a mom in tennis shoes had been dismissive, patronizing, and insulting—all the things the men on the Senate Judiciary Committee had been to Anita Hill. "I might not fit the standard people expect a U.S. Senator to be, but I'm used to fighting the odds," Murray would say. Her official campaign slogan—"The choice for real change"—was edged out bit by bit as Murray was increasingly identified as the "mom in tennis shoes."

Murray's staff worried that the nickname would hurt her. They thought she needed to be more senatorial. But Murray resisted her staff's attempts to change her style and message. She knew that the once-insulting phrase had transformed into a trophy. The mom-in-tennis-shoes label emphasized Murray's gender, middle-class origins, and outsider status—three things that played to her political advantage in 1992.

Murray's use of the mom-in-tennis-shoes story on the campaign trail was only partly legitimate. She was a genuine, down-to-earth suburban mom. At the same time, she had organized thousands of citizens to lobby the state, she had been elected school board president, and she had doggedly knocked on every door in her state senate district. Once in the state senate, Murray had been appointed to a whip position and named one of the top five freshman state legislators in 1990 by the *Seattle Times*. Not *just* a mom in tennis shoes: Patty Murray was also a politician.

In June, the campaign conducted a poll that showed Murray's name recognition at only 8 percent. But 60 percent of the respondents recognized the "mom in tennis shoes." Murray's campaign consultant Beth Sullivan later recalled, "When we found out that the mom in tennis shoes was much better known than Patty Murray, we knew that we couldn't afford to make her more senatorial."

Murray's campaign advisers considered the fact that her "slogan" could work both for and against her: voters might assume that Murray's duties as a mother would compromise her ability to represent the state. The advisers also worried about her children. Should they appear with the candidate on the trail? It was an issue of appearances. How could a U.S. senator have time to raise two children, ages twelve and sixteen? Naturally, if the candidate were a married man, the question would be moot. Voters would never assume that caring for children would get in the way of a man's political responsibilities. "I'm running to show that you can do *both*," Murray told her staff. "My family comes with me on the campaign trail and to Washington." Murray wanted her children to share the campaign experience with her and learn from it. Murray explained later, "I was putting my life and their lives on the line and I thought, If they go through it, win or lose, at least they'll get something out of it."

During the campaign, Murray's husband, Rob, went on working as he had for fifteen years, as a computer systems designer at Stevedoring Services of America. He rarely campaigned with Patty, supporting her on the sidelines instead. Rob drove Patty to headquarters in the morning, helped the campaign with its computers, and kept track of the campaign's finances, but he stayed out of the spotlight, giving no more than two interviews to reporters. Sara, twelve, spent her summer vacation stuffing envelopes and answering the phone at campaign headquarters. Opinionated, curious, and devoted to her mother, Sara went everywhere with the candidate. Murray's instinct had been right. On the campaign trail, men and women alike told her that they respected her for being both a mother and a candidate. Murray's children made her slogan come alive.

Murray called Don Bonker a "recycled politician and lobbyist": Bonker had spent fourteen years in Congress before running unsuccessfully for the Senate in 1988. But Bonker's problem was more complex. Typically, when men run against women, they are uncomfortable going negative for fear of looking like bullies. That September, however, Bonker ventured into negative campaigning by portraying Murray as an intellectual lightweight who lacked his experience and expertise.

As a matter of fact, the two agreed on most issues; their difference was in style. Bonker was a congressional insider; Murray knew close to nothing about how Washington, D.C., worked. "He strongly believed being a member of Congress was an asset," marveled Sullivan. In fact, it was political suicide that summer: Congressional popularity was at an all-time low; the public was enraged by the House Bank check-overdraft scandal. Murray, who had only been to Washington, D.C., once, on a family vacation, jumped at every chance to stress her outsider credentials. During her first debate with Bonker, Murray discovered the perfect symbol for her message. After catching a glimpse of Bonker's watch during the debate, Murray noticed that it was set three hours early. Near the end of the debate, Murray dryly said, "I'm laughing because my opponent's watch is at four-thirty, on D.C. time." In fact, Bonker's watch was broken, but the impression remained: Don Bonker was in sync with Washington, D.C., not Washington State.

Murray won the primary. It wasn't even close. With 28 percent of the vote, she finished 8 points ahead of Republican Rod Chandler and 9 points ahead of Don Bonker. She had trounced ten candidates from both parties in Washington State's open, "jungle" primary, where candidates from both parties participate. No one had predicted that Murray would lead the pack. No polls published before the election showed her in the lead. That night, as Murray claimed victory, only one elected official bothered to come to the party.

Murray had raised $550,000. EMILY's List had supplied $150,000, which paid for all of the campaign's television advertising. Murray's campaign ads ran during shows like *Murphy Brown*, targeting women between ages twenty-five and forty-five. A telephone poll conducted the weekend before the election showed that most people supported Murray because she was a woman. The poll also found that 15 percent of the voters said that all things being equal, they would vote for a woman over a man for office this year. The specter of the Hill-Thomas hearings had made a profound impact on the electorate, and Murray's message that women could bring fresh, real voices to the Senate had resonance. She became the eleventh woman to win the nomination to the Senate in 1992.

The day after the primary, Rod Chandler, her Republican opponent in November, mocked Murray by carrying around a pair of tennis shoes. Political experts in Washington, D.C., called with congratulations but begged her to drop the "hokey" slogan and start acting more like a senator. Murray refused to change: her primary victory had proved the point that women candidates no longer had to act like men to get elected. "I've watched women come into politics thinking they had to become a man to succeed," Murray said. "What I am is a different role model. This mom in tennis shoes is what I really am."

Rod Chandler did look more senatorial than Patty Murray. A former television anchorman and five-term congressman, Chandler had a deep baritone voice and thick white hair. He had spent $1.5 million dollars in the primary, and now, in his first television ad, Chandler, a moderate Republican, came on strong. He had no compunctions about negative campaigning, attacking Murray for being a liberal and lacking knowledge of the issues. The candidate modeled himself as a sensitive male and spoke about his struggles with alcoholism and his wife's breast cancer.

Murray had become the front runner. She had out-polled Chandler in the primary even in the conservative eastern parts of the state. But Murray still looked like the underdog. Her financial support came from teachers, labor unions, and environmental and women's groups. Individual donations to her campaign came mostly from women—teachers and retirees. The average contribution was $45. Murray called for guaranteed health insurance, improved public education, middle-class economic relief, and a $100 billion cut in the defense budget. She attacked Chandler for voting for a congressional pay raise and sending out $120,000 of taxpayer-funded franked mail. On September 24, Murray's campaign tracking polls showed her 16 points ahead of Chandler.

A few weeks later, she prepared for her four debates with Chandler. With the help of a researcher flown in from the Democratic Senatorial Campaign Committee, she educated herself on the issues and studied the language of Washington. In spite of all the preparation, Murray's staff was still concerned. They thought she needed a power suit. Patty Murray owned only three suits—one royal blue, one navy blue, and one red. In 1988, Murray had been sworn in to the state senate wearing the red suit, which had been made for her on a friend's home sewing machine. Murray's limited wardrobe and unsophisticated haircuts had been ridiculed in the Seattle papers, so her mostly female campaign staff decided to act as Murray's fashion police. "We wanted her to have a suit for the debate that would make her look as powerful as Rod Chandler," said Murray's friend and campaign adviser Kennie Endelman. Endelman asked a friend who owned a boutique to open her store at midnight so Murray could shop there secretly, out of sight from reporters. Murray and Endelman picked out a dark-blue pinstripe, which would later become known inside the campaign as the "debate suit."

By the end of October, however, the Murray campaign had run out of money, power suit or no. Murray refused to take a mortgage out on her house to pay for TV airtime, so the campaign went "black" for ten days—Chandler was on the air, Murray wasn't. Chandler put a woman on TV who said she wanted to support female candidates in general, but she couldn't vote for Patty Murray because the candidate was "just not ready." True, Murray had made some mistakes. She had told the Rainbow Coalition that she supported the idea of making Washington State a nuclear-free zone and then changed her mind. When she couldn't answer every question posed by a newspaper editorial board, she promised to "come back in a year and tell you what I've learned." The *Seattle Post-Intelligencer* ran an editorial about Murray stating that she was "obviously shaky in her understanding of major issues." Murray's campaign tracking polls showed that Chandler was chipping away at her lead—the gap had narrowed from 16 to 9 percentage points. The *Seattle Times* endorsed Chandler. The *Post-Intelligencer* endorsed Murray.

Then, at the end of the second debate, Chandler did something strange. For the previous hour, he had aggressively attacked Murray, repeatedly accusing her of not being specific enough. Murray had fought to keep her composure, but her voice had cracked with emotion. Chandler had appeared confident, condescending, and arrogant. By all accounts, he had soundly beaten Murray. Murray made her closing remarks.

Then it was Chandler's turn. Without any explanation, Chandler began to sing. In his smooth baritone, he serenaded Murray with an old Roger Miller song, trying, as he said later, to make Murray smile. It was an odd selection, a rambling ballad about a philanderer who spends all his money and abandons his wife and child: "Dang me, dang me," Chandler sang. "They ought to take a rope and hang me—hang me from the highest tree. Woman would you weep for me?" The audience sat silent in disbelief, and as soon as Chandler finished, Murray returned fire: "That's just the kind of attitude that got me into this race, Rod."

On election day, 1.2 million people in the state of Washington voted for Patty Murray. One million voted for Rod Chandler. Murray secured 54 percent of the vote, Chandler 46 percent. Murray had spent $1.2 million ($270,000 raised from EMILY's List); Rod Chandler, $2.5 million. Women had come out to vote for Murray, producing a 7-point gender gap; 58 percent of women and 51 percent of men had voted for Murray.

At her victory party, surrounded by her family, Murray told her supporters that she had won because she was an outsider. She said, "[People know] that I am like them, and they know that when I'm on the floor of the Senate, I will be saying the same things that they will." All the Democratic officials who skipped Murray's primary victory party showed up this time.

Patty Murray didn't eat or sleep all night. Between 2:00 A.M. and 4:00 A.M., she shuttled from camera setup to camera setup, giving interviews on all three network morning shows. Then she went to campaign headquarters, where she took phone calls and even reviewed job applications. Finally, she went home. As she walked through the door at 203rd Place, the phone there was also ringing. When she picked it up, a familiar, slow, soft voice spoke to her. It was Anita Hill, congratulating Murray and thanking her for having the courage to run. Murray, who had never met Anita Hill before, replied that it was Hill who had inspired her to run, and Hill who deserved the thanks.

2

The McKinneys

On October 11, 1991, as Anita Hill took the stand in the Senate Judiciary Committee hearings, Cynthia McKinney stood at the farthest fringes of power in the Georgia political hierarchy. She was a thirty-six-year-old black woman who represented Georgia's Fulton County district in the mostly white, mostly male Georgia general assembly. Running for Congress, however, would not be as far-fetched for McKinney as it had been for Patty Murray. McKinney had politics in her blood, and the Year of the Woman offered her a singular opportunity. Here was the chance for the daughter of a civil rights warrior to succeed where her father had failed.

In 1948, when Cynthia's father joined the Atlanta Police Department, James Edward "Billy" McKinney was only the ninth black man in Atlanta to wear the uniform. When Billy McKinney started work, he found that the police department was as segregated as the city it served. Black officers couldn't arrest white criminals. Black officers couldn't wear uniforms when they testified in court. They had to work the 6:00-P.M.-TO-2:00-A.M. shift. They weren't allowed to use the locker room at police headquarters and had to change in and out of their uniforms in the basement of the Butler Street YMCA.

Billy McKinney rebelled. In the early 1950s, McKinney filed suit in federal court protesting segregation in the police department. He lost the suit, and for the next fifteen years, conditions at the police department remained the same. McKinney took to the streets with a picket sign, alone. Because of his "agitation," McKinney would never be promoted during his twenty-one years with the police department.

Cynthia, Billy McKinney's only child from his second marriage, was born in 1955. As soon as Cynthia was old enough to walk, Billy swept her into the civil rights movement. In the late fifties and sixties, as McKinney participated in sit-ins and protests across the South, Cynthia came along perched on her father's shoulders. In the summer of 1963, when Martin Luther King led 200,000 civil rights protesters to the nation's capital, Billy McKinney, a member of King's Southern Christian Leadership Conference, had wanted to bring eight-year-old Cynthia along. Cynthia's mother Leola worried that Billy, caught up in the passion of the march, would lose Cynthia in the crowd. She put her foot down, and Billy went to Washington alone. Cynthia watched Dr. King's "I have a dream" speech on TV. It was one of the last times Billy McKinney would represent the family in Washington without Cynthia.

Cynthia Ann McKinney was born the year after *Brown v. Board of Education* outlawed racial segregation in public schools. Her father sensed that in some important ways his daughter's life would be easier than his. She would not suffer the indignities of segregation. She would not be shut out of the political system. But Billy McKinney vowed that even if his daughter, a child of Atlanta's black middle class, would have better opportunities, she would not grow up ignorant of the struggle. "My dad made sure that if I moved up, I would not move out," Cynthia remembered.

In those days, Cynthia walked the creek behind her house to an all-black Catholic girl's elementary school, St. Paul of the Cross. When her class stood in line every day to go to lunch, the students ritually held out their bare arms and compared skin tones. The lighter the skin, the more beautiful the girl. Dark-skinned girls, like Cynthia, were "automatically ugly."

But by 1968, Cynthia's status as a dark-skinned girl had changed. Black had become beautiful. Cynthia adopted James Brown's anthem, "Say It Loud, I'm Black and I'm Proud," which was banned on local radio stations after the 1966 Atlanta race riots. In the eighth grade, against her mother's wishes, Cynthia became the first in her class to wear an afro.

At St. Joseph's High School, McKinney sat in her first desegregated, coed classroom, one of only ten black students in the whole school. She graduated from St. Joseph's in 1973 near the top of her class. Neither of her parents had college degrees, but Cynthia won scholarships at Marquette and Emory Universities. She decided instead to go to college in California—she wanted to expand her horizons, see the country, get out of the South. In Los Angeles, McKinney moved in with her mother's sister and enrolled at the University of Southern California, where she majored in international relations and graduated in

1978. Two years later, Cynthia took her master's and completed her Ph.D. course work in international relations at the Fletcher School of Law and Diplomacy. After working in Washington, D.C., for Senator Herman Talmadge for a period of time, she married and moved to Jamaica. Cynthia made her first move toward politics in 1986. Actually, it was made for her: Cynthia's father signed her up for her first race.

Billy McKinney had represented House District 35 in the Georgia general assembly since 1973. He had started his political career after losing a race for the city council and one for county commissioner. Three times, Billy McKinney had also run for the U.S. Congress in Atlanta's 5th District; three times he had lost. In 1986, without Cynthia's knowledge or consent, Billy literally entered her name on the rolls as a write-in candidate for the Georgia general assembly. "I just went down there and forged Cynthia's name," Billy McKinney later said. "I ran Cynthia."

Only afterward did father tell daughter that she was a candidate. Later, Billy's reasons emerged: he had a personal vendetta against Barbara Couch, the incumbent state legislator. Earlier that year, Couch had beaten Billy in a contest for vice chair of the nineteen-member Fulton County delegation. Now he retaliated by running his only available understudy, his thirty-one-year-old daughter, against Couch.

At the time, Cynthia was in Jamaica. She had married Coy Grandison, a Jamaican political organizer for whom she had high expectations. Grandison, she believed, could be the politician in the family, running for Parliament in Jamaica while Cynthia stayed home and raised their child. In 1985, she had given birth to a son, Coy Jr.

Billy McKinney's secret plan, therefore, found Cynthia at one of the more ambivalent moments of her life. On the one hand, she was flattered. She wanted to fulfill her father's hopes. She had worked as gofer and, later, assistant press secretary on her father's three losing races for Congress. She had a sense of humor and of family pride about the prospect of running for elective office, and Billy's signing her up for the race was just "Billy up to his antics again." On the other hand, Cynthia wondered if being a politician was the future she really wanted.

Cynthia stayed in Jamaica and never came home to campaign. She lost at the polls, but not without discovering something important. Twenty-eight thousand voters in Fulton County had recognized and voted for a McKinney.

By 1988, Cynthia had separated from Grandison. She discovered that her political ambition had outstripped her husband's. As she later described it, Grandison habitually acted as a political adviser. He "talked a big political game, but in the end he never had the guts to run himself."

Cynthia moved back to Atlanta with her son to teach political science at Clark Atlanta University. That year, Barbara Couch decided not to run for reelection. Cynthia felt embarrassed by her lack of effort in 1986, and realizing that her fate might just be tied to her father's after all, she jumped at the chance to prove herself. This time, she signed herself up and beat seven opponents in the primary to win the election. Her Fulton County at-large district stretched 75 miles long, the largest district in the Georgia general assembly. It had a population of 640,000, half of it black. In one stroke, she had surpassed the boundaries of her father's career in the general assembly.

Billy McKinney, now sixty-one, had once again been reelected by the 35,000 constituents of House District 35.

In 1988, running uncontested and winning in the 35th didn't quite seem enough, however. Billy McKinney overstepped his boundaries and also took credit for his daughter Cynthia's victory. "If her name were Grandison, she wouldn't have gotten ten votes," he told the local newspaper. "Her name is what put her in this office, because she has forty years of civil rights and political participation, by me, preceding her." Billy McKinney was showing the first signs of strain at being outdistanced by his daughter.

The fact that Cynthia was a daughter, not a son, proved threatening for Billy. "Being the chauvinist that I am, I would rather have had one of my sons decide to be a politician rather than my daughter," he once told reporters, adding, "but I am no less proud of Cynthia and what she is doing." The McKinneys became the only father-daughter state legislature team in the nation. Cynthia lived at home, where she and Billy shared an office in their wood-paneled basement. Although father and daughter were close, Cynthia did not always follow Billy's political lead. Billy was known as the "black redneck" of the Georgia general assembly, and he voted conservatively on issues like the death penalty, gay rights, and welfare, while Cynthia usually took a more liberal stance. In 1990, Cynthia described her complex relationship with her father: "We're friends. We're just political enemies."

In April 1991, Cynthia considered running against her father because her at-large seat would be abolished in 1992. "I have a different constituency," Cynthia told the press. "Mine is a little bit younger and able to knock on more doors." Cynthia later said that her remark was just off the cuff. She never did run against her father, but she had put him on notice.

For over a century, Georgia systematically denied blacks political rights. In 1908, the Georgia legislature passed its Disenfranchisement Act, which limited voter registration to men who had served in the Confederate forces, were descended from confederates, had "good character," could read and write English, or owned forty acres of land. The law was specifically designed to prevent blacks from voting, and it worked. For example, by 1958, in Terrell County, which was 64 percent black, only forty-eight blacks were registered to vote. There were 2,810 whites on the rolls.

On August 6, 1965, the day Lyndon Baines Johnson signed the Voting Rights Act, 27 percent of the voting-age population in Georgia was black, but there were only three black elected officials in the state. Less than a third of the blacks in the state were registered to vote, and in the twenty-three counties where the majority of the voting-age population was black, 16 percent of blacks and 89 percent of whites were registered to vote. By 1980, as a result of the Voting Rights Act, 69 percent of the black voting-age population had registered to vote. By 1990, there were 495 black elected officials in Georgia.

When the Voting Rights Act became law in 1965, the Democratically controlled Georgia state legislature tried to fight it by redistricting to maximize Democratic and white political power while minimizing black influence. In 1971, they divided Atlanta's large metropolitan black population between the 4th and the newly created 5th Congressional District, to guarantee that the 5th District's population would have a white majority. Then they purposefully drew Representative Andrew Young's and Maynard Jackson's houses outside of the 5th District. Young's and Jackson's houses sat one block from the new district line, at a symbolic disadvantage. Georgia has no residency requirement, so Young was able to run in the 44 percent black 5th District, and he won in 1972. Young's ability to gain 25 percent of the white votes in the 5th District became one of the few examples of a black politician in the state of Georgia winning an election in a district with a white majority.

In almost every other election in the state, white voters continued to reject black politicians. Racial-bloc voting was the norm in Georgia. A 1989 survey showed that 86 percent of whites voted for white opponents of black candidates. When Andrew Young ran for mayor of Atlanta in 1981 against a white opponent, he gained only 8.9 percent of the white vote, but because Atlanta's electorate had a black majority, he won.

When it came time for redistricting, in 1981, the general assembly again attempted to dilute black voting strength. Julian Bond, then a Georgia state senator, offered legislation that would make Atlanta's 5th District 6y percent black. The Democratic leadership rejected Bond's plan, and the chairman of the House Reapportionment Committee, Mack Wilson, said at the time, "I don't want to draw nigger districts." But Wilson and his racist colleagues had no choice. They were forced by the Justice Department under the guidelines of the Voting Rights Act to make the 5th Congressional District 65 percent black.

Ten years later, when the 1990 census showed that 27 percent of Georgia's population was black, civil rights activists had new ammunition in their arsenal—the 1982 amendment to the Voting Rights Act, which prevented states from diluting the black vote. With this law in mind,

Cynthia McKinney set her sights on redistricting. The only way to give black citizens a voice, McKinney believed, was to elect African Americans to public office, and the only way to elect blacks in Georgia was to draw black-majority districts.

In July 1991, Cynthia, as a member of the legislature's reapportionment committee, introduced the maximum-black plan, or "Max Plan." Her plan rewrote district lines, significantly expanding the number of state legislature and congressional districts with a population that was more than half black, assuring the election of a black candidate. The Max Plan carved three majority black congressional districts out of a total of eleven, approximately the same number of districts that the black population represented. In 1992, only one out of the ten Congressional districts had a black-majority population.

The Georgia Democratic party resisted Cynthia's plan. In the past, the Georgia state legislature ensured white, Democratic victories by packing congressional districts with large black populations. The almost unanimously Democratic black vote was distributed in approximately 30 percent parcels to each district. A 30 percent black population would hardly ever be big enough for black candidates to win elections, but it ensured white Democratic victories in districts where white voters no longer provided reliable party-line votes. Black-majority districts, on the other hand, created lily-white neighboring districts, which tended to vote Republican.

Reapportionment committee members had made a pact with one another not to second McKinney's motions, and as a result, her redistricting proposals were rarely voted on. Half the black caucus in the general assembly supported the Democratic leadership rather than McKinney.

The Max Plan threatened some black incumbents by creating more black-majority state representative districts,
which decreased the percentage of black populations in
each district. In some cases, black-majority districts that
were formerly 85 percent black were redrawn with only a
60 percent black margin. Some of McKinney's black
opponents were also political insiders who had gained
leadership positions or committee chairmanships and
therefore had a personal stake in toeing the party line.

Democratic leaders wanted Cynthia silenced, and they
asked Billy to intervene. For twenty years, the assembly leadership had deliberately punished Billy by never giving him
a committee chairmanship. Billy was near retirement, and
tired of being a renegade. He wanted power, a title, something to give him some recognition before he bowed out.
The leadership dangled the possibility of a chairmanship.
Billy took the bait, but he realized he was speaking from
his own experience as he lectured his daughter. He warned
Cynthia that if she didn't compromise, she would become
an outcast. "I'm labeled a radical and a troublemaker," he
told Cynthia. "I want you to excel, to do more than I did,
to be bigger in politics than I was. If you challenge the system like I did, it will stymie your growth." Despite Billy's
warnings, Cynthia went on following in his footsteps. A
year later, after the reapportionment fight was over, Billy
shook his head in proud disbelief: "God, white folks hate
her. They hate her guts."

Cynthia didn't back down from the Max Plan, nor did
she listen to Billy. "I couldn't tolerate him trying to shut
me up," she later recalled; besides, she could afford to
make enemies. She wasn't running for reelection to the
general assembly, so she had nothing to lose. She didn't
need the Democratic leadership to help her get ahead.

Cynthia also bore a personal grudge: fiercely loyal to Billy, Cynthia was bent on exacting retribution. "Everything I did in the general assembly had to do with my father," she would later explain. "There was no way I could walk into the House chamber and look at [Speaker] Tom Murphy and not remember what he did to my dad. Murphy is the protector of the old order of the South. He is the protector of those who prize prejudice. Murphy kept my dad down."

Cynthia didn't hesitate to use her gender to full advantage. Her male colleagues called her "abrasive" and "nit-picking." In a man, her confrontational style would have been considered even more explosive. Cynthia wasn't always taken seriously by her Southern gentleman colleagues—an insult that served as an asset. "It's a lot easier for men to mistreat other men intentionally than it is for men to mistreat a woman intentionally," McKinney would later reason. She reveled in the freedom that her gender gave her to challenge the status quo. "If a black man did the same things I did, he would be six feet under." The men in the Georgia statehouse didn't know how to defend themselves against this young, smart, black, aggressive, well-educated woman who was shaking up their political system. McKinney would continue to employ these assets as a congresswoman.

Cynthia loved to lord her knowledge of the Voting Rights Act over her less sophisticated colleagues. She knew Georgia's demographics better than anyone else on the reapportionment committee. She had spent the past six months poring over census data, working with the ACLU, finding pockets of populations, and drawing intricate district lines. It didn't take long for Cynthia to be labeled "a good ol' boy's worst nightmare."

In August, just weeks after McKinney unveiled the Max Plan, the reapportionment committee approved its first redistricting map. The plan created only six more black-majority state legislature seats and one new black-majority congressional district. "It's good ol' boy politics as usual," McKinney said at the time. She threatened to slap a lawsuit on the general assembly if the U.S. Department of Justice didn't reject the plan first.

As McKinney had hoped, the Department of Justice, which by law must approve redistricting plans in sixteen states, including Georgia, rejected Georgia's first proposal. The DOJ sent the plan back to the general assembly and asked them to do just what McKinney had proposed—draw more black-majority districts. The Justice Department also rejected the state's second plan, which drew only two black-majority congressional districts, claiming that the plan submerged significant concentrations of black population. Democrats in Georgia cried foul, blaming the rejection on a Republican conspiracy. President George Bush's administration's interests were not civil rights, but Republican political gain in the South, the Georgia Democrats said. They accused Cynthia and the civil rights community of acting as Republican pawns. In fact, the Voting Rights Act did help the interests of both blacks and Republicans, and Cynthia had secretly made use of the Republican party's computer system when she drew up part of the Max Plan. But McKinney never worked directly with Republican legislators, and Republicans on the reapportionment committee did not support the Max Plan and rarely voted with her.

When the Justice Department rejected Georgia's second redistricting plan, Cynthia knew that the state would have no choice but to draw three black-majority congressional districts. McKinney's notoriety on the reapportionment committee had made her famous statewide and very popular in the black community. She feared that black politicians who had not advocated three black-majority congressional districts would take advantage of the new seat, so she went to Representative Tyrone Brooks, her forty-six-year-old mentor and partner on the Max Plan. McKinney asked Brooks to run for Congress, but Brooks refused. His candidacy would be divisive, he said. White voters wouldn't support him because he was too much of an outspoken civil rights advocate. Brooks encouraged McKinney to run instead: she deserved the seat because she had fought to create it, and she, better than he, could bridge the gap between black and white voters. Brooks also told McKinney that she should run because she was a woman. "It's about time for us black men to take a back seat to black women," Brooks told McKinney.

But not everyone agreed with Tyrone Brooks. Many members of the African-American community in Georgia were angry that a black woman like Anita Hill would betray her race and try to impede a black man's chance to sit on the nation's highest court. McKinney sympathized with Hill. "I believed every word Anita Hill said," McKinney later recalled. "People will do anything to discredit someone who is telling an unpleasant truth. I've been there."

Anita Hill provided a moral context for McKinney's decision to run for Congress. "Anita Hill's strength gave me strength," McKinney said. "The Hill hearings made me feel that it was my time." Because of the divided feelings about Hill in the African-American community, McKinney would not mention Anita Hill's name on the campaign trail. But she took Hill as her own guardian angel, and no one could avoid the comparison: McKinney, like Hill, was something new in the political landscape, a young, highly educated, well-spoken black woman challenging the white male political establishment.

On December 26, 1991, Cynthia McKinney officially announced that she would run for the U.S. Congress in Georgia's newly created 11th District. In April 1992, the Georgia general assembly acquiesced to the Justice Department's requirement that it draw three black-majority congressional districts. McKinney left the reapportionment fight a victor and hit the campaign trail.

In the beginning, Cynthia's campaign was nothing more than a mom-and-pop shop. Billy McKinney served as campaign manager and treasurer, and his campaign cochair was Margie Pitts Hames, Cynthia's close friend and a feminist activist. Cynthia's boyfriend, Muhammad Jamal, was assistant treasurer. Campaign headquarters consisted of an empty room in a former Pizza Hut building. Two filing cabinets and a piece of plywood constituted the campaign's one desk.

Adam Hames, twenty-three, a 1991 graduate of American University and Margie Pitts Hames' son, became the campaign's first volunteer. Stealing a campaign slogan from Texas Governor Ann Richards, Hames painted signs that read: "Vote for Cynthia McKinney on July 21st—Why Not a Woman?" Every morning during Atlanta's rush hour, Hames and the campaign's four other volunteers would stand on a hill near the Panola Road exit of I-20 in Lithonia and wave their signs at commuters. For three months, Hames' signs remained the campaign's only advertising.

In the overwhelmingly Democratic 11th district, with a population that was 64 percent black, the African-American candidate with the most votes in the July 21 Democratic primary would be the likely winner in November. No one believed McKinney had a chance against her toughest opponents, state representative and black caucus chairman Michael Thurmond, and state senator Eugene Walker, and as a result, no one gave Cynthia money. Walker, who was chairman of the Senate Reapportionment Committee, had been endorsed by Governor Zell Miller. But McKinney's advantage was grassroots support. Her reapportionment campaign had galvanized the black community, who organized for her in churches, neighborhood groups, and local civil rights organizations. McKinney organized the grass roots by tirelessly touring the unwieldy 256-mile-long district, which stretched from the Atlanta suburbs across former plantation country to coastal Savannah.

The woman that pundits expected to represent Georgia in the U.S. Congress was Cathy Steinberg, a state legislator running in Georgia's 4th Congressional District. Steinberg demonstrated that women candidates could raise serious money. EMILY's List would raise $133,531 for Steinberg, who ultimately lost her race. But in a Catch-22 characteristic of first races, EMILY's List refused to donate money to Cynthia's campaign before the July 21 primary because Cynthia had not raised enough money to prove that she was a serious candidate. "We were trying to figure out, is there a campaign there?" EMILY's List president Ellen Malcolm later explained. "One way to find out is by how much money the candidate has raised. A lot of candidates have grassroots support, but it's hard to get a sense of what's going on in a rural district where you have such low-budget campaigns."

On a typical day on the campaign trail, Cynthia walked from one crumbling apartment to another at a public housing project in rural Screven County, a predominantly white community, talking to people about their concerns and encouraging them to register to vote. She spoke at three churches there and used the same opening lines each time: "My name is Cynthia McKinney. First let me state the obvious. I am a woman. I am an African American. And I am a candidate for Congress. What you may not know about me is that I am a fighter." She soothed the county's resentment of being included in the 11th Congressional District, invoking images of the Los Angeles race riots of late April. "I am the only candidate in this race that can bring a healing touch to our state and to our nation," McKinney said. "Throughout history, it has always been the women who bound up the wounds of the soldiers, who cared for the sick, who raised the children and taught them the difference between right and wrong. I am a candidate for Congress because I want to bring healing to Georgia, and I want your help." McKinney stressed domestic issues in her speeches. Her priorities were to improve education, health care, and economic development for the poor and disfranchised.

Despite her conciliatory stump speech, Cynthia's advisers worried that the conservative rural voters in the 11th District would be turned off by her image. In the South, the word "feminist" was a term of contempt. Feminists were perceived as radicals, as man haters, and McKinney's image verged on militant. According to a poll the McKinney campaign conducted in June, voters in the 11th District thought Cynthia was "aggressive," "outspoken," and a "change agent." Though McKinney was as charming and flirtatious as she was fearless and confrontational, voters clearly didn't know her softer side.

Part of her image problem may have been attributed to her personal style. As an adult, Cynthia had always worn her hair in a crown of braids, refusing to take the more conventional route of straightening it. Her father and other campaign advisers worried that voters would not get past Cynthia's hairstyle, and that she would "scare white folk." In her 1988 state legislature campaign, Cynthia had bowed to pressure from her father to straighten her hair and wear conservative clothes. After winning the '88 election, she again wore her hair braided, and in 1992 refused to change, ignoring her advisers' counsel. "White people know I'm black and there's nothing I can do about it," Cynthia explained. "Why can't you be natural and proud of who you are and what you look like, and not be threatening?"

In early July, two weeks before the primary, the campaign had only $2,000 in the bank. Bill Fletcher, the media consultant, needed $20,000 to air a series of radio ads that would target black voters. The campaign had set its sights on McKinney's two black opponents, Thurmond and Walker, in hopes of capturing the largest percentage of black votes to guarantee McKinney a place in the runoff. In Georgia, if the winner of the primary wins less than 50 percent of the vote, the top two contenders must hold a runoff election. Bill Fletcher had advised McKinney to ignore the white candidate, funeral director and former Waynesboro Mayor George DeLoach, because Georgia's pattern of racial-bloc voting assured that white Democrats would vote for DeLoach. McKinney could take on DeLoach in the runoff when she had a monopoly on the black vote.

But in order to air radio commercials, the campaign needed money. The Women's Campaign Fund and NOW had donated a few thousand dollars to McKinney, but EMILY's List had determined that McKinney's candidacy was too great a long shot and hadn't given her a cent. In a last-ditch effort, Margie Pitts Hames called her clients. In 1972, Hames had argued the Georgia companion case to *Roe v. Wade*—known as *Doe v. Bolton*—in front of the Georgia supreme court. Now Hames worked as the legal counsel to Georgia's abortion clinics. Hames gave the clinics a hard sell on Cynthia. Cynthia, she argued, was the only candidate in the race who would stick her neck out for a woman's right to choose. Eugene Walker and Michael Thurmond were pro-choice, but they weren't as committed to the issues as Cynthia was. Some of the clinics owed Hames legal fees, which she forfeited in return for contributions to McKinney's campaign. Within a week, fifteen $1,000 checks had arrived in the mail.

On July 14, seven days before the primary, the McKinney campaign bought $14,000 worth of airtime on black radio stations in Atlanta, Augusta, and Savannah during drive time and gospel hours. Two messages were transmitted: one soft, aiming to increase McKinney's "positives," followed by an attack ad. Andrew Young, the civil rights leader, was featured in both. Young had not always been a fan of Billy McKinney's. But he had watched Cynthia McKinney develop as a politician over the past four years, and he believed she had star potential. So when Cynthia asked Young to endorse her candidacy, he agreed.

The attack ad hit McKinney's opponents right where the campaign's poll showed they were the most vulnerable: "I've always been a fighter for civil rights, for jobs, and for justice," Young's voice-over said, "and that's why I'm supporting Cynthia McKinney. . . . When the state tried to limit black influence by drawing only two black-majority congressional districts, Cynthia McKinney fought the state plan and helped force the creation of a third district.

"Her opponents were too quick to compromise and supported the state plan, which the Justice Department rejected. Cynthia McKinney is the only candidate in the race who has been consistent in her support of the three black-majority districts."

A week before the primary, the McKinney campaign aired an even tougher radio spot that was designed to take advantage of what Bill Fletcher called "the trust gap"—the voters' tendency to trust female candidates more than they trust men. "You can tell a lot about a man by the way they act when they think no one is watching," the ad began. "And what we can tell about Senator Gene Walker and Representative Mike Thurmond is that they can't be trusted. . . . Walker and Thurmond sold out black voters by going along with the good old boys who wanted to limit our influence by drawing only two black-majority congressional districts instead of the three we deserved.

"Gene Walker and Mike Thurmond sold out their black constituents in return for political support and campaign contributions. . . ."

Thurmond and Walker avoided negative radio and television ads. Neither man wanted to fall into the trap of looking as though they were beating up on the only woman in the race. McKinney's damaging radio ads dominated the airwaves for five crucial days before the primary, but on primary day, she was still the underdog. Eugene Walker had spent $154,676, Michael Thurmond had spent $36,268, and McKinney trailed with $33,694. Pundits predicted that she would come in third out of a field of five candidates. Eugene Walker rented a hotel ballroom for his victory party, where all the Atlanta television stations set up their camera crews. Only one reporter came to McKinney headquarters at the former Pizza Hut in South De Kalb County. By midnight, the television crews had missed the story. Walker came in third behind George DeLoach, a white candidate who had garnered most of the district's white vote. Cynthia led the pack with 31.2 percent of the vote.

Billy McKinney couldn't bring himself to give his daughter credit for her upset victory. "She beat a man who had the governor, all of the bankers, all of the money," Billy would say in an interview a year later. "It was a race between Billy McKinney and Eugene Walker and Michael Thurmond. It wasn't about Cynthia, it couldn't be about Cynthia." Cynthia, knowing that Billy could not have won the election, shrugged off her father's wounded ego. True, she had benefited from his name recognition and reputation in the black community, but she brought more to the campaign. Cynthia attracted white female voters because of her gender, and white gay supporters because of her liberal stand on gay rights. Her charm, her smarts, and her sophistication had given her an entrée into a political arena that had been out of reach for her father.

Two days later, on July 23, EMILY's List donated $10,000 to McKinney's campaign. On August 11, capturing 56 percent of the vote, McKinney won the runoff against DeLoach. Her victory was tantamount to winning the general election.

That night, every microphone seemed to have Billy McKinney's name on it. "Can you believe we won?" he exclaimed over and over. "I'm ecstatic," he exclaimed, and when the first person didn't quite seem adequate for the historic occasion, he declared: "This is Billy's dream." Cynthia, meanwhile, had arrived at campaign headquarters to give her acceptance speech. She was radiant. Billy stood by her side. Cynthia announced that her congressional campaign would be dedicated to her father—to his three failed congressional bids. She told supporters, "Daddy never gave up after twenty years of fighting. I guess it really has come full circle."

In the next six weeks, she raised over $100,000. Pat Schroeder and Rosa Parks campaigned for Cynthia, as did Governor Zell Miller. In just one month, McKinney had advanced from a "solid underdog to the darling of the party establishment." The *Atlanta Constitution* called McKinney's campaign a "reversal of fortune."

On November 3, with a stunning 73 percent of the vote, Cynthia trounced Republican Woodrow Lovett, a white farmer. She had outspent Lovett ten to one, and most of all had benefited from being a black Democrat in a heavily black and Democratic district. But the truest measure of the reversal of the McKinneys' fortunes came weeks later, when Cynthia hired Andrea Young, the thirty-seven-year-old daughter of Andrew Young, to be her administrative assistant on the Hill. Through years of struggle in the civil rights movement, Andrew Young had been the coolheaded leader and Billy McKinney the hotheaded rabble rouser. Now, with Andrea Young working for Cynthia McKinney, the McKinneys were, for the moment, leading the way.

On election night, in a live television interview at campaign headquarters, Billy told the Atlanta viewing public, "This is my seat." To which Cynthia responded graciously, "Yes, but I'm going to be sitting in it."

3

The Women's Caucus Convenes

Never before had women's numbers in Congress increased by more than five in one election year. The Hill-Thomas hearings served as a reminder that Congress was inhabited by men capable of belittling women and their concerns. The firestorm of anger that the hearings ignited propelled women into the political arena. Not only did more women run for national office, but more money was raised for women candidates, and more women voted for women candidates than ever before. The Year of the Woman had made false starts in 1972, 1984, and 1988, but 1992 finally produced the goods. In 1990, only 70 women had run for Congress in the general election. Two years later, 224 women ran for the House in the primaries, 108 in the general election.

In the months following Anita Hill's Senate appearance, organizations that funded women candidates saw their coffers swell. EMILY's List proved the most dramatic example. The donor network increased its membership rolls from 3,000 at the time Hill testified to 24,000 on election day, one year later. The List donated $6.2 million to women candidates in 1992; it had given away $1.5 million in 1990. Anita Hill's impact on the public's perception of the scarcity of women in Congress had single-handedly turned EMILY's List into a campaign powerhouse.

All told, political action committees that gave to women candidates in 1992 increased their combined giving from $2.7 million in 1990 to $11.5 million, allowing half the female congressional candidates to outspend their opponents. In 1992, for the first time, women candidates could compete financially with men.

More women candidates and more money to fund them coincided with another important political factor: there were 91 open seats in the House, four times more than in the previous election year. New seats had been created by the decennial redrawing of district lines following the 1990 census, and by a rash of resignations due to the House Bank scandal. The House had not been open to so many newcomers since 1948.

Thirty-nine women candidates, in 1992, ran for open seats, thus avoiding the challenge posed by well-funded incumbents. In 1990, only seven women had run for open seats. But in 1992, twenty of the twenty-four freshwomen House members won in open districts. Two female candidates also beat incumbents in the Democratic primaries, and two in the general election. Women also benefited from the fact that 1992 was the first post–Cold War election, and domestic issues like education, health care, and jobs dominated the debate. This rare confluence of political circumstances reached a crescendo on Election Day, when women voters constituted 54 percent of the voting public and women voted for female candidates in greater numbers than in any previous election.

The small basement hearing room, usually subdued, buzzed with women's voices. The date was January 6, 1993. Men appeared only on the walls: a gallery of three-piece suits, mustaches, and grave expressions painted in crisp brush strokes—committee chairmen of congresses past. Today, Pat Schroeder, the fifty-two-year-old "dean" of the congresswomen, made quite a different picture.

She was tall, a big-boned woman with a broad, handsome face. She had high cheekbones, thick salt-and-pepper hair. Sitting at the head of the table with Olympia Snowe, Schroeder's Republican cochair of the Congressional Caucus on Women's Issues, Schroeder looked as though she had arrived at the pinnacle of her political power. This year, the congresswomen's ranks had increased from 29 to 48 in the House, and from 2 to 6 in the Senate. After winning a special election, Kay Bailey Hutchison would later bring the number of women in the Senate to 7. Women could now act as a voting bloc, powerful enough to sway the outcome of a piece of legislation. More women in Congress meant more clout for Schroeder: more votes and more voices supporting the issues she cared about. Schroeder's chief power base, the women's caucus, had doubled in size, with freshwomen making up 22 of its 42 voluntary members. But for Schroeder there was a downside: she would now have to share the spotlight.

The women's caucus was on the brink of its most successful congressional session ever. On this January morning, along with familiar faces like Illinois's Cardiss Collins,

New York's Nita Lowey, and Jan Meyers of Kansas, there were many new ones. Into the room walked San Francisco's fifty-five-year-old media darling Lynn Woolsey, a former welfare mother turned personnel executive. Nydia Velazquez, a thirty-nine-year-old Puerto Rican who had snatched her New York district out from under nine-term congressman Stephen Solarz, followed. Next came Carrie Meek, of Miami, who had worked her way through college as a domestic servant and the first African American to represent Florida in 129 years. Here was Karan English, whose foray onto the basketball court in the men-only congressional gym would be chronicled in the *New York Times,* and North Carolina's Eva Clayton, the president of the 110-strong freshman class, had become a leading mouthpiece for the celebrated class of '92. Karen Shepherd, the fifty-three-year-old Democrat from Salt Lake City, arrived cool and collected. Virginia's daring Leslie Byrne entered next, followed by Cynthia McKinney, who bounced into the room wearing gold tennis shoes.

Here was the new species of women delivered to Congress by the Year of the Woman. They were feminists and proud of it. They were elected in their own right, not as fill-ins for their late husbands. They had come to represent women, and they were comfortable being women in a man's institution. In the past, "women members would go around saying I'm not *just* a woman," Schroeder recalled. "They were always a little hesitant about how much time they were spending on women's issues, because they didn't want people to think that that was all they were doing." What encouraged Schroeder about the new women was that they had come to Congress ready to take a stand on women's issues.

The freshwomen filled the room with energy and direction, eager to work together to empower the caucus. In December, they had held a press conference to announce they were all pro-choice. All twenty-four freshwomen (three of whom were Republicans) declared that they supported the Family and Medical Leave Act, as well as full funding of Head Start and an end to sexual harassment in Congress. The group vowed to work together to pass the Freedom of Choice Act, codifying *Roe v. Wade*. Incredibly, in its sixteen-year history the women's caucus had never taken a position on abortion. But today, the new women in the room were all pro-choice.

Pat Schroeder had helped elect many of these women. She had flown to their districts, starred in their fundraisers. She had stepped up to every microphone and said: *Congress would be a better place if more women were elected.* In the previous Congress, Schroeder had had a virtual monopoly of the airwaves. Reporters gravitated to Schroeder for a pithy quote, interviewing her when they needed a story about women, children, or military issues. She was a sharp-tongued critic who could speak in nonstop sound bites. Washington recognized Schroeder more for her glibness than her intellect. She would always be better known for coining the phrase "Teflon president" during the Reagan years than for authoring the Family and Medical Leave bill in 1985. The average American hardly knew there *were* other women in Congress. Women like Louise Slaughter, Barbara Kennelly, and Connie Morella found themselves essentially anonymous outside their home districts and beyond the Beltway.

Schroeder had become a spokeswoman for all feminist women across the country. After twenty years of hard work, she was the most high-profile, quotable female politician in the nation. But now here were the freshwomen of 1992 on ABC, on CBS, on CNN—all of them getting credit for changing Congress twenty years after Schroeder had broken the ice for women on the Hill.

Pat Schroeder's childhood prepared her well for politics. Patricia Nell Scott was born in Portland, Oregon, in 1940. Her family moved six times before she graduated from high school in Des Moines, Iowa. Tall for her age, with thick eyeglasses, Pat was habitually the awkward newcomer in town. Each time her family moved, she would line her toys up on the sidewalk in front of her new house in hopes of attracting the interest of neighboring children.

Pat's mother, a schoolteacher, always worked. Her father, a pilot, opened his own aviation insurance business. Both of Pat's parents had grown up on Nebraska farms during the Depression; they brought independent thinking to their parenting. "I was raised in a family where no one said, 'You can't do that,' " Schroeder remembered. As such, she earned her pilot's license at the age of sixteen. While working to pay tuition, she graduated Phi Beta Kappa from the University of Minnesota in three years. Pat's parents didn't blink an eye when she told them she wanted to go to law school. In 1961, she enrolled at Harvard Law School as one of 19 women among 554 students. On her first day of class, the two men sitting on either side of her demanded that their seats be changed. They complained that they had never sat next to a girl in their entire academic careers and didn't plan to start at Harvard Law. Schroeder found

Harvard Law good preparation for Congress: when she first arrived on the Hill, she was one of 15 women among 535 men.

A few weeks after Schroeder was first elected to Congress, in 1972, Bella Abzug called to welcome Schroeder to the 93rd Congress. Abzug could not resist asking: How would Schroeder manage to do her job with two young children at home? At the time, Schroeder's daughter was two and her son was six. She was the first woman with young children to serve in Congress.

Abzug knew that on Capitol Hill there was no time for anything but the job. Congresswoman was no nine-to-five position—it absorbed one's entire life. But Schroeder refused to abandon her family. "My bottom line was, you always figure that when the train stops, and you gotta get off it, the only people in the station will be your family," she said. "Anybody who thinks this job is permanent and forever has missed the point. If you shove your family out the door, and haven't done a good job with them, then what have you really accomplished?"

Schroeder was determined to be both a good mother and a good member of Congress, even if it meant being torn. As late as 1993, Schroeder came late to an interview because she was buying traveler's checks for her daughter, Jamie, who was on her way to teach English in China. When Jamie was younger, Schroeder had missed more serious appointments. One former staffer remembers being very upset when Schroeder skipped an important subcommittee hearing because she had to take Jamie shopping for shoes. "She was always in a lot of emotional turmoil over these choices," said the staffer. "She spent so much time worrying about her duties as a mother."

Schroeder rarely revealed the guilt she suffered in those early years. She tried instead to include her children as much as possible in every phase of her life on the Hill, bringing them to press conferences, holding birthday parties in her office while the House was in session, and even toilet-training Jamie in the office bathroom. She brought both children along on official overseas trips, taking them to Geneva for the SALT Disarmament Conference in 1973. She signed up for congressional delegation trips to Thailand, where her husband had business, and to China, where her daughter lived.

Schroeder always managed to present the lighthearted view of the life of the congresswoman as mother. "After I was elected, I realized I had to set priorities," she remembered. "And I did: my family and my job. I stopped worrying about other details." Cooking, she said merrily, had never been her strong suit, and her favorite recipe was "Domino's phone number." Schroeder learned that her children didn't care who made the beds, who did the laundry, or who did the grocery shopping. "In fact," she added, "they don't care if anyone does it."

Pat and her husband, Jim, a lawyer whom she met at Harvard Law School, had live-in help. They split child-rearing duties. "Where do we get this notion," Schroeder asked, "that we have to be there all the time entertaining our children?" Schroeder still believed in the concept of quality time. The mystery was why "we think that our breathing the same air in the same house is going to make their lives different."

Schroeder's early decision to tweak the establishment in Congress, starting with her *Redbook* interview, came partly from her belief that she would never be let inside. "I suppose some women think they have penetrated the club. I mean, you can get things done, but you're never in." But by the mid-eighties, Schroeder's complaints of clubbiness and institutional sexism had become an excuse. The real reason Schroeder had not become an insider was that she herself resisted compromise. In a system that operates on the credo "I'll scratch your back if you scratch mine," Schroeder seemed habitually unable to do any scratching. She became a loner, making enemies of the very people who should have been her natural allies.

In 1985, Schroeder shot herself in the foot when she voted against a pro-labor plant-closing amendment. Her vote alienated the chairmen of the Post Office Committee and the Education and Labor Committee, Augustus Hawkins and William Ford. Schroeder had just recently introduced the Family and Medical Leave Act, and Hawkins and Ford were just the men Schroeder needed to help her pass it. But the chairmen felt betrayed by her vote against their pet bill, which had been narrowly defeated. She became a pariah in those two committees, and in turn, the family-leave bill languished.

When it came to working with the Democratic leadership, Schroeder's independent streak made her incapable of being a team player. Whenever the most politically volatile issues of pay raises, perks, and franked mail came up, Schroeder almost uniformly voted against them. Since she was considered to have one of the safest seats in Congress—she won reelections by margins as large as 70 percent—Schroeder's refusal to make a seemingly principled political sacrifice looked self-serving to her colleagues. In 1989, Schroeder voted against a pay raise and ethics package that increased congressional salaries by 40

percent but prohibited members from pocketing honoraria given to them by special interests. Vic Fazio, a liberal
Californian and an ally of Schroeder's on abortion and
other issues, had put a compromise package together.
Schroeder, who annually earned among the highest
amounts of honoraria in Congress, looked hypocritical
when she took the holier-than-thou position of opposing
the pay raise. "I've always been hard to paper-train,"
Schroeder said later about her relationship with the
Democratic leadership.

Schroeder's stubborn independence often got under the
skin of her peers. Her vote against Fazio looked as if "this
is a woman who was so self-righteous that she couldn't give
an inch to someone who came up with a reasonable compromise," said a former senior Democratic leadership aide.
"It just stuck in everybody's craw." *Roll Call*, the Capitol Hill
newspaper, listed Schroeder on its "Dishonor Roll," accusing her and others who voted against the measure of
"political cowardice." The Democratic caucus also denounced Schroeder. Schroeder went back to Denver and
portrayed herself to the local press as an innocent victim
of a corrupt power structure. "I'm not sure if she voted the
way she did because she was principled as much as it was
good press," said a former Schroeder staffer.

Among the Democratic leadership, Schroeder developed a reputation for being unreliable and undepend-
able, a "high-maintenance" member who had to be
lobbied heavily on pay and perk bills. "She alienates the
Democratic party leadership because she won't vote with
them," said a former leadership aide. "She trashes the
leadership in the press and then asks them for favors."

Yet Schroeder's refusal to "go along to get along" may
have been the best thing she could have done for her

career. It bolstered her public persona both nationally and in her district, where she had never been challenged by a serious opponent. Her sheer staying power became the ultimate sign of her true success, because it helped her achieve power by an alternate route: seniority.

Schroeder's resistance to team play soon became evident at the January women's caucus meeting.

Abruptly, no more than eight minutes into the meeting, Schroeder signaled the vote for caucus officials. Some of the women were still finding their seats. Some had not yet arrived. Following Schroeder's lead, Marilyn Lloyd, a sixty-four-year-old conservative Democrat from Chattanooga, raised her voice over the clatter of conversation and made the motion to reelect last year's leadership slate: Schroeder and Snowe as cochairs, Cardiss Collins as secretary, and Marcy Kaptur as treasurer. Connie Morella, a liberal Republican from Montgomery County, Maryland, seconded the motion. Freshwoman Marjorie Margolies-Mezvinsky was expected to join Morella, but she was nowhere to be found. With a low-pitched "aye," the caucus agreed to the motion. For the twelfth year, Pat Schroeder would keep her place at the head of the table. It would be Olympia Snowe's tenth year in the job.

And yet the meeting had literally just begun. How had this all happened so fast? Margolies-Mezvinsky arrived minutes after the vote had been cast. Justifiably stunned, she would later argue, "No one gets to those meetings on time." Cynthia McKinney, too, was amazed. She wanted to reelect Schroeder, but she had also hoped to participate in the caucus. The whole affair reminded McKinney of how things operated in the Georgia general assembly—deals cut in smoke-filled rooms behind closed doors.

Cynthia McKinney and her fellow freshwomen had just spent the month of December acquainting themselves with Congress and its strict seniority system. Although some freshwomen got plum committee assignments—Carrie Meek pulled Appropriations, and Marjorie Margolies-Mezvinsky, Lynn Schenk, and Blanche Lambert snatched Energy and Commerce—they all found themselves on the bottom of the seniority ladder. At the very least, it would take even the most successful of the freshwomen ten to twenty years before they would see real power in the House. Frustrated, the freshwomen had hoped that the women's caucus would be different. Women, they believed, would not buy into antiquated rules. McKinney, for one, had faith in her fellow women members. Women, she felt sure, would be more democratic, less hierarchical.

Freshwoman Leslie Byrne heard the message loud and clear. Schroeder and Snowe seemed to be saying, "This is the way we've done it in the past, and this is the way we're going to do it now." Byrne had had higher hopes for this momentous first meeting, hopes that had been briefly encouraged by Louise Slaughter.

Slaughter, a sixty-three-year-old Democrat from Rochester, New York, arrived late and sat down next to Byrne. Full-figured with a head of wavy auburn hair, a square jaw, and sparkling blue eyes, Slaughter gave the thirteen new faces at the table a long, hard look. Then she breathed a sigh of relief and whispered to Byrne, "I feel like the cavalry has just arrived."

After the rapid-fire elections, Karen Shepherd piped up. No one had voiced objections yet. Shepherd complained that the caucus leadership should include freshwomen. Nancy Pelosi, a fourth-term Californian, asked if the by-laws could be reviewed and discussed at the caucus's next meeting. Her question posed a direct threat to Schroeder, because the women's caucus did not have "rotating" chairs. Other caucuses rotated their chairmen every two years so most members had a chance to serve in the top position. Maxine Waters, a two-term black Californian, ob-served the need for more racial diversity in the caucus's leadership and all-white staff. Cynthia McKinney agreed. There had been only four black women in the caucus in 1992; now there were nine.

Pat Schroeder was taking hits from every side: all of the caucus's constituent groups felt hoodwinked, and they all wanted a piece of Schroeder's job. She tried to appease them by appointing Maxine Waters to head a task force on changing the caucus bylaws. Changing the bylaws, everyone knew, would dethrone Schroeder in the next Congress. This came as no surprise to Schroeder, who ear-lier had resigned herself to the fact that this would be her last term as caucus cochair.

She found this new power struggle ironic. Until now the chairmanship of this caucus had been a thankless job, as Schroeder's twelve-year tenure had coincided with a twelve-year Republican reign in the White House. During the Reagan years, the caucus met only once with the pres-ident—before he took office. Both Reagan and Bush had stiff-armed the women.* Issues that the caucus pro-

*Ronald Reagan met with the women's caucus once, at Blair House, before he was sworn in as president. The caucus sent four letters of request to the White House to meet with President Bush. All were rejected.

moted—family leave, equal pay, day care, and protection from sexual harassment—were at odds with the Republican agenda. When the congresswomen attended a ladies' lunch with Nancy Reagan, they were instructed by the White House not to discuss issues.

With Bill Clinton in the White House, Schroeder knew that issues the congresswomen cared about would be endowed with newfound legitimacy. The women's caucus would at last have a chance to meet with the president in the Oval Office and take its agenda straight to the top. They would work with the president to pass family-leave, medical-leave, and pro-choice legislation that had been stalled for years. They would talk to Clinton about women's health care coverage and funding for breast cancer research.

In 1993, the women on the Hill would also meet with Hillary Rodham Clinton. Politics and policy would be the subject of their discussion, but when the *Washington Post* published a story about the caucus's first gathering with the First Lady, the story ran on the front page of "Style," the section devoted to lifestyle features and cultural happenings. Schroeder was incensed. "The First Lady met last week with forty members of Congress who happen to be female, and the story appeared in the 'Style' section," Schroeder pointed out to Leonard Downie Jr., the *Post*'s managing editor. "The First Lady met several weeks before with a group of members of congress [the black caucus and the hispanic caucus], who happen to be male, and the story appeared in the 'A' section. . . . What gives?"

Although the women's caucus had always been a political backwater, Schroeder had enhanced the caucus's power by forcing bills through resistant committees, onto the front pages of newspapers, and into the hands of naysaying presidents. "We spent the last twelve years beating our heads against a brick wall," said a caucus staffer. "People weren't interested in being caucus cochair because our issues weren't winners." After twelve years of building an expert staff and writing dozens of pieces of legislation, Schroeder, in her independent fashion, had made her job into something worth fighting for.

In 1973, when Pat Schroeder first came to Congress, there was no women's caucus. Nor, to Schroeder's surprise, did the congresswomen meet regularly to discuss women's issues. Ten years after the publication of the feminist movement's manifesto, *The Feminine Mystique,* and six years after the formation of the National Organization for Women, the women's movement had scarcely reached Capitol Hill. The fifteen congresswomen were divided on feminism, with New York's Bella Abzug and Missouri's Leonor Sullivan representing polar opposites. In Congress, Abzug's famous feisty style proved to be a liability; her abrasiveness alienated fellow representatives, as well as the more old-fashioned of her female colleagues.

Leonor Sullivan was the quintessential old-fashioned congresswoman in the tradition of Margaret Chase Smith. She was a senior Democrat from Missouri, elected to fill her late husband's seat in 1953. By the mid-seventies, she had become a powerful insider, chairing the Committee on Merchant Marine and Fisheries. Sullivan had been the only female member of the House to vote against the ERA. She explained her no vote by saying, "There are differences between male and female roles in our society and I hope there always are."

Naturally, Sullivan and Abzug clashed. "Each had a firm idea of what a woman should be," one observer noted, "and the gulf between these views simply couldn't be bridged." Sullivan believed that bringing attention to gender harmed women's chances of gaining respect from their male colleagues. Abzug believed just the opposite, and imposed her feminist agenda on her colleagues. In 1976, Sullivan retired, at seventy-two. That same year, Abzug left the House to run for the Senate, losing to Daniel Patrick Moynihan. The remaining women in the House were free, finally, to launch the women's caucus.

Unlike Schroeder, Louise Slaughter was an unabashed insider. Her seat on the powerful Rules Committee had made her one of the most influential women in the House. Slaughter's maternal manner and her air of warmth belied her ambition and tough political know-how. "She's a combination of Southern charm and backroom politics," an observer once said, "a Southern belle with a cigar in her mouth."

Louise McIntosh was born in 1929 in the steep hill town of Lynch, deep in the heart of eastern Kentucky's Appalachia. The McIntoshes prided themselves on having family roots reaching back to Daniel Boone and Abraham Lincoln. Louise's father, Oscar, worked in the U.S. Steel coal mines and supplemented a meager wage by playing pool. Louise, a child of the Depression, learned to live on a daily diet of beans and corn bread. All the children in town had to line up for typhoid shots because there was no refrigeration for the vaccines, she remembers—there was no electricity.

The Roosevelt administration's New Deal brought dams, electricity, and clean water to Harlan County. The United Mine Workers brought medical care. Louise was born with a rare disease called hemorrhagic purpura, which caused internal bleeding. A UMW doctor saved her life. Louise's older sister, though, was not as lucky and died of pneumonia at age seven.

In 1935, the McIntoshes escaped Harlan County, moving west and out of the mountains to the small town of Monticello, near the Tennessee border. Oscar McIntosh set up his own machine-and-welding shop, leaving the poverty of coal-mine life behind. But Louise never forgot her first five years in Harlan County. Her political outlook was shaped by a strong belief that the federal government and labor unions can be good forces in needy people's lives. "I've always been very keen on government," recalled Slaughter. "If the government hadn't come into eastern Kentucky and brought us wiring and clean water, we probably would have died."

Louise attended the University of Kentucky, where she earned her B.S. in 1951 and her master's degree in public health in 1953. At UK, she worked for the student health service as a technician, drawing blood samples from patients. Louise dreamed of being a doctor, but it was "out of the question back then." No women were enrolled in the University of Kentucky's Medical School. In those days, doctors were men, women were nurses. Louise bitterly remembered that when she worked at the UK hospital in 1954 she had to get off the elevator with all the other nurses whenever a doctor walked on. "It really burned me up."

After college, Louise, who had never been north of Cincinnati, traveled across the country, interviewing suburban housewives as a market research representative for Procter & Gamble. Wearing a dress, a hat, and white gloves, Louise walked door to door asking women to compare different brands of laundry detergent and cake mix.

The job proved to be good preparation: twenty years later, Slaughter would get her start in politics by making strangers feel comfortable—shaking hands, knocking on doors.

During her travels with Procter & Gamble, Louise met Bob Slaughter, an Air Force officer, at a hotel swimming pool in San Antonio, Texas. Within ten months, they had married and moved north to Rochester, New York, where Bob went to work for the American Can Company, and later, Kodak. Slaughter settled down to fifteen years as a housewife and mother of three girls. "I was a Southern woman," she said. "I understood the perfect order of things: men were in charge and were most certainly better, and they needed a lot of attention."

Slaughter took her role as housewife seriously. She knew every recipe in *The Betty Crocker Cookbook*. She filled dozens of mason jars with pickled vegetables, took flower-arranging classes and guitar lessons, played the piano, and learned to tailor. Slaughter sewed all her daughters' clothes, including their winter coats. She sewed Bob's ties and jackets, and she knitted sweaters. She pushed her daughters to fulfill her own unrealized dreams. "I really wanted my middle daughter to be a doctor," Slaughter said. "But I think I pushed too hard and she rebelled."

By the 1970s, Slaughter began realizing some of her own ambition. In 1971, she and Bob led a citizens' campaign opposing the development of a fourteen-acre forest of rare beech trees across the street from their house. The effort failed, but that year, aided by the momentum of the tree-saving campaign, Slaughter ran for the Monroe County legislature. The local newspapers described her as an "ecology-minded housewife." She lost, but ran again, managing the campaign from her kitchen, staffing it with women from the neighborhood, and financing it with garage sales.

On her third try, in 1975, she was elected to the county legislature and found her voice just as the feminist movement swept the nation. When Slaughter won a seat in the U.S. House of Representatives, in 1986, she was fifty-seven and an old hand at local politics. Her husband Bob would soon retire from his job at Kodak, and the Slaughters' marriage would undergo a role reversal: Louise would become the primary breadwinner as Bob took charge of their family's domestic life.

By the time Slaughter came to Washington, she had defeated three incumbent male politicians for three different offices over the course of eleven years. Slaughter had served on the county legislature, and as a political appointee in Governor Cuomo's administration. She had run Cuomo's campaigns for governor and Morris Udall's campaign for president in Monroe County. She had served four years in the New York Assembly in Albany. Slaughter had become a political animal.

At the January women's caucus meeting, she proposed that for the first time in its history, the women's caucus adopt a pro-choice position on abortion. Loud shouts of agreement answered Slaughter's motion. The freshwomen, some of whom had been elected precisely because they were pro-choice, considered "choice" a critical civil right for women. It stunned them that the caucus, as a group, had never taken a position on choice.

Slaughter, Schroeder, and the other veteran women in the room knew why. In the last two congressional sessions, most of the women in the caucus were pro-choice, with two important exceptions: Lindy Boggs and Mary Rose

Oakar. Boggs, the venerable representative from New Orleans and the widow of former majority leader Hale Boggs, was pro-life and Catholic. So was Oakar, a tough insider from Ohio who between 1985 and 1989 had been the only female member in the Democratic leadership. These two popular women had earned so much clout in the House and the women's caucus that no one dared fracture the women's solidarity over an issue on which they disagreed. After serving in Congress for seventeen years, Boggs retired in 1990. Oakar lost her bid for reelection in 1992; she had overdrawn her account at the House bank too many times, and was eventually indicted. With Oakar's exit from the scene, many congresswomen privately rejoiced. As one congresswoman's staffer put it, "we were dancing in the streets." The women could now make abortion what it should be: a woman's issue.

The decision to be pro-choice was a given. The real challenge was resolving where the caucus should stand on the Freedom of Choice Act. The bill, known as FOCA, would ensure a woman's right to an abortion in every state in the nation by writing *Roe v. Wade* into law. During the Reagan and Bush administrations, an increasingly conservative Supreme Court had allowed states to apply more and more restrictions to abortion availability. FOCA was first introduced in 1989 in reaction to *Webster v. Reproductive Health Services,* a Supreme Court decision that allowed the state of Missouri to ban public facilities and employees from performing abortions. For four years, FOCA had been the main focus of pro-choice interest groups in Washington. Candidate Bill Clinton supported it, and so had the freshwomen and most pro-choice members of Congress. By 1992, the bill had gained momentum, picking up 131 co-sponsors in the House and 31 in the Senate.

At the beginning of the 103rd Congress, FOCA was the front-burner bill for pro-choice advocates.

Louise Slaughter announced that the caucus should develop a consensus opinion on the bill and suggested that a delegate from the women's caucus meet with abortion-rights leaders Vic Fazio and Don Edwards so the women could have an early impact on the legislation. With Slaughter's mention of the word "FOCA," the room erupted into a confusion of conversations as the women tried to determine who was "on" FOCA as a co-sponsor, who was not, and why not.

Twenty-four hours earlier, Don Edwards, the fifteen-term liberal congressman from San Jose, California, had stealthily introduced FOCA as House Resolution 25. Before "dropping" the Freedom of Choice Act, Edwards failed to consult with Pat Schroeder. Schroeder, who served on the Judiciary Committee with Edwards, was insulted that he would introduce the bill without consulting her on the compromises that he chose to include. She would later say that Edwards' move was a perfect example of how the opinions of women members were being overlooked on important legislative decisions pertaining to women. The congresswomen could be counted on to appear at pro-choice press conferences as "skirts," as Schroeder would say. But in reality, four men had always called the shots on abortion strategy: Les AuCoin, Bill Green, Edwards, and Fazio.

Edwards had introduced FOCA at the earliest possible date because he thought the election of Bill Clinton, the first pro-choice president in twelve years, would help the bill pass quickly. Edwards included a key compromise: allowing states to require parental notification for minors. Parental notification was a very popular restriction that had the support of most pro-choice members of Congress, and Edwards knew that its inclusion would be the key to FOCA's swift passage. Schroeder, who hadn't been consulted by Edwards partly because she was less willing to make deals, was opposed. She believed H.R. 25 should be introduced "clean," and if the parental-involvement measure had to be included, it should be in the form of an amendment that could be used as a bargaining chip when the bill came to a vote.

By January 6, Slaughter and Schroeder had come to an agreement. At the caucus meeting, everything went according to plan. Slaughter delivered her talking points without missing a beat. Discussion over FOCA heated up. The women admitted that Edwards had caught them by surprise. His swift introduction of FOCA had left them confused over the bill's fine print.

Then the plan began to go awry. Nita Lowey, a three-term congresswoman from New York's Westchester County, had begun to explain the pros and cons of the complex piece of legislation. As her colleagues tried to make up their minds on parental notification and federal funding, Lowey guided the chaotic discussion. The parental-notification specifications had been included as an amendment to FOCA last year, Lowey explained. This year, Edwards included the compromise provision in the original bill. All at once, it seemed as though everyone in the room had an opinion on FOCA.

Pat Schroeder had no trouble making herself heard. "It's obvious," she announced, "that we need to have a pro-choice task force meet to discuss the caucus's position on FOCA before the caucus meets with Vic Fazio and Don Edwards." The chairwoman of this newly created task force, she indicated, would be appointed now. Louise

Slaughter sat up a little straighter. Here was her big moment. The appointment she and Schroeder had agreed upon would now be hers. But all of a sudden, her pleasant sense of anticipation turned to shock. "Nita," Schroeder said, turning to Nita Lowey, "why don't you head it?"

Slaughter kept her best poker face and didn't flinch. She knew what none of the other congresswomen in the room yet knew. To everyone else, Nita Lowey appeared the obvious choice for chairwoman, and in truth, she had overshadowed Slaughter with her deeper grasp of the facts of FOCA. It would take Slaughter several days to unravel the real reasons Schroeder had stabbed her in the back that morning. At the moment, burning in her seat, bewildered, Slaughter began to see that everything she had done to create the pro-choice portfolio for herself—the December 1992 lunch meeting her top staffer, Elaine Ryan, had called with Schroeder's two aides to propose the pro-choice task force; her own conversation with Schroeder; the interoffice memos outlining the plan—had been a direct threat to Schroeder's power and authority. This was the first time that Schroeder had delegated an important, high-profile issue to a fellow congresswoman, and although the task force had actually been Louise's idea, Schroeder clearly did not trust her with the power to run one.

In the three months preceding the January meeting, Schroeder had heard the rumors: Slaughter wanted to mount a campaign against Schroeder for caucus Democratic co-chair. Word had it that Slaughter thought Schroeder wasn't doing a good job. Then there was the Violence Against Women Act. Schroeder, the only woman on the Judiciary Committee, wanted control over the $1.8

billion bill that would help curb domestic violence and was bound to pass in the 103rd Congress. But Schroeder knew that Slaughter had persuaded her ally Barbara Boxer, the bill's chief sponsor in the House, to pass the legislation on to Slaughter when Boxer moved over to the Senate. To make matters worse, Slaughter had also let Schroeder know that she didn't plan to help Schroeder save the Select Committee on Children, Youth and Families, which Schroeder chaired, from the cost-cutting chopping block.

Four floors above, Louise Slaughter's administrative assistant, Elaine Ryan, awaited news from the meeting. At 10:30, Slaughter walked in the door.

"Honey," Slaughter exclaimed, "what the hell was that?"

When Slaughter told Elaine what had happened, Ryan was shocked. Only days earlier, Ryan had told Slaughter, "Walk the plank and they'll have a coronation for you, they'll be feeding you grapes." Now Ryan snapped up the phone and called Schroeder's office. She asked for Andrea Camp.

At about the same moment, down the hall, Lesley Primmer, executive director of the women's caucus, also called Andrea Camp. She, too, wanted to know why Schroeder had chosen Lowey instead of Slaughter.

Ryan got through first: "Schroeder was supposed to commend Slaughter for having the courage to do this," Ryan blurted. "What chapter did I miss?"

Next it was Primmer's turn to ask Camp, "How did that happen?"

Camp, who had not been at the meeting, said she didn't know.

With no further revelations coming from Pat Schroeder's office, Primmer stalked down the hall to

Slaughter's office to powwow with Elaine Ryan, who was understandably angry. Primmer had a peace offering in mind. Before leaving her office, she paused to check the caucus bylaws and was relieved to find that Schroeder was well within her powers to appoint Slaughter to another task force chair.

In Ryan's office, Primmer proposed that Slaughter head a task force on women's health. Ryan liked the idea. Slaughter had worked hard on women's health, and besides, everyone was for improving women's health. No one opposed breast cancer funding, unlike funding for abortion. Primmer and Ryan discussed the plan with Camp, who suggested that, to mollify Slaughter, Schroeder could ask Lowey to chair a women's-health task force instead, turning abortion back over to Slaughter. Schroeder, apparently, was willing to take the knife out of Slaughter's back. Ryan broached the offer to Slaughter, who was a proud woman. Despite her tough edge and hot temper, Slaughter still preserved some of her self-effacing Southern manners. At that moment, it was clear to Slaughter that a graceful solution was needed.

"I can't take abortion away from Nita," Slaughter said. "And besides, maybe I want women's health." In 1992, she had helped push through a $500 million budget earmark for breast cancer research at the National Institutes of Health (NIH). In the long run, she believed, women's health might turn out to be a better issue for her conservative district than abortion.

Later that day, after the staffers had set the stage for the negotiation, Schroeder herself called Slaughter and offered the chair of the newly created women's-health task force. Within a week, Slaughter called Schroeder to discuss the Violence Against Women Act (VAWA). Realizing that she had nothing to gain in a turf battle, Slaughter offered Schroeder control over VAWA, but Slaughter would still remain one of the bill's chief co-sponsors. Schroeder announced that she had been working on VAWA for years. Even though Slaughter believed that Boxer had done all the hard work on the bill, she didn't challenge Schroeder. Bitter but resigned, she knew the fight was lost. "I'm not a bill poacher," she told Schroeder. "The most important thing is to get it passed. Why don't you take it?"

4

---◈---

Initiation

She was an attractive young woman with dark, almond-shaped eyes, a toothy smile, and plaited hair. She did not resemble 98 percent of her colleagues, and not only because she wore gold sneakers to work. Out of 435 House members, only nine in the 103rd Congress were black women. Just three years earlier, only one black woman served in Congress.* Cynthia McKinney was thirty-seven, in a House where only 47 out of 435 members were under forty. Long after she moved into her office, hired her staff, and began making speeches on the House floor, McKinney would continue to be mistaken for support staff. Over a year would pass before Capitol policemen and elevator operators would allow her to pass unquestioned.

---

*Cardiss Collins was elected in 1973 in a special election to fill her husband's seat after his death. Maxine Waters, a California Democrat; Eleanor Holmes Norton, a Democrat from Washington, D.C.; and Barbara-Rose Collins, a Democrat from Michigan, were all elected in 1990.

Congress has often been called "the last plantation," and the term still applied in 1993. For decades, the institution had exempted itself from most of the civil rights and worker-protection laws that it imposed on the private sector. Most of the African Americans employed on the Hill held clerical and manual-labor jobs. They were in charge of the labyrinth of tunnels that constitute the small town of congressional beauty parlors, barbershops, restaurants, stationery stores, newsstands, post offices, credit unions, and cavernous boiler rooms.

At age fifty, Lillie Drayton had operated members-only elevators on Capitol Hill for twenty-two years. So when a gray-haired member of the U.S. Congress stepped onto Drayton's elevator in wing-tipped cordovans one afternoon, Drayton didn't hesitate. She didn't need to ask which floor. It was mid-January, the House had just started its 103rd session. Drayton greeted her new passenger with a slight twang of Georgia in her voice, "Hello, Mr. Chairman."

"Hello, Lillie," replied Chairman George Miller.

Drayton pressed three. Moments later, the elevator doors parted, Chairman Miller stepped out, and another figure stepped in.

The new passenger was a black woman, like Drayton, though a generation younger. She wore a white silk pants suit, a floppy green ribbon holding her braided hair, and gold sneakers.

"Excuse me," said Drayton, but the younger woman continued walking into the elevator. "Excuse me," Drayton repeated, "members only."

"Yes," came the reply, "thank you."

Drayton regularly gave the gate to tourists, lobbyists, and summer interns. But this young woman, she would later recall, "was just bouncing right along."

Drayton spoke slowly and clearly: "The elevator is *only* for members."

The passenger pointed to a genuine congressional membership pin, which she wore on a gold chain around her neck instead of the customary spot on a suit lapel. Drayton stood there and stared. During the ride to the ground floor she would discover that this iconoclastic woman was Drayton's own representative from Georgia's 11th District, as well as one of the few African-American congresswomen Drayton had served on her elevator.

"You see," said Cynthia McKinney, "we now come in all shapes and hues."

After the 1992 elections, the number of African Americans in Congress swelled from twenty-six to forty. Southern blacks like McKinney had waited an especially long time to get to Congress. Five Southern states sent blacks to Congress for the first time since Reconstruction. Black members from Northern cities, however, had built up considerable seniority and power by the start of the 103rd Congress: three were full committee chairmen and sixteen chaired subcommittees.

For a hundred years, whites had had a monopoly on Congress in the South. In 1972, Andrew Young of Georgia and Barbara Jordan of Texas became the first blacks elected from the South since 1901. John Lewis, the civil rights hero and founder of the Student Non-Violent Coordinating Committee, eventually filled Young's Atlanta seat in 1986. Cynthia followed in Lewis's footsteps as the fourth black person and the first black woman ever to be elected to Congress from Georgia.

The gold sneakers made great copy: in early March, they made the front page of the *New York Times,* when Maureen Dowd wrote about McKinney as "a 37-year-old former college professor and single mother from Atlanta with uncommon poise and a decidedly unpinstriped wardrobe." The story automatically put McKinney on the national map, a rarity for a representative. *U.S. News & World Report* and *The National Journal* published profiles of Cynthia. CBS covered her for their morning-show special on the new freshmen, and *Newsweek* began chronicling her first year in office. In March, the *Christian Science Monitor* would pick up the story: "Black, female, and young, newly seated Congresswoman Cynthia McKinney is part of the forward guard of a new generation infiltrating the corridors of traditionally white male power." McKinney seemed to embody the sense that Congress would never again be quite the same place.

Her popularity created chaos: Some five hundred résumés flooded McKinney's office for the seven positions she had to fill in D.C.; it seemed as if every young, idealistic staffer on the Hill wanted to work for her. It fell to Andrea Young, McKinney's newly hired administrative assistant, to find a press secretary. The office needed someone to answer the flood of interview requests. *USA Today* was calling about photographing all of the new freshwomen, as was *Vogue*. The office didn't have computers yet. Constituent mail arrived in huge canvas bags five times a day. The phone rang behind every conversation. The fax machine churned out notices, hate mail, and invitations twelve hours a day. Lobbyists from industries and interest groups Cynthia had never heard of wanted to meet with her.

In her first months on the job, McKinney spent most of her time sitting in the House chamber, observing. She would often choose a seat in the third row, near her friends Carrie Meek and Maxine Waters. Her first impression of House debates was that they were much more civilized and less inflammatory than those in the Georgia general assembly. It was impossible, McKinney decided, to get mad at someone when you used antiquated, stilted language and called the enemy "the gentleman from California."

In addition to observation, McKinney soon saw there were plenty of questions to ask. For a month she studied the movements of the Mace. a 46-inch-tall ebony pillar, with a silver eagle perched atop a globe. It looked like an American colonial version of a totem pole. Each day, McKinney noticed the sergeant-at-arms, a distinguished white-haired man who policed the House floor, move the Mace from one rose-colored marble pedestal at the right of the speaker's chair to another pedestal on a lower dais of the speaker's rostrum. One day, McKinney asked the sergeant-at-arms what the various positions of the Mace signified. Werner Brandt explained that when the House is in session, the Mace sits on the speaker's right. When the House is in the "Committee of the Whole," during which it can only vote on amendments, it is moved to a lower dais. McKinney later realized that "asking about the Mace was like asking what an axle is if you're on the Transportation Committee."

When McKinney asked the sergeant-at-arms her question, she happened to be wearing a baseball cap the chairman of the Agriculture Committee had just given her. Werner Brandt told McKinney that she was violating a House Rule: wearing a hat in the chamber. She would have to take the cap off or leave the floor immediately. Embarrassed, McKinney quickly removed the cap.

Adjacent to the House chamber stood the Speaker's Lobby. Crystal chandeliers hung from ornate ceilings. High-backed leather chairs and dark Oriental rugs gave the room the atmosphere of a men's club. This was where members of Congress gave interviews to the press between votes, and where Susie Rodriguez first interviewed with Cynthia McKinney for the job of press secretary. Impressed by McKinney's relaxed appearance and demeanor, Rodriguez took to her instantly.

McKinney asked her several questions, but foremost "Can you write with passion?" Rodriguez thought she could. She felt strongly about the causes McKinney championed—civil rights for blacks, equal rights for women, economic help for the poor and underprivileged.

McKinney warned Susie that working for her would be much more than a nine-to-five job. "I want your life," McKinney told Rodriguez. Rodriguez started at $23,000 a year in early February.

When Rodriguez started work a month after McKinney's swearing-in, the computer system still hadn't been installed. In one corner of the four-room office suite sat Adam Hames, twenty-four, the legislative correspondent, piles of letters from hundreds of McKinney's constituents cluttering his desk.

Despite the chaos in the office, McKinney had set strict rules. Proper Southern manners combined with twelve years of a Catholic schoolgirl's education had given her high standards. For the women in the office, bare legs were forbidden, pantyhose required. Phones were to be answered before the third ring. Everyone in the office had to answer the phone, even McKinney, with the following greeting: "Good morning. Congresswoman Cynthia McKinney's office. How can I help you?" The staff reported to work at 8:00 A.M. and rarely went home before 8:00 P.M. Each aide rotated evening duty with McKinney, which required driving her to receptions or eating pizza with her in the office during late votes.

Every morning, McKinney began the day with a hug for each of her staff members. She didn't believe in hierarchy and took everyone seriously, regardless of title or age. She encouraged dissent. She felt that commitment was more important than skin color or gender. Two-thirds of the staff was African-American, and half was female. Every other Friday was "girls' early day off." The following week, the "girls" rotated with the "boys."

Back in December, McKinney had asked Speaker Tom Foley and Majority Leader Richard Gephardt if she could be appointed to the Rules Committee. She argued that her four years in Georgia's state legislature made her fluent enough in politics and parliamentary procedure for the job. There was just one problem: no vacancies on the powerful Rules Committee.

At the time, most freshmen were vying for the money committees—Appropriations, Ways and Means, and Energy and Commerce. Appropriations allowed members to funnel money and "pork" projects to their districts; Ways and Means had jurisdiction over taxation and was popular with big-business PACs; Energy and Commerce controlled over 40 percent of all of the legislation in the House. A seat on any of these committees practically guaranteed a member's reelection because it helped fill campaign coffers with early donations that would scare off future opponents.

McKinney wasn't interested in money. She wanted power. The Rules Committee decided which bills reached the floor, which amendments could be attached to the bill, and how many minutes of debate were permitted. Even if a bill passed through a committee and was ready for referral to the full House, the Rules Committee could prevent it from ever being voted on. The Democratic and

Republican leadership handpicked Rules Committee members, who were chosen for their loyalty and dedication to the party. Because they were in the majority in 1993, Democrats stacked the deck nine to four so that Republicans had virtually no influence.

In mid-December, as she expected, McKinney didn't get Rules. Instead, she drew the Agriculture and Foreign Affairs Committees. McKinney and Eva Clayton of North Carolina would be the first black women ever to serve on the Agriculture Committee. McKinney would also be the second black woman ever to serve on Foreign Affairs. Neither was a "power" committee, but they made sense for McKinney, as her district included farm country—cotton, peanuts, soybeans—and, in addition to being a Ph.D. candidate in International Relations at Tufts University's Fletcher School of Law and Diplomacy, she had majored in International Relations at the University of Southern California. Next to the politics of equal rights, international relations was McKinney's passion. But McKinney feared she wouldn't be taken seriously by the foreign policy establishment, one of the last of Washington's white-shoe male bastions.

She was, at least initially, correct: when she walked in, characteristically late, to her first Western Hemisphere Subcommittee meeting, the nine other subcommittee members, scattered in small cocktail-party clusters, went right on talking. McKinney happened not to know any of them, and she felt nervous and shy. She sat down at a long table alone. Just then, Ileana Ros-Lehtinen, a third-term Republican congresswoman from Florida, told the others that she wanted to take a group picture. She corralled the members together, handed her camera to a staffer, and stepped into the picture. Nine members of the Western Hemisphere

Subcommittee smiled for the camera. Meanwhile, on the other side of the room sat the tenth, uninvited.

At the long table, No. 2 pencils, notepads, and agendas sat squared in front of each seat. As soon as the group seated itself, someone made an inside joke that everyone but McKinney understood. The chairman, New Jersey Democrat Robert Torricelli, known as "The Torch," was more interested in hazing the freshmen and putting them in their place than making them feel comfortable. Freshmen, as far as most committee chairmen were concerned, were meant to be seen and not heard. Today, Torricelli gave McKinney the silent treatment: as papers were passed around, decisions made, schedules discussed, McKinney was ignored entirely. At last the meeting adjourned, and still no one had introduced himself or herself to McKinney.

On February 17, President Clinton strode into a packed House chamber to address a joint session of Congress. The new president had come to deliver his first State of the Union message. By custom, the president advanced down the center aisle to the speaker's rostrum. On both sides of the aisle, standing shoulder to shoulder, Democrats and Republicans, senators and representatives, jockeyed to shake the president's hand. In this split-second transaction, as the executive smile met the Capitol grin on national television, the congressperson could expect to be noticed by millions of Americans.

Typically, the president would shake some fifty hands, all on the aisle. A touchy-feely president like Clinton would occasionally reach back into the ranks, but the only way to guarantee the televised handshake was to nail down an aisle seat. Aisle seats were given to senior members and committee chairmen. For a freshman, there was but one way to the aisle, and Cynthia McKinney was determined to take it. By 10:00 A.M., McKinney had seated herself in the center aisle, five rows up from the chamber door. For the next ten hours, McKinney left the seat only for a bite to eat and two bathroom trips. This was her seat and no one was going to take it from her.

As prime time approached, McKinney was joined by her friend and fellow freshwoman, sixty-six-year-old Carrie Meek. Beside Meek stood another Democrat, William Natcher, of Kentucky, who at eighty-four seemed to have come from a different epoch. Meek introduced Natcher to McKinney, and the three talked about the budget deficit, discussing how Congress should cut its operating costs. McKinney had an idea. "Instead of cutting my sixteen staffers," she said, "why not cut some of the committee budgets?" In 1993, the Appropriations Committee's operating budget was $20 million a year; it employed over two hundred staffers. Why not eliminate Appropriations?

Natcher had come to Congress two years before McKinney was born. He nodded politely, then turned away to greet other colleagues. "You better be quiet," Carrie Meek whispered in McKinney's ear. "That man is the chairman of the Appropriations Committee." As it turned out, Natcher never forgave McKinney for her naïve blunder, and McKinney was too proud and stubborn to apologize.

Minutes later, President Clinton walked down the center aisle of the House Chamber, preceded by a parade of dignitaries—Supreme Court justices, members of the Cabinet. Standing, clapping, shouting, the 103rd Congress gave Clinton an enthusiastic welcome, and the president responded characteristically, shaking every hand in sight.

He grasped members' hands, pounded their backs, remembered their names. But when Clinton came to the fifth row, he did something different: Clinton not only shook Cynthia McKinney's hand, but in an overt display of favoritism, the president hugged her.

The presidential bear hug was McKinney's first sign that she had "arrived." It gave her hope for a chance to be taken seriously, to get things done for her district. The president needed McKinney's vote, McKinney needed the president's support, and Clinton's hug sealed the deal on a new relationship between two ambitious Southern Democrats.

5

Family and Medical Leave

With Bill Clinton in office, it looked as though family and medical leave would finally have a future. America was the only advanced industrialized country in the world without a national family- and medical-leave law. Employers were completely within their rights to give their female employees who had just given birth only a few weeks of temporary disability leave. Labor laws were out of sync with dramatic changes that had taken place in American society in the past thirty years. In 1965, over one-third of mothers with children under the age of eighteen worked outside of the home. By 1992, the percentage of working mothers had almost doubled, to 67 percent—making the housewife the exception rather than the rule. The structure of the American family had changed while laws remained the same.

In April 1985, Pat Schroeder introduced the Family and Medical Leave Act. Her bill called for employers with five or more workers to give employees up to twenty-six weeks of unpaid family leave. When Schroeder introduced H.R. 2020 in the second session of the 99th Congress, her name stood alone on the bill for almost six months. No one would co-sponsor the legislation. "People thought I was nuts," Schroeder recalled. "It was like wearing a bathing suit to church." Schroeder committed her sin at the altar of free-market capitalism. In 1985, laissez-faire prevailed in Washington. Women's-rights groups and labor organizations were behind Schroeder's bill, but the Chamber of Commerce, a powerful business lobby, vehemently opposed it. So did the Reagan administration. At the time, only nine states had laws that required employers to hold jobs for women with newborns.

For the following eight years, the Family and Medical Leave Act lurched through the dance of legislation. Republicans rejected the bill because they opposed government regulation of business. Pro-family, new-right conservatives opposed the family-leave bill because they thought it was "anti-motherhood" and encouraged women to work. The feminization of the workforce was a clear threat to social conservatives who tried to turn back the clock in the eighties and wipe out advances the women's movement had made in the previous decade.

Supporters of family leave argued that parental leave should be a minimum labor standard, like health and safety, child labor, and minimum-wage laws. In 1978, Congress had passed the Pregnancy Discrimination Act, which prohibited employment discrimination against pregnant women and required employers to cover pregnant employees under their health insurance and temporary-disability plans. Despite this law, working women were not guaranteed job safety after they recovered from childbirth, and they still routinely experienced discrimination by their employers.

Parents did not have a guaranteed right to stay at home for any minimum length of time with their newborn or sick children. As more and more women entered the workforce out of financial necessity, they were compelled to make the choice between their jobs and their families. Poor women were punished most by lack of parental-protection laws. Their jobs were often the only thing that kept their families living above the poverty line, and their unskilled positions were the easiest to find replacements for.

In 1987, a Supreme Court decision gave the family- and-medical-leave bill a boost. In *California Savings and Loan v. Guerra,* the Court's decision—that states can require private businesses to grant unpaid leave for new mothers—gave Democrats in Congress new impetus to push for passage of the bill. By 1987, women accounted for more than 62 percent of the increase in the civilian labor force since 1979.

In November 1987, the House Education and Labor Committee approved the family-leave bill. Republican congresswoman Marge Roukema, of New Jersey, negotiated a crucial compromise with Democrats that exempted small businesses with fewer than fifty employees from the legislation, making the bill politically palatable for moderate Republicans. The new cutoff exempted 95 percent of the nation's employers from the law, but it still included 42 million people—39 percent of the nation's workforce.

In 1990, the Family and Medical Leave Act passed in both the House and the Senate, only to be vetoed by President Bush in June. The House failed to override Bush's veto. At the time, 71 percent of female members of Congress and only 52 percent of male lawmakers voted to override the president's veto. Meanwhile, companies that had voluntarily installed family-leave laws reported good results. Aetna Life and Casualty Company claimed that its new family-leave policy saved the company $2 million in 1991 because it reduced employee turnover and cut hiring and training costs. A survey found that taxpayers paid $4.3 billion a year in unemployment to support workers who lost their jobs because they didn't have medical leave.

Again, in 1991, the House and Senate passed Family Leave with bipartisan support. Moderate Republicans—including Roukema, Nancy Johnson of Connecticut, Olympia Snowe of Maine, and Connie Morella of Maryland—supported the bill. "This is not about working families getting rich, it's about working families getting by," said Roukema, whose advocacy for the bill was partly motivated by her son's death from leukemia.

The bill, which gave twelve weeks of unpaid leave to workers for the birth or adoption of a child or the illness of a close family member, became the Democrats' trump card to the Bush campaign's religious-right "family values" message. Hoping to heighten the perception that the Republicans were insensitive to women and working families, the Democrats deliberately waited until September 1992—during the heat of the presidential campaign—to send the bill to the White House for George Bush's signature. Bush handed down his second veto. The veto came on the heels of the Republican National Convention in Houston, where the religious right controlled the platform that called for a constitutional amendment to ban abortion, and the women's movement was denounced by Patrick Buchanan and Marilyn Quayle. Women who cherished both their families and their equal rights outside of the home were especially angered by Marilyn Quayle's oft-quoted remark: "Most women do not wish to be liberated from their essential natures"—motherhood.

In late September, the Senate voted to override the president's veto, 68 to 31. Fourteen Republicans broke rank to vote for the override, but the House could not reach the two-thirds majority it needed, and Bush's veto was sustained. Again, women lawmakers of both parties supported the legislation in overwhelmingly larger numbers than their male colleagues. By 1992, only 37 percent of all businesses in America provided maternity leave for mothers, and only 18 percent allowed for paternity leave for fathers.

In the summer of 1992, the Year of the Woman had occurred almost exclusively in the Democratic party—three times as many Democratic women were running for office than Republican women. Twelve women Senate candidates and seventy candidates for the House were celebrated at the Democratic National Convention in New York City. At the convention, Al Gore heightened the Democratic ticket's commitment to the family-leave issue when he gave a spellbinding speech recounting his son's near-death accident and the painful weeks his family had spent watching over his son's hospital bed.

Public opinion polls showed strong support for family-leave legislation, and the "forgotten middle class" and working women overwhelmingly supported Bill Clinton's election. A 4-point gender gap helped elect Bill Clinton, who received 45 percent of the women's vote as opposed to 41 percent of the men's vote. George Bush had only garnered 37 percent of the women's vote. Two weeks after being sworn into office, Clinton was eager to sign into law the bill that so perfectly defined his differences with the Reagan and Bush administrations.

When the congressional leadership made Family and Medical Leave, H.R. 1 and S. 5, the first bill that the 103rd

Congress passed, it marked the beginning of the end of the 1980s backlash against women's gains. The twenty-eight new women members of Congress had been an important factor in the leadership's decision to put family and medical leave on the fast track. "The women drove it," a House Democratic leadership aide said about the legislation. "There was never a doubt that the bill was going to fly with all of the new women. It was put on the agenda first partly because there were so many new women who could lock up family leave."

Both Congress and the White House could hardly wait to prove to cynical and disillusioned voters that the days of gridlock—and President Bush's forty-six vetoes—were over. Choosing this major piece of social legislation as the first law the new regime would pass marked a clear recognition of both the feminization of the American workforce *and* the feminization of Congress.

The family-leave legislation would bring together all the women on the Hill for the first time in the 103rd Congress. Their advocacy of an issue that was integral to women's rights in the workplace sent a strong message about what their priorities would be in the two years to come.

In the Senate chamber on February 2, 1993, Patty Murray rose to make the second speech of her Senate career. Standing only five feet tall behind her shiny mahogany desk, Murray, the youngest woman ever elected to the Senate, looked more like a Senate page than a senator. She had been assigned to desk No. 62, a 174-year-old relic on the far left aisle, three rows above the Senate well. Sixteen years earlier, Murray had been a secretary who took shorthand, typed a hundred words a minute, and had no choice but to quit her job when she became pregnant. Few of the men in the Senate chamber—twenty of whom were millionaires—knew what it was like to get their boss coffee and take dictation for a living.

Murray told her colleagues that she had been twenty-six years old, newly married and working as an executive secretary in Seattle, when she became pregnant with Randy, her first child. Patty and Rob Murray didn't have a nest egg to fall back on, and they needed both salaries. "A family-leave policy would have enabled me to devote my attention to the changes in my family," Murray said. "It would also have given me a very important message about our country: That our families are as important as our jobs." Murray told the Senate that her boss had asked her to quit her job.

The family- and medical-leave bill had been handed to Patty Murray on a silver platter. Unlike Pat Schroeder and Marge Roukema, Murray had done virtually no legislative spadework on the bill. But Murray was a veteran of family-leave battles in the Washington state senate. For what better law could Murray cast her first vote than family leave?

After the speech, Murray sat down, flushed and relieved. To her surprise, other senators came to her desk to congratulate her. One senator told her that he had never before heard anybody talk like that in the Senate chamber. Compared with the usual male senator, who delivered speeches in booming, stentorian tones, Murray had spoken with simplicity and from the heart. She used the word "care" eleven times.

California's Dianne Feinstein, one of the four newly elected Democratic women senators, spoke next. Like Murray, Feinstein had also experienced job discrimination because of her pregnancy. "Thirty-five years ago, when I was pregnant with my daughter, Katherine, there was no maternity leave," said Feinstein. "I left my job to have my child."

These speeches, and their subsequent approval ratings, substantiated Murray's belief that women could reform Congress by simplifying the elevated diction used on the floor: Constituents could feel more connected to a government that spoke to them. "I think women talk in language and in terms that people understand more clearly," Murray said later. "If you listen to the men, they debate economic theory. The economic theory is important, but what really makes people understand what's in a bill is when you talk about what it really means to you." For the rest of the 103rd Congress, Murray would continue to take to the Senate floor with personal anecdotes about her life, her family, and her friends. Her staff would label the senator's style "Patty-speak."

Murray's speech on the Senate floor became the denouement of her four-year struggle on the issue of family and medical leave. In 1989, as a freshman state senator, Murray had a good friend whose sixteen-year-old son was dying of leukemia. At the time, Washington State's law required employers to give their workers six weeks of parental leave to care for a newborn child, but there was no protection if an employee's child fell seriously ill. Murray's friend asked her boss for time off so that she could take care of her son, who only had a few months to live. When her employer told her that they wouldn't guarantee her a job when she returned, she quit. As a result, she lost her health insurance and watched the medical bills pile up. "It was awful," recalled Murray, her eyes brimming with tears. "You shouldn't be forced to choose. It was so *wrong*."

When a family-leave bill was introduced in the Washington state senate that extended parental leave from six to twelve weeks, Murray attached an amendment including medical leave. Powerful business lobbies and the Democratic leadership begged her to drop the amendment. Murray refused to retreat. "The members of the Senate and the House then didn't have a sense of the issue," Murray recalled. "A lot of them were older men whose children were grown up, or who had wives at home to take care of their kids for them." At the time, Murray was the only senator who was a mother with young children. None of her colleagues wanted to be on record voting against a law that allowed parents with terminally ill children to take time off from work without losing their jobs. After Murray gave an impassioned floor speech, her amendment passed. "Man, I was impressed," a lobbyist told the *Seattle Times*. "She wants to change the world, and she makes you believe there's a good chance she can do it."

When Murray arrived in Washington, D.C., she made a point of setting an example as an enlightened, caring employer. Murray acted on her philosophy that "if you care about your employees as people with lives separate from here [the office] and allow them to have that, they can do a better job." She instituted a strong family-leave policy—ten weeks of paid leave. Then she hired a thirty-three-year-old woman who was seven months pregnant with her first child.

Pam Norick had been born and raised in Seattle, and she had a master's degree in foreign relations and five years of Hill experience. Norick was smart, hardworking, and committed; Murray described her as a "dynamo." When Murray interviewed Norick for the job of Murray's national security adviser, she asked Norick how she planned to do both—be a Senate staffer who would be on call around the clock seven days a week, and be a mother.

Norick knew that she would need a flexible work schedule, but before she could bring it up herself, Murray did. To make Norick's life easier, Murray suggested that she could work at home on Fridays. Norick gratefully accepted Murray's offer and became an employee whom Murray mentioned in speeches and interviews as proof of her mandate.

But hiring Norick did not come without its risks. A year later, a senior female staffer without children of her own complained to Murray that she didn't like Norick's special arrangement and thought Norick should be fired if she didn't change it. The complaint incensed Murray. She called a meeting of the entire staff and defended Norick in an inspiring speech. Murray explained that each employee had different responsibilities outside of the office and that everyone's needs were being treated equally. She emphasized that the office had to work as a team and support one another. Thanks to Murray, Norick's job remained secure— but only, as it turned out, for the time being.

Until February, Murray had been overloaded by the trials of moving to a new city and starting a new job. In Seattle, the family had left their sky-blue clapboard house, their friends and neighbors. Sam, their 90-pound golden retriever, was too old to make the move. The day after Christmas, Murray had driven cross-country with her husband, Rob, and her thirteen-year-old daughter, Sara, in the Ford Taurus they had bought for the trip, which took five days. A moving van with all their furniture followed them to Arlington, Virginia, where the Murrays had rented a three-bedroom house. The movers arrived late, and Murray spent her last night before becoming a U.S. senator in a sleeping bag on the floor.

Patty Murray, the youngest woman ever elected to the Senate, was short and slight—a size-10 extra-petite whose shirtsleeves crept close to her knuckles. The wedding ring on her left hand was a simple gold band. Her short light-brown hair was cut straight as a paintbrush. The desk in her office was so long it almost seemed to have a vanishing point, and as she sat there, under the Hart Building's cavernous sixteen-foot ceilings, she looked not unlike the comic book character Richie Rich, dwarfed—and amused— by her own power. "The ceilings have to be this high," she said, "so they can fit the large egos of the senators."

Murray used her height to accentuate her populist appeal. In a March 30 floor speech supporting Clinton's doomed economic-stimulus package, Murray surprised everyone with her candor: "When I was in high school, I never dreamed I would become an elected official, much less a United States senator. I always thought senators had to be tall and rich and male . . . but my parents always told me that the little guy was just as important as the big guy. And I believe that. It's easy to forget about the little guy . . . but I can't." She added: "You see, the highest-paying job I had before I came to Washington, D.C., paid twenty-three thousand dollars a year." Senator Murray now made $133,600.

The senator could not count the times Capitol Hill guards had asked to see her identification. Unlike the 435 members of the House, senators have famous faces. The one hundred members of the "upper chamber" are not issued ID pins. Guards are supposed to *know* the senators, then step aside deferentially. Murray took the guard's officiousness as a compliment, because she didn't want to look like a typical senator: "I wasn't elected to be a senator with a capitol S, somebody who makes people bow and scrape."

She succeeded. One day, on the way back to her office from the Capitol, Murray stepped into an empty "Senators Only" elevator in the basement of the Hart Building. She pushed the button for the third floor, and as the doors began to close, a man jumped into the elevator. With a sneaky grin, he turned to Murray and said, "Aha! You're pretending to be a senator, too!"

Among her fellow female senators, Murray was sui generis. Dianne Feinstein, the former mayor of San Francisco, who had also run for governor, looked and acted like a corporate CEO. Barbara Boxer had served in the House for ten years. Carol Moseley-Braun, the only African-American member of the Senate, was a lawyer and a county government politico. That was why the press loved the "mom in tennis shoes." The national and international media all wanted a piece of Murray. Camera crews lay in wait outside the newly installed Senate women's bathroom to capture Murray exiting on video. Murray's press secretary, Rose Berg, fielded between sixty to eighty interview requests a day and began to feel more like a switchboard operator than a spin doctor.

In early January, Murray appeared on ABC's *This Week with David Brinkley,* where she successfully faced off against Sam Donaldson and George Will over the proposed middle-class tax cut. But she would refuse most other offers to appear on national television. French TV, the *Today* show, children's magazines, and *Mirabella* all wanted to know what it was like for a former volunteer preschool teacher to be a senator. Murray declined the interviews. She believed that she would learn her job by doing her job, and appearing on television as the "mom-in-tennis-shoes" senator would only turn her into a caricature of herself. A booker for the *Today* show kept on calling. Senators rarely turn down a chance to reach five million viewers, and eventually, the *Today* booker exclaimed, "Do you know who you're talking to? This is the *Today* show!"

Murray's fears about not being taken seriously proved to be well founded. When the senator paid a courtesy call on Speaker Tom Foley in December, Foley was nonplussed, and remarked to an aide after the meeting that Murray proved all you need is a "schtick" to get elected these days. In fact, the remark revealed more about Speaker Foley. What he could not yet see in those first days of the 103rd Congress was that Patty Murray had come to office by virtue of the very thing the Speaker had lost by being there, something the Speaker would be seen to sorely lack in two years: the common touch.

In the House, on February 3, the congresswomen dominated the family-leave debate. They rose one after another to make their first official statements of the congressional session. Marjorie Margolies-Mezvinsky was joined by Leslie Byrne and Jolene Unsoeld, Pat Schroeder and Patsy Mink, Connie Morella and Barbara-Rose Collins, Eva Clayton and Nancy Pelosi. Thirty-seven out of the fifty-four women on the Hill spoke to the merits of H.R. 1, not only as legislators but as working mothers—mothers with sixty-seven children, all told. Their speaking styles were personal and powerful. Patricia Ireland, president of the National Organization for Women, applauded them, noting that their performances were emblematic of the difference women were making on the Hill: "Women bring a different set of priorities," she said.

That day, the U.S. House of Representatives passed the Family and Medical Leave Act by a vote of 265 to 163. The next day, despite Republican filibuster threats, the bill passed in the Senate 71 to 27. All but six of the forty-eight congresswoman and one of the six women senators voted in favor of the bill. A gender gap persisted: 87 percent of all women members of the House voted for the bill, versus 59 percent of all congressmen. All the Democratic congresswomen and half of the Republican congresswomen voted for the legislation. Only 20 percent of Republican men in the House supported the bill.

For the few Republican congresswomen who voted against the family-leave bill, like Representative Deborah Pryce, of Columbus, Ohio, fiscal responsibility prevailed over gender solidarity. Pryce supported family leave in principle; she was a working mother of a two-year-old girl. But she was a fiscal conservative. On the campaign trail, she had called for a balanced budget, more jobs, and less government regulation. Her opponent, Democrat Richard Cordray, in an irony typical of conservative Republican women, was the "women's-issues" candidate.

Her Republican roots went back to Warren, Ohio, where Pryce's father owned a chain of drugstores. Pryce, the oldest of five children, "literally grew up in a small business." Like Patty Murray, Pryce was a pure product of Main Street, with one crucial difference. Patty Murray's father had always been an employee; Deborah Pryce's father had owned the drugstore. As a Republican, and true to her background, Pryce sympathized with business owners. With a vote pending on the Family and Medical Leave Act, she balked at forcing the "heavy hand of government" on businesses. She favored giving companies tax incentives for offering family leave to their employees. Pryce thought the bill would cause the loss of jobs and provoke employers to think twice before hiring women of child-bearing age.

By the time the family-leave bill was signed into law, it became clear that Deborah Pryce's first allegiance would be to the Republican party, often leaving women's issues aside when they conflicted with the Republican party position. Pryce alienated Democratic and moderate Republican congresswomen when she spoke out forcefully on the floor against the bill. "Even if you have to vote no," Schroeder would later complain, "why give the speech?" Pryce refused to join the women's caucus, allying herself instead with the Conservative Opportunity Society, a Republican group. Never one to "just hang out with the girls," Pryce soon began to feel unwelcome in the Capitol building's plush, peach-colored Lindy Boggs congressional women's reading room, which, since the 1992 elections, had acquired the atmosphere of an elegant women's club room.

By contrast, the passage of the Family and Medical Leave Act was a personal triumph for Patty Murray. It affirmed her choice to be a working mother. Sometimes the job would have to give. Sometimes her family would have to give. Murray tried to find the middle ground.

Voting in the Senate takes place at night so often that being a senator could almost qualify as a night job. In the middle of the week, Murray's family would drive up to the Hill to eat dinner with Patty at restaurants in Union Station, a three-block walk from her office. By day, Murray tried to make herself as accessible to her family as possible, giving them the phone number for her direct line. During staff meetings, Murray made a practice of giving her family's telephone calls top priority. On Fridays, when the Senate was out of session, Murray asked her staff not to schedule any appointments so that she could work from home, communicating with the office via the telephone and e-mail from her laptop computer.

Murray even gave her children priority over the White House. In the fall of 1994, White House staffers were stunned when Murray arrived thirty minutes late for a high-level health care reform meeting with Hillary Rodham Clinton and a group of senators. No one aside from the president himself is late to White House meetings, especially not for the reason Murray gave: a parent-teacher conference at her son Randy's school. In the beginning of Randy's junior year, Murray had already rescheduled the conference twice. She refused to let Randy down a third time. Murray was surprised when she discovered that the reason for her tardiness had not been greeted as merely routine. "I thought it was perfectly normal," Murray said afterward.

But it was often hard to be normal and a U.S. senator at the same time. Murray longed to spend even an hour with people who were just her friends and nothing more. She remembered returning to Seattle and running into friends whom she hadn't seen in a long time. Gratefully relaxing into a conversation that she hoped would include old, familiar topics such as kids and schools, Murray was brought up short when one of her old friends said to her, "I'm so glad I ran into you! My husband wants money for this project—can you help him?"

Murray tried to maintain a semblance of normalcy in her household. She shunned the active cocktail and dinner-reception circuit that occupied the evenings of most senators and members of Congress. She turned down all breakfast invitations, except for those sponsored by the Washington State congressional delegation. On Saturdays, she drove her daughter Sara to soccer games, rotating "Orange Mom" duty—the mother who brings the plate of orange sections—with the other parents. When Sara needed to bring brownies to school for a bake sale, Patty would find herself, after a twelve-hour day on the Senate floor, breaking out the Duncan Hines in her kitchen.

In spite of Murray's efforts, her children were devastated by the move to the capital. Separating from their schools, their friends, and their extended family made them homesick. Three months after the family had moved to Arlington, Randy took the family car in a fit of rebellion and tried to drive back to Seattle. But his escape was foiled by the Washington Beltway. Randy drove around and around D.C. in circles, unable to find the right exit heading west.

Murray missed Sara's fourteenth birthday party because of late votes, but she vowed to be there for Sara's fifteenth—a promise that required asking favors of the Senate majority leader. Murray told George Mitchell that Sara's birthday constituted an "emergency" situation and asked if there was any way that he could see to it that the Senate could close up shop at a decent hour or predict for her when the votes would be. Mitchell could not oblige. As the clock ticked closer to cake time, the endless quorum calls looked as though they would stretch far into the night. Murray decided to take the risk and drive home, hoping against hope that she would not miss a vote. She was lucky that night. There were no votes.

When it came to public exposure, Murray protected her family like a nervous mother hen. Reporters' requests for interviews with Patty's husband Rob, or Sara and Randy, were automatically denied. The Murrays' house remained "sacrosanct," as Murray's press secretary put it, off limits to both the press and Murray's staff. As a result, Patty often had to inconvenience herself. One afternoon, she needed to give an interview to the CBS Seattle affiliate, but she had already gone home and had promised to pick Sara up from school. Unwilling to break her promise to Sara, and equally unwilling to allow the television crew to come to her house, Murray decided to do the interview in a park near Sara's public school.

On February 5, 1993, a sunny, cool morning, 150 Washington pro-family activists gathered at the White House. Patty Murray and Pat Schroeder were among them. They sat in eight rows of white folding chairs on the Rose Garden's soggy bright-green grass. Leafless cherry tree branches framed the stage where President Clinton stood poised to sign the Family and Medical Leave Act

In the sixteen days since the inauguration, the administration had been transformed. Six out of Clinton's twenty-one cabinet members would be women, and 37 percent of his first five hundred political appointees were women, the highest number in history. In George Bush's Washington, two women served in the cabinet. Bill Clinton's White House already seemed a friendlier place. And yet, for all the excitement, President Clinton and Vice President Gore stood flanked by the same old faces: Senators Ted Kennedy, Chris Dodd, and George Mitchell and Representatives Bill Ford, Bill Clay, Pat Williams, and Tom Foley. These were the men who had made the Family and Medical Leave Act law—the congressional leadership and the chairmen of the committees and subcommittees that had the power and official jurisdiction over H.R. 1 and S. 5.

"I am proud that the first bill I sign as president truly puts people first," Clinton said, echoing his campaign theme. "It took eight years and two vetoes to make this legislation the law of the land."

And yet, in the second row, Pat Schroeder had been seated behind Hillary Clinton, Tipper Gore, and Marian Wright Edelman. Schroeder was not alone in feeling that she should have been on the stage with the men. But White House protocol dictated who was on stage; committee chairmen and the leadership had to be there. Bill Clinton needed those men standing behind him. They were the ones who he hoped would help him fulfill his ambitious legislative agenda in the 103rd Congress.

The signing of the bill was a victory for Schroeder, but her seat in the second row signified defeat. Although neither a committee chairman nor in the top ranks of the congressional leadership, Schroeder was, for all intents and purposes, the bill's godmother. She remembered how difficult it had been to convince some of the powerful congressmen on the stage to take an interest in her bill back in the eighties, when family leave was unpopular. Now, in the early months of 1993, family leave had virtually no enemies. The men with power had finally embraced the bill: in the macho, high-noon language of lawmaking, these men had won "bragging rights" to it. Schroeder had been outgunned. "When a bill becomes a big deal," she concluded, "boys grab it." The Year of the Woman had proved itself to be exactly that—one election year. It would take many more before women would be able to break the strictures of seniority.

6

Parliamentarians

For twenty years, Pat Schroeder had been fighting the battle over abortion rights, and as the summer of 1993 began, she found herself for the first time in charge of the troops. As the most senior woman in Congress, Schroeder would take the lead in the debate over providing federal funding of abortion for poor women. The showdown would be the congresswomen's first defeat, and it would be an important moment in their political education. The debate over the Hyde Amendment would expose Schroeder's strengths and weaknesses, illustrating her ability to negotiate intricate parliamentary intrigues, as well as her inability to forge and sustain coalitions among her own ranks. It would also reveal the deep racial divisions underlying much of the abortion debate.

The stakes couldn't have been higher. Six months earlier, on the twentieth anniversary of *Roe v. Wade,* the Supreme Court decision legalizing abortion, President Clinton signed an executive order to make good on a campaign pledge to overturn the "gag rule" that banned abortion counseling in federally funded family-planning clinics. He reversed the Department of Defense policy barring abortions in overseas military hospitals. He also reversed the "Mexico City" policy, which denied U.S. aid to international family-planning organizations that provide abortion services, and he lifted the fetal-tissue research ban. Clinton also directed the FDA to investigate lifting the import ban on the French abortion pill, RU-486.

With the stroke of a pen, Clinton did what Schroeder and other pro-choice members of Congress had fought to do for more than a decade. On January 22, twelve years of steady pro-choice defeats in Congress were wiped out. Clinton's executive orders had dramatically reshaped the landscape of abortion politics, but they had also created high expectations for even greater pro-choice victories in Congress. Clinton had done his part; it was now time for Congress to produce.

When Schroeder walked onto the House floor on the morning of June 30, she had no reason to doubt that she would emerge victorious. Mastery of esoteric parliamentary mechanics would decide the day's fight, and the women of the House had developed an unbeatable strategy to defuse Henry Hyde's amendment to restrict Medicaid funding for abortions.

For weeks, Schroeder had met with House parliamentarians, the nonpartisan officers who referee floor action. Nita Lowey, the chairwoman of the pro-choice task force, would be Schroeder's co-manager on the floor. Together, in meeting after meeting with the parliamentarians, they had taken pains to disentangle the knotty, often restrictive legislative rules that would regulate the floor vote. Schroeder's and

Lowey's key staffers on abortion had also grappled with the parliamentarians. Members from the women's caucus pro-choice task force had unraveled the rules as well. For the first time in the history of the Congress, congresswomen would be in control of an abortion fight.

They had the rules on their side. "Parliamentary-wise," as Schroeder put it, the women found themselves that morning facing an opponent who would not be allowed to introduce his amendment because it was against the rules. The amendment Schroeder expected Henry Hyde to introduce would change the meaning of the Labor/Health and Human Services appropriations bill. In parliamentary terms, it constituted "legislating" on an appropriations bill, something that could be done only in committee, not on the House floor. Schroeder planned to object to Hyde's amendment because it violated parliamentary procedure. With a single "point of order," Pat Schroeder planned to silence Henry Hyde.

Nita Lowey would later point to the meetings with the parliamentarians as the start of their troubles. Again and again, as Schroeder and Lowey reviewed each of Hyde's possible moves, the women had asked the parliamentarians, "Are you sure there's nothing else he can do?" Again and again, the answer had been no. Then on June 29, the night before the vote itself, they got a different reply. One of the parliamentarians, straining to remain impartial, answered, "Motivated people can be very creative."

Henry Hyde had been fighting—and winning—this battle since 1977. The central idea behind the 1977 Hyde amendment was the proposition that the federal government should only allocate the nation's tax dollars for an abortion when a pregnant woman's life was in danger. In

1977, the last year before the Hyde Amendment became law, Medicaid paid for about 320,000 poor women's abortions. Hyde's initial amendment put a stop to that. Unbeknownst to Schroeder and Lowey, Hyde's 1993 amendment included a new compromise provision to allow funding if the mother had been the victim of rape or incest. If enacted, Hyde's provision would slightly expand the number of abortions Medicaid would pay for. But the expansion, although a significant step in the right direction, would not be enough for some congresswomen, who wanted Medicaid to pay for all poor women's abortions.

Hyde's measure raised questions for poor women, a disproportionate number of whom were black and would suffer simply because of their inability to pay for an abortion. For veteran Congresswoman Cardiss Collins of Illinois and newcomers Cynthia McKinney and Carrie Meek, who felt strongly about helping poor black women in their districts, Hyde would be a watershed vote.

Now, at ten o'clock in the morning on June 30, Pat Schroeder marched onto the House floor, dressed in a scarlet suit. Across the aisle, her opponent's large white head of hair caught the light from the TV cameras. Henry Hyde was a big, affable man. If Capitol Hill had an official greeter, it would certainly have been Hyde. But earlier this morning, the proverbial Jekyll-Hyde metamorphosis had taken place. In his first speech, Hyde had sermonized on the evils of abortion: "My amendment forces us to confront whether we want to coerce . . . people to subsidize the triumph of King Herod, the slaughter of the innocents, and what is more innocent than an unborn child in the womb? It is not a chicken, not a tumor, it is not a diseased appendix. This is a tiny member of the human family."

Schroeder, in the aisle, had meanwhile been stopped cold. "You're not going to believe what we've just heard," Rachel Gorlin, an Appropriations Committee staffer, told Schroeder. If anyone knew what was going on behind the scenes, it was Rachel Gorlin, who was a veteran of every House fight on abortion in the eighties and had worked for former Oregon representative Les AuCoin, a pro-choice legislative expert. Every Thursday morning at 8:30 A.M., as recently as the summer of 1992, Gorlin staffed the strategy sessions for the pro-choice task force, paying for refreshments out of her own pocket. This morning, feeling a little as though she was in the wrong place at the wrong time, Gorlin thrust a piece of paper into Pat Schroeder's hand. On it, Gorlin had written a single sentence: ". . . none of these funds appropriated under this Act shall be expended for any abortion except when it is *made known* to the official. . . ."

Schroeder puzzled over the words. She found it hard to believe that she had not seen this until now. Like it or not, this was brand-new language from the latest version of Henry Hyde's amendment. It had been sitting on a parliamentarian's desk for five days, deliberately hidden from Schroeder's camp.

Schroeder blurted, "What does this mean?" But even without an answer, she understood that this one obscure sentence could be the undoing of all her preparations.

Rachel Gorlin left the chamber and returned a few minutes later with a huge book under her arm: volume seven of *Cannon's Precedents*. Here, on page 687, was the key: a reference, dating to 1908, citing Nebraska congressman Gilbert M. Hitchcock's amendment to an appropriations bill. For the first time in history, the Hitchcock precedent had used the "made known" phrase, which parliamentarians at the time deemed an acceptable "limitation" on the appropriations bill, not illegal "legislation." The use of the passive "made known" language allowed Henry Hyde to set limitations of the use of funds—funds that would pay for abortions—in the appropriations bill. Because Hyde's amendment would not give *new* responsibilities to federal officials, it could not be challenged as "legislating."

Curiously, the House parliamentarians of 1993 knew that eighty-five years earlier the gentleman from Nebraska had made a precedent of questionable merit, but in an effort to prove to Republicans that they were nonpartisan, the parliamentarians kept this precedent from Schroeder and the others—the very same precedent that Henry Hyde was about to use.

But there was still more that Pat Schroeder had not known until now. Worse, it was coming at her from within her own party. William Natcher, the eighty-four-year-old Democratic chairman of the Appropriations Committee and a staunch abortion opponent, had sided with the Republicans, and stabbed his own party in the back. The unmistakable smell of an old boys' deal hung in the air.

In his black mortician's suits and unusually festive neckties, Chairman Natcher made a ghostly presence in the chamber. The night before, Steny Hoyer, Vic Fazio, and Nancy Pelosi, all Democratic Appropriations Committee members, had talked to Natcher. Even though they were members of his party, he gave them no hints about what was to come in today's session. Natcher knew that everyone needed him. All members of Congress wanted something from the Appropriations Committee for their own district—a few million for the courthouse, the new water project, the library. The Democratic leadership couldn't touch Natcher. Even the Clinton administration was reluctant to pressure him.

Clinton had promised in his campaign to lift the Hyde Amendment. In April, the administration sent Congress a "clean" bill, with no Hyde language, in its budget request. But the administration's efforts to prevent the Hyde Amendment from passing stopped there. The White House did not lobby Natcher on the Hyde issue. Instead, the White House sent signals that they were uneasy about overriding state laws on Medicaid funding for abortion, and wanted to find a way for states to have flexibility. Arkansas, for example, had a constitutional amendment that forbade the use of state funds for abortions.

In June, the Secretary of Health and Human Services, Donna Shalala, sent Natcher a nimbly worded letter stating that the administration was opposed to the Hyde Amendment but wanted to "work out an approach . . . consistent with both state and federal law." Pro-choice members of the Appropriations Committee thought the letter hurt more than it helped their argument, because it exposed the administration's lack of commitment to the issue.

That morning, in his most gruff, warlike voice, Natcher had announced that he planned to allow a vote on Hyde's amendment by doing something committee chairmen never do on their own bills. Natcher was going to allow new amendments to be added to his bill by voting *against* the "motion to rise." This would mean that Hyde could now do exactly what Schroeder had been told that Hyde could not do: put up his amendment for a floor vote. In one move, Natcher had snatched back the control Pat Schroeder had until this moment been sure was hers.

For Schroeder, now doubly in the dark, the big question was, Why hadn't anyone told her about *any* of this? Rachel Gorlin had heard a rumor as early as the day before, but she had chosen not to warn Schroeder. Instead, she telephoned Joanne Blum, the lobbyist for Planned Parenthood; Blum had been her comrade in the pro-choice battles of the eighties. Blum had not passed on the tip to Schroeder either. Blum had been lobbying members of Congress that day not to vote against the Hyde Amendment, but to vote for the Freedom of Choice Act, a bill that Pat Schroeder did not fully support. Moreover, pro-choice groups like NARAL and Planned Parenthood had all but exempted themselves from this morning's fight. But the truth was, neither Gorlin nor Blum felt they owed the congresswomen any favors. Pat Schroeder had long been known as a loner. If pressed for an explanation, many of her colleagues would privately agree: Pat Schroeder, a true pioneer, had never been much of an organizer.

Until now, after all, the men of Congress had been in charge of the abortion issue. Before the 1992 elections, congresswomen as a group had never found a unified voice on abortion. Women teamed up with liberal prochoice congressmen like Les AuCoin, Don Edwards, Vic Fazio, and Bill Green. The men had more clout and political expertise than their female colleagues. They also had seniority, leadership positions, chairmanships. With their staffs, the men had been doing the heavy lifting on abortion for more than twelve years.

The addition of twenty-four new pro-choice women in the 103rd Congress had shifted the balance of power. Les AuCoin and Bill Green had lost their elections, leaving room for new leadership. The new congresswomen wanted to make abortion rights a priority in their congressional careers, and the pro-choice task force of the women's caucus became the vehicle for their influence. The congressmen, by default, backed off. Speaker Foley had not reappointed the pro-choice task force that Les AuCoin and Don Edwards had steered through the previous Congress.

The congressmen had also withdrawn from the abortion issue because of a feud boiling behind the scenes during the spring of 1993. At issue was the Freedom of Choice Act. Planned Parenthood, NARAL, and Don Edwards championed the legislation designed to write *Roe v. Wade* into law and prohibit states from passing certain restrictions on abortion availability. They had insulted Schroeder and her female colleagues by introducing the bill in January without consulting the women first. Some congresswomen—among them Schroeder, Slaughter, and McKinney—were skeptical about FOCA's merits, because it failed to address what they saw as the most important issue of the day: public funding for abortions. They believed the bill should be a lower priority with Clinton in the White House, since the threat of the Supreme Court overturning *Roe v. Wade* no longer loomed. Several liberal pro-choice groups also shared the view that FOCA could be a step backward.

Away from the public eye, the fight over FOCA bitterly divided the pro-choice community. The pro-choice members of Congress and the dozen groups devoted to the cause, no longer arrayed against a common enemy in the White House, had split off into factions, scrapping among themselves over what the movement's new offensive strategy would be.

By now, it was 2:30 in the afternoon, and Cynthia McKinney had been listening to the arguments over the

Hyde Amendment with mounting disbelief. Inspired by her anger, she hurriedly scribbled a coda to her prepared speech. She gathered her papers together, walked to the well, and faced her colleagues.

The contrast was a shock. To her left sat the over-whelmingly white male Republicans; to the right, the Democrats, more than half of them women, including eight African-American women. The scene, one of the Democratic congresswomen would later recall, looked like "a bad high school dance, with all the girls huddled in one corner and all the boys in another."

Cynthia now had one minute to make her argument about why poor women should receive Medicaid funding for abortion. "Mr. Chairman," she began, in her high, fluty voice, "for far too many women in this country, the legal right to choose is meaningless, because they have had no practical access to the full range of reproductive services. The real choice for low-income women becomes carrying their pregnancy to term or finding alternative funding—that is, for rent, food, or clothing, or money for unsafe and sometimes self-induced abortions."

Fighting for composure, she went on: "During the past sixteen years of the Hyde Amendment, the unintended pregnancies have not gone away. All available data con-firm that what Hyde has succeeded in doing is creating devastating consequences in the lives of low-income women. The Hyde Amendment is nothing but a discrim-inatory policy against poor women who happen to be dis-proportionately black. . . ."

McKinney seemed to have just started when, behind her, standing on the third—and highest—dais of the speaker's rostrum, the chairman, Representative Philip Sharp, gaveled once, then again. He reminded McKinney her time was up. McKinney drew back slightly from the lectern. She stopped reading her prepared remarks, but she did not stop speaking. Her voice rising, she suddenly said, "Quite frankly, I have just about had it with my colleagues who vote against people of color, vote against the poor, and vote against women." McKinney turned and marched up the aisle to her seat. The blood in her ears was so loud, she couldn't hear the hissing from across the aisle.

Hissing or no, Henry Hyde needed cover. He had taken hits from both parties, almost all of them from women. He needed a woman on his side. Before using the last of his allotted time to close out the morning's debate, he turned to Barbara Vucanovich, the seventy-two-year-old conservative Republican from Nevada. Without ever taking her own place at the microphone, Vucanovich leaned over and spoke into a microphone held open to her by Hyde. "I urge a no vote on the motion to rise, and I strongly support the Hyde Amendment," she said.

Now came Hyde's turn. Eyes flashing, Hyde pointed a finger at the Democratic women. He seemed at first to be taking them seriously. "I want to say to my friends on the other side, especially those that debated opposite my position, that I am sincerely glad that they were born and that they avoided being aborted." His tone turning fatuous, he added, "I am delighted they are here. They have added to the civilization we live in."

Next he replied to Cynthia McKinney: "About those people that say the poor are discriminated against, you know what we do?" Hyde again began to preach, thrusting his index finger in the air. "We tell poor women, 'You can't have a job, you can't have a decent place to live . . . I'll tell you what we'll do, we'll give you a free abortion because there are too many of you people, and we want to kind of refine—refine the breed. . . ."

From the far side of the chamber: hisses.

"And I tell you," Hyde went on, "if you read the literature, that is what is said, and that is what is done. . . ."

Cardiss Collins, the sixty-one-year-old Chicago congresswoman, looked as if she were about to explode. In a deep, even voice, she roared, "Mr. Chairman, will the gentleman yield?"

"I do not have the time," Hyde flung back dismissively.

"I am offended by that kind of debate," Collins flared.

Behind Collins, Democrats clapped and cheered their support. Representative Carrie Meek was by now so angry her eyes began to stream with tears. "Just let me at him," she cried. "I'll get him by the you-know-whats."

Eight times, the chairman banged the gavel, trying to silence the increasingly chaotic House. "The committee will be in order!" the chairman commanded.

But Hyde wasn't finished. Pointing his finger at Collins, Hyde announced, "I am going to direct my friend to a few ministers who will tell her just what goes on in her community."

This time he had gone too far. Beyond patronizing, beyond fatuity and self-righteousness, this was outrageous behavior for a member of Congress. Henry Hyde had no business telling Cardiss Collins how to represent her people. Collins had served the 7th District of Illinois, abutting Hyde's district and 66 percent black, since 1973. She did not need Henry Hyde's "friendship."

The Democrats erupted into a chorus of loud jeers and boos. Collins, with Carrie Meek and Cynthia McKinney standing behind her, requested that Hyde's words be "taken down"—a disciplinary measure censuring offending comments that are directed specifically toward a colleague. Collins' request was denied by the parliamentarian. Later that day, Hyde would apologize to Collins and erase from the *Congressional Record* his two most offensive remarks, about "refining the breed" and directing Collins to clergymen in her district. He would also tell the *Washington Post* that he was frightened by the showdown. "It is intimidating to have five or six women all glaring at you. It was like lighting a firecracker."

Schroeder had one minute to end the debate. She felt queasy. Her voice was shaky, her breath short, her speech unfocused. She seemed uncertain about how to proceed. The women in the debate, she pointed out, were "being made to develop and debate an amendment we did not see, we did not know about, on an appropriation bill where the rules of this House say it does not belong."

As for Henry Hyde, "I say to the gentleman from Illinois, women are not beasts, and that is what we are really hearing here. . . . It seems to me that when the 19th amendment passed, we should have been equal beings. But we are hearing that we have got to go through these incredible procedural backflips to try to put all these restrictions on because women of America can't be trusted."

The following week, reporters would ask the black congresswomen if they were going to drop out of the women's caucus because the white congresswomen did not defend Cardiss Collins on the House floor. Because Schroeder had not come to Collins's aid in her speech, much less yielded her own time at the microphone to Collins, she would leave the impression that she was out of touch with the passions of the moment.

In truth, the congresswomen grew even closer because of June 30. "What we realized that day is that we can only count on each other," said McKinney. Privately, however, McKinney ventured that "white women don't know how to fight" as well as black women do. McKinney felt right at home in the fight. "It felt like the Georgia legislature," she later said. "Because there was a touch of racism. There was disdain for the position of women."

But the day was not over. Now came the Hyde Amendment itself. Essentially, members were being asked to choose between voting for slightly relaxed restrictions on abortion funding or no restrictions at all. "It was an impossible vote," said a congresswoman's abortion-rights staffer. The new and improved Hyde Amendment gave political cover to the "mushy middle," a majority of members who were pro-choice but also supported some restrictions on abortion. Hyde, for a change, represented the middle ground. The women looked like the radicals of the debate. William Natcher, feeling more and more uncomfortable under the hostile gaze of the Democratic women standing next to him, wanted to get it over with, and the amendment was put to a vote.

The House agreed to the Hyde Amendment 255 to 178. The voting told a great deal about the political realities of the 103rd Congress: 77 percent of all women members and 37 percent of all men voted against the Hyde Amendment. Eighty-six percent of Democratic women and 58 percent of Democratic men voted against the amendment. Fifty percent of Republican women and 6 percent of Republican men voted against Hyde. The vote count proved that both Republican and Democratic women were significantly more pro-choice than Republican and Democratic men. Eleven women sided with Hyde—five Republicans and six Democrats, all from conservative districts.

After the votes were counted, something interesting happened. Hyde turned to a woman who all day long had been sitting quietly behind him to say, "I just want to thank you. Without your suggestions, this wouldn't have happened."

The woman was Deborah Pryce. Sitting silently behind Hyde through much of the day, Pryce had nonetheless influenced the Republican victory. She had been one of the class of '92's twenty-four pro-choice congresswomen. In her campaign, she had received donations from pro-choice political action committees like Republicans for Choice, WISH List, and the Women's Campaign Fund. At the time, Pryce passed the Women's Campaign Fund's litmus test. She filled out a questionnaire saying that she supported federal funding for abortion. Now she was all but going against her word.

Abortion had always been a sticky issue for Pryce. During her '92 campaign, she had been accused of flip-flopping on the issue. She had been able to win a close race for the Republican party nomination because she led pro-life Republicans to believe that she was also pro-life. Pryce, who was an infertility patient for ten years, adopted a baby girl in August of 1990. The ordeal of infertility and adoption changed her opinion on abortion. She was no longer staunchly pro-choice. Now she was "personally opposed" to abortion, she told her fellow Republicans.

After Pryce received the Republican party endorsement, she resigned from the bench, where she had been a municipal judge, and was free to discuss her political opinions for the first time. Just one week after Pryce received the Republican party endorsement, she announced that while she was personally opposed to abortion, her politics were decidedly pro-choice. Pryce's perceived betrayal infuriated the right-to-life movement, who retaliated by running their own pro-life candidate in the race.

Now, as a member of Congress, Pryce calculated correctly that most taxpayers did not want their money spent on all abortions. At the time, thirty-one states, including her home state, Ohio, had laws allowing for Medicaid funds to pay for abortion only if the mother's life was in danger.

Pryce played a role in expanding the Hyde Amendment to include rape and incest. She and Republican freshwoman Tillie Fowler of Florida agreed that they couldn't vote the party line unless the Hyde Amendment was expanded to include rape and incest. A month before the vote came up, the two women approached Hyde on the House floor and asked him if he would consider including rape and incest. Hyde brushed them off. But two weeks later, after his vote count showed that a pure Hyde Amendment was in trouble, Hyde came back to Pryce and Fowler. "We made it clear that as Republican women we wouldn't be much help to him," said Pryce. "We told him that the amendment would have a lot better chance of passing" if rape and incest exceptions were included.

The next day, when Pat Schroeder called a press conference, she had no talking points to guide her. But as one aide would later reveal, an unofficial "spin strategy" had been worked out to "avoid the 'stupid' angle." Schroeder and the others had worked long and hard with the parliamentarians, who weeks later would apologize and admit that they were wrong not to show the women the precedent. Even if certain victory had become a waterloo, none of the women deserved to be tagged "stupid" about House procedures. They chose instead to "make it a 'sexist' angle." Ten women sat at a large square table with reporters, rehashing Hyde but mainly venting their anger. What the reporters saw was more confession than polish.

Cynthia McKinney admitted, "We have some learning to do."

Louise Slaughter seemed to agree: "We really showed them that we could be had. It was a terrible setback and we really have to take a look at what we're doing here."

When Nita Lowey admitted that the women had been outmaneuvered, her press secretary, Howard Wolfson, cringed. Afterward, he took Lowey aside and unbraided her for being too self-effacing. In their anger, the congresswomen had perhaps been too candid. A staffer, looking back on it later, would admit, "we should have waited until everyone had cooled down."

"It seems to me that these men don't realize we're equal partners in this House of Representatives," said Cardiss Collins, still seething over her floor fight with Hyde. "They don't run the whole show."

Anna Eshoo, a freshwoman from California, said, "My own view is that we were rolled from the inside."

Schroeder complained that when it had been clear that Hyde and Natcher had tricked them, Foley and the Democratic leadership should not have left the women hanging—they should have pulled the bill off the floor. But the leadership did not want to cross the all-powerful Natcher. In charge of abortion strategy for the first time, the women had been left holding the bag.

Some members revealed how new they were to the institution. "I was shocked to learn that this is not a pro-choice Congress," said first-term Representative Lynn

Schenk of San Diego, who was the vice chair of Nita Lowey's pro-choice task force. "With all the hype of the Year of the Woman, I was lulled into a false sense of change." Afterward, longtime pro-choice experts would mock Schenk's remarks. "Honey," said one staffer, "get a clue. I'm not responsible for your inability to count [votes]."

One of the congresswomen's legislative assistants seemed to speak for them all when she observed, "Women take loss differently. They blame themselves more. If Chuck Schumer had lost on a big bill, the last thing he would have done is hold a press conference afterward to tell everyone how horrible he felt."

The next day, *The New York Times* said the women looked "naïve, unprepared and inept." They got pounded in the other major dailies, too. As it all began to sink in, Pat Schroeder realized that the press conference had been a mistake. The women had ignored a cardinal political rule: You're not hit until you *look* hit.

7

The Squeaky Wheel

The women in the House were still licking their Hyde Amendment wounds when Senator Carol Moseley-Braun made a surprising announcement. She planned to take her name off the co-sponsorship list of the Freedom of Choice Act. Moseley Braun's disclosure constituted the second major blow to the pro-choice community in only two weeks. This time the firepower came from inside the pro-choice ranks; once again, race and class were at issue. Moseley-Braun exposed the heart of the debate over FOCA when she said that the legislation "discriminates against young and poor women" because "it trades off the rights of some women for the promise of rights for others."

Moseley-Braun's announcement, coupled with the Hyde Amendment floor fight, which had featured African-American congresswomen, revealed a trend: For the first time in the history of the U.S. Congress and the twenty-five-year abortion-rights struggle, black female lawmakers were leading the debate.

The National Organization for Women and the National Black Women's Health Project had urged Moseley-Braun to publicly announce her opposition to FOCA. By doing so, the liberal pro-choice groups declared war on the more politically moderate pro-choice organizations like NARAL and Planned Parenthood, who had made FOCA the centerpiece of their legislative agenda.

After Moseley-Braun's announcement, all eyes turned to the African-American women in the House. Would they join Moseley-Braun and drop off FOCA? Cynthia McKinney found herself in an intoxicating position of power. She and her fellow black congresswomen held the fate of FOCA, and of the pro-choice movement, in their grasp. McKinney had co-sponsored FOCA in May, but she had had second thoughts about the legislation. She agreed with Moseley-Braun's analysis that the bill was an "unacceptable compromise."

McKinney wanted funding for poor women's abortions to be a greater priority of the pro-choice movement, and FOCA did not address this issue. McKinney also thought that Moseley-Braun's announcement served as a needed wake-up call that forced pro-choice groups, many of whom sat out the Hyde Amendment debate, to start taking the issue of abortion funding more seriously. McKinney's choice was clear. She could either follow Moseley-Braun's public protest against FOCA, or she could play her cards more subtly and work behind the scenes.

By mid-year, McKinney had begun to learn the ropes and become a player. Shedding her early naïveté, she no longer found herself unknowingly insulting powerful committee chairmen. She knew her way around and didn't have to ask dismissive guards for directions. Elevator operators knew her by name. More important, the president and the Democratic leadership knew her by both name and reputation. She had gained recognition and respect among her colleagues as an activist and a party loyalist.

Carol Moseley-Braun's announcement placed McKinney at a crossroads. By nature, McKinney felt comfortable as a dissenter: she was Billy McKinney's daughter, and her early political education consisted of confronting conservative Southern politicians in Georgia. The political climate in Washington, however, was much more attuned to McKinney's liberal, progressive views. She knew that if she wanted to become an effective legislator, she would have to put down her dukes and start making friends.

For the past six months, the job of finding a consensus on the Freedom of Choice Act had fallen to the chair of the pro-choice task force, Nita Lowey, a fifty-five-year-old mother of three who had been elected to Congress in 1988. When Lowey first ran for Congress in 1987, one of her political opponents described her as a "schleppy, giggly, uninformed housewife." But by 1994, Lowey had become a skilled negotiator. During February and March, her task force met every two weeks to discuss whether or not the women's caucus should endorse FOCA. The task force listened to all sides of the argument, meeting with pro-choice groups who both opposed and supported the bill. Lowey convinced the congresswomen to keep their differences over FOCA under wraps. If news that the women were not behind FOCA leaked to the press, Lowey knew the bill would die instantly.

For the freshwomen, the two-page Freedom of Choice Act was the first congressional bill many of them had read closely. The meetings in February and March were about more than just analyzing a piece of legislation—they were about the fundamental question of what being pro-choice in 1993 meant. Just believing abortion should be legal was no longer good enough. With Clinton in the White House, the boundaries had shifted, moving the pro-choice definition to the left. To be truly pro-choice required supporting federal funding of abortions for low-income women and opposing parental notification for minors. The Freedom of Choice Act compromised this pure position because it failed to address funding and condoned parental-notification laws.

In April, the women's caucus quietly announced that it would endorse FOCA as a group. Lowey had persuaded the congresswomen to endorse FOCA in exchange for adopting a broader abortion agenda and focusing equally on three fronts: funding, FOCA, and clinic violence. Kate Michelman, NARAL's president and FOCA's chief sponsor, was so overjoyed by the caucus's announcement that she sent Nita Lowey a dozen yellow roses.

Now, in one fell swoop, Carol Moseley-Braun had undone the fragile consensus Lowey had worked so hard to achieve. Lowey immediately called McKinney and the other African-American congresswomen and pleaded with them not to follow Moseley-Braun. She knew that if the black women in the House dropped off FOCA, it would seriously damage the credibility of the entire pro-choice movement. Lowey believed that Moseley-Braun's protest fueled the flames of a divided women's movement.

After listening to both sides of the issue, McKinney decided to stay on as a co-sponsor of FOCA and to use her leverage from the inside. "I didn't want to become a tool of those whose ultimate goal is to divide white women and women of color," she said. McKinney bargained with the pro-FOCA groups. She wouldn't make a public display of her differences with the bill if they in turn would make funding for poor woman a top priority. Carol Moseley-Braun had already delivered the protest. Now McKinney could pick up where Moseley-Braun left off and push for change.

Hoping to deflect negative news stories about the stinging Hyde defeat and schisms within the pro-choice ranks over FOCA, McKinney decided that the woman's caucus needed a new cause to rally behind. As it happened, Jocelyn Elders, an Arkansas pediatrician, had just been nominated by Bill Clinton for surgeon general. Dr. Elders was the first African-American woman to be considered for the job, and her work on preventing teenage pregnancy and preventive health care for children appealed to virtually every member of the women's caucus. The Elders nomination was under attack from the right—she had been labeled the "condom queen" because of her outspoken advocacy of sex education and condom distribution in high schools.

McKinney, as the newly appointed chair of the caucus's task force on children, found herself in the perfect position to take a stand on Elders. The Monday after Moseley-Braun's announcement, McKinney shot off a memo to all the women in the caucus. She urged them to sign a letter of support for Elders. Next, McKinney organized a press conference. McKinney wanted the women's caucus to present, once again, a unified front. McKinney's press secretary, Susie Rodriguez, held a meeting with other press secretaries in which she stressed that the message of the press conference should be "unity." The press conference would be another step in Cynthia McKinney's initiation.

On July 15, twenty congresswomen came to show their support. The Capitol's small radio-TV gallery overflowed with reporters; the excess people were sent to an ante-room where they could listen to the proceedings on a loudspeaker.

McKinney spoke first. She announced that Elders was an excellent choice for surgeon general because she had been a "strong voice for those in need, from education programs to preventive care, from women's health to children's needs." McKinney noted that America ranked twentieth in the world in infant mortality and thirty-first in the world in low-birthweight babies—a trend that had worsened in the 1980s and a trend that Elders, who had turned the tide for low birthweight babies in Arkansas, was qualified to address.

Next came Maxine Waters, Barbara-Rose Collins, Patsy Mink, Blanche Lambert, Nydia Velazquez, Carrie Meek, and others. An unusual sense of camaraderie prevailed. No one played to the cameras, no one hogged the credit. Each congresswoman thanked McKinney for organizing the press conference.

She had dressed for the occasion in a hot pink silk jacket and a green-and-pink matching silk dress. Her hair was arranged in a crown of tight braids, and everyone said she looked terrific. Her colleagues' compliments were more than small talk: they revealed something about the way this class of woman politicians was able to do business with one another. At a typical Capitol Hill press conference, the accepted manner is squash-court competitive; congressmen angle for position, the best sound bite wins. But these women weren't afraid to talk about the things women talk about, or to display themselves as women. In one another's company, at one another's press conferences, they no longer felt they had to be men.

The press conference worked. Press coverage the next day demonstrated that the women's caucus was a force to be reckoned with. In September, Elders' appointment was confirmed by the Senate, although her outspoken style would lead to her ultimate dismissal by President Clinton in 1994. The Freedom of Choice Act was scarcely mentioned again. Overshadowed by pro-choice legislation that provided funding for new populations of women, FOCA would not reach the House or Senate floor for a vote in the following year and a half of the 103rd Congress.

One week later, Carol Moseley-Braun made another bold move. Taking the floor, Moseley-Braun convinced twenty-seven senators to change the votes they had cast only three hours earlier to reject Jesse Helms' amendment granting a patent extension to the United Daughters of the Confederacy. The patent had become a matter of Senate tradition. First issued in 1898 to protect the UDC's insignia—a stylized flag of the Confederate States of America—the patent demonstrated, by 1993, how out of touch the Senate had become. It took Carol Moseley-Braun to tell the Senate that this was a vote about "racial symbols, the racial past, and the single most painful episode in American history." In a dramatic, emotional floor speech, Moseley-Braun single-handedly sensitized the Senate to a matter of racial history that its all-white members had not considered in a hundred years. Moseley-Braun's stand against the symbolism of the Confederate flag and against Jesse Helms, the Senate's most conservative, antiquated Southerner, proved that old habits could be broken.

Carol Moseley-Braun's courage to take on the Senate inspired Cynthia McKinney. McKinney's Georgians were some of America's most politically neglected constituents—

rural, poor, black, many of them victims of intimidation and discrimination by mayors, school boards, and city councils. McKinney was the first African American to represent them in the U.S. Congress.

McKinney's passion to improve the lives of her constituents was genuine, verging on the holier-than-thou. But the path that she took in order to deliver on her promises to her district was far from holy, or even selfless. As one of McKinney's closest aids said, "Her agenda is to achieve power first, and then to achieve her goals once she has the power." Real success would involve pushing and shoving, self-promotion and compromising.

McKinney represented a new generation of black politicians. The original civil rights activists, like her father, had broken the initial barriers. Billy McKinney's generation opened the door for Cynthia's. Her job was to go through that door and do what it took to stay inside. So when the White House telephoned McKinney's office on May 5 to invite the congresswoman to join the president for an early-morning jog, McKinney knew she was on her way.

All that spring, as Washington had grown greener and greener, Clinton had been asking members of Congress to jog with him. The four-mile, early-morning runs along the Mall or down by the Potomac at Haines Point had given the president a chance to stay in shape—his waistline continued to be fodder for cartoonists and late-night comedians—but also to twist arms. In the next three weeks, his budget bill would come to a vote in the House, and he needed as many supporters as possible.

McKinney hadn't exercised in five years. She never jogged, and she didn't own running shoes. McKinney's fellow freshwoman Lynn Schenk of California had turned down her invitation to jog with the president for similar reasons. Lynn Schenk just wasn't a runner, nor did she think of herself as a "photo-opportunity kind of person," which was, actually, the point of the whole endeavor. The sight of bulky President Clinton, smiling from under his latest baseball cap and accompanied by several members of Congress, sporting extra-large T-shirts and short running shorts, had become the capital city's daily press release. Running with the president was the swiftest way onto the local news or front-page wire photo back home.

Still, some members had refused. Who, after all, would suddenly try running four miles on a warm May morning, let alone four miles while talking policy with the president? "I am at an age," said Lynn Schenk, "where I have better sense than to make a fool of myself."

McKinney never hesitated. She accepted the president's invitation immediately. To McKinney, any access was good access. She wanted to show Georgia that she was playing the game in Washington, that she had power and credibility. That she was being taken seriously and could get things done.

The next morning, suited up and ready to schmooze, McKinney arrived at the White House at the appointed hour—6:50 A.M. Within ten minutes, the president's party had been bused to Haines Point and set down under the bright-green leaves of early May. First came the advance Secret Service detail, followed by the president, who was flanked by three members of Congress—Sanford Bishop of Georgia, Mike Kreidler of Washington, and McKinney— all followed by an ambulance, a Secret Service van, and pairs of motorized policemen.

This procession moved slowly around the grassy peninsula. For the first half-mile, everything was fine. McKinney found herself happily running and chatting beside Clinton, who was relaxed and friendly. It felt like the sunniest May morning of her life.

McKinney followed the president another half mile. As they jogged, they talked about the Clinton economic stimulus package, about health care, and about the House gym—Clinton was amazed to hear that women weren't allowed to use the members' gym. But now it was getting harder to run and to talk at the same time. McKinney had begun to pant noticeably. Then, all at once, she felt clobbered by dizziness. The president, meanwhile, chatted on easily, showing no signs of fatigue. McKinney struggled on a few more steps, her knee-length T-shirt and ankle-length stretch pants feeling as though they were made of chain mail, her running shoes as though they were made of lead.

Falling off the pace, she realized that she could save herself from a total washout by flagging down the Secret Service van. For the next three miles, as the president jogged, and as McKinney's Georgia colleague Sanford Bishop bit his lower lip to keep from sucking air, McKinney rode in air-conditioned Secret Service comfort. Then, as the procession neared the end of its Haines Point loop, McKinney saw that the moment of truth was at hand. The pool of TV cameras and photographers, which until now had been kept quarantined from the presidential entourage, had been given clearance to photograph the president as he swept by to finish the run.

In a flash, McKinney leapt from the van. At a comfortable trot, she resumed her place in the procession, neatly reattaching herself on the president's right flank. Her tim-

ing couldn't have been better. A year and a half later, after Clinton's popularity had plummeted, pictures of the
president jogging with Democratic members of Congress
would be used against them by Republicans in the 1994
congressional elections, but for McKinney, the jog with
Clinton only made her star shine brighter. The next morning, the Georgia papers carried exactly the picture that
McKinney had gone running for: Congresswoman
McKinney on a bright May morning chatting easily with
the president. Susie Rodriguez immediately sent out a
press release touting the jog.

It had been only five months since she had saved herself
an aisle seat at the president's first State of the Union Address. Becoming a staunch Clinton supporter had been
the first step in McKinney's strategy to gain access and
power. She spoke out in support of Clinton's initiatives.
She faxed her speeches and press releases to the White
House congressional liaison office. She had been an easy
"yes" vote on the stimulus package (which failed) and the
Budget-Reconciliation Act (which passed by only one
vote). And although she did not require intensive lobbying and favors from the administration in return for her
votes, she was often the first person, as one White House
aide put it, to "have her hand out."

In March, McKinney had flown to Georgia on Air
Force One with the president. She used her access to
Clinton to ask for help in her district. McKinney explained that a poor neighborhood in Augusta called
Hyde Park had become a toxic waste dump. The Southern Wood Piedmont plant had shut down its operation
there and left the soil and water in the surrounding

neighborhood contaminated. About forty people in the community had died in the last two years from pollution-related diseases.

McKinney told the president that she wanted the Environmental Protection Agency to intervene and designate Hyde Park a Superfund site. The next day, the EPA called McKinney's office. Eight months later, the Agency for Toxic Substances and Disease Registry issued a report labeling the neighborhood "a hazard to public health."

Six months later, McKinney had another crisis in her district for which she needed the administration's help. Sixty percent of the world's kaolin supply is mined in Georgia, and most of the state's "kaolin belt" resides in the 11th Congressional District. The clay, which is called "white gold," is used in the manufacture of hundreds of products, including ceramics, magazine paper, toothpaste, and latex paints. One billion dollars' worth of kaolin is strip-mined from Georgia's poorest counties every year by large multinational companies that drastically underpay landowners. Some landowners get as little as a nickel a ton for kaolin, which, after refining, sells for up to $700 a ton. Unlike the coal-mining companies in Kentucky, the kaolin-mining companies pay no mineral severance tax, depriving the state of about $65 million a year (if the tax were 5 percent).

After the *Atlanta Journal-Constitution* published an exposé of the kaolin industry in May of 1993, McKinney began to hear complaints from landowners in her district who claimed they had been forced by the kaolin-mining companies to lease their land for long periods of time, from fifty to ninety-nine years, at very low rates. McKinney met with her constituents and learned that members of state government had been influenced by the powerful industry and refused to challenge the status quo. In September, McKinney wrote a letter to Attorney General Janet Reno asking the Justice Department to investigate allegations that the kaolin companies had conspired to fix prices and use "fraud and trickery" to prevent landowners from receiving fair value for the kaolin on their property. The Justice Department never responded.

In November, Cynthia met Janet Reno at a White House reception, where she buttonholed the forbidding, six-foot-one-inch-tall attorney general to ask her why the Justice Department hadn't responded to her letter. Within hours, Reno called the head of DOJ's congressional liaison office and asked for immediate action on the kaolin case. An aide in the department would later explain that Reno, the first woman attorney general, often "responds better to women than she does to men." But there was another reason, too: Reno asked the department to look into the case so that McKinney would stop "haranguing" her.

Four months later, in February 1994, officials from the Justice Department paid Cynthia a visit. They told her that a preliminary check showed some serious violations of antitrust law. Justice, they said, would consider investigating Georgia's kaolin industry. Seven months later, it became official. The antitrust division of the Justice Department began conducting an open investigation of the kaolin industry. "The squeaky wheel," said Cynthia, "gets the grease."

After the presidential jog in May, McKinney's collegiality with Washington's power brokers widened. By late July 1993, she had broken from the Congressional black caucus during the budget debate on the Earned-Income

Tax Credit. The two chairmen of the House Ways and Means Committee and the Senate Finance Committee were in the midst of conducting a secretive conference committee on the budget, reconciling the Senate and House versions of the bill. McKinney had heard a rumor that the Earned-Income Tax Credit (EITC), which gave taxed revenues back to low-income workers (an average of about $3,000 to families and $300 to childless workers), was about to be decreased from the president's proposed $28 billion to $17 billion, and that childless workers would be cut out of the Earned-Income Credit entirely. The EITC and an antipoverty program, Empowerment Zones, were competing for the same pot of money, and it looked as though the Empowerment Zones would win.

Charles Rangel of New York City, the dean of the black caucus and a senior member of the Ways and Means Committee, favored the Empowerment Zones. McKinney believed that part of Rangel's enthusiasm had to do with the fact that his Harlem district would be a likely recipient of at least one of the ten zones. McKinney feared that her rural district would be less likely to benefit from Empowerment Zone projects. The small towns and cities in Georgia's 11th District could easily be overlooked, while big cities like New York, Chicago, and Los Angeles, with their impoverished neighborhoods, might get most of the money. The EITC, on the other hand, gave money to all low-income workers, regardless of their geographic location.

In order to press her agenda, McKinney had to talk to the two men who were single-handedly managing the budget bill in congress: Dan Rostenkowski and Daniel Patrick Moynihan. She found Rostenkowski on the House floor, at the head of a long line of congressmen. McKinney took her place at the end of the line and waited her turn. Rarely shy, McKinney couldn't help feeling intimidated by the idea of asking favors from this larger-than-life Chicago pol. When she finally came face to face with Rosty, she got it all out in one breath: "Mr. Chairman, we've got to protect childless workers, we've got to keep the EITC at $22 billion. Please do that for me!"

Lifting his eyebrows and his right thumb, the chairman gave a nod.

A few days later, in a Senate office building hallway, McKinney ran into Senator Moynihan. She had never met him before. Not missing a beat, she asked the chairman of the Senate Finance Committee if she could have a meeting with him to discuss the Earned-Income Tax Credit. The senator agreed. McKinney marched into his office on a hot July night at 6:00 P.M. with four freshman members of the Congressional black caucus.

McKinney and Moynihan instantly discovered that they were both graduates of Tufts University. Pleasantries aside, McKinney announced that she was staging a coup. "We are not speaking for the whole black caucus," she told Moynihan. "The black caucus has spoken, but we would be happy to take some Empowerment Zone money and transfer it into real money."

Moynihan, the most learned and experienced antipoverty expert in Congress, agreed with the substance of McKinney's argument. He had always favored the EITC over Empowerment Zones, but the black caucus, and especially Charles Rangel, held the political chips on the issue. McKinney's support would give Moynihan the cover he needed to increase funding for the EITC. "It was very important to Moynihan that his doubts about the way the pie was cut up were shared by some members of the black caucus," said a Moynihan aide.

On August 5, when Pennsylvania freshwoman Marjorie Margolies-Mezvinsky cast the dramatic 218th vote to pass the omnibus Budget-Reconciliation Bill, McKinney's wish came true: the Earned-Income Tax Credit was funded at $21 billion. From then on, the elder members of the black caucus started taking McKinney seriously.

By the time the North American Free Trade Agreement (NAFTA) came to Congress in November 1993, McKinney's relations with the White House had been fortified by a series of loyal party-line votes. Not only had McKinney learned how to gain favor, she had learned how to use it. McKinney had watched as the fence sitters on the budget votes were heavily courted by the administration with visits from Clinton to their districts and various legislative concessions. McKinney discovered that "holding your gunpowder" until the last minute would give you more leverage to get what you wanted from the White House.

The North American Free Trade Agreement would eliminate trade barriers and tariffs among the United States, Mexico, and Canada. Even though free trade had generally been a Republican issue, Clinton enthusiastically endorsed it. Most liberal Democrats, with close ties to labor, opposed the treaty. Cynthia knew from the very beginning that she would not vote for NAFTA, but she decided not to tip her hand too quickly.

For weeks before the November 17 vote, McKinney's name remained on the "undecided" list. Cynthia entertained a host of pro-NAFTA lobbyists. Ross Perot stopped by her office. Jimmy Carter called. Energy Secretary Hazel

O'Leary also called. McKinney patiently listened to O'Leary's reasons for why she should vote for NAFTA. Then she asked O'Leary if the Energy Department could look into two toxic-waste problems in her district—Hyde Park and the Savannah River nuclear power plant.

On the day of the NAFTA vote, O'Leary sent McKinney a long-stemmed red rose with her business card attached by a white ribbon. A note on the back of her card said: "Thanks for listening. Fondly, Hazel."

President Clinton, meanwhile, was doing more than sending out roses. The day before, November 16, Clinton's vote count still looked too close to call. The time had come to call in all votes. Clinton had reserved his evening to meet with members of Congress who his staff had assured him were in the "if needed" category. As a matter of courtesy, and because they didn't want to waste the president's time, several members of Congress who knew they were going to vote against NAFTA turned down invitations to the White House that night. But McKinney was still officially on the "undecided" list, and she accepted the president's invitation to meet with him in the Oval Office.

It was a cool November evening. In the Oval Office, the thick, beige curtains were drawn. Only one White House staffer was in the room. Protocol for private meetings with the president called for members of Congress to come alone. Cynthia did not know this, and she brought a member of her staff, Mario Chapman, as well as her fiancé, Muhammad Jamal, who had flown up from Atlanta just for the occasion. Before the first exchange with the president, Cynthia had already made a crucial blunder: her entourage was larger than the chief executive's. It appeared to the White House as though McKinney's friendly relations with the president had gone to her head. In light of what was to come, she seemed not so much naïve, which in fact she was, but willing to take advantage of the president's goodwill in order to impress her fiancé by parading him around the White House.

Clinton began the meeting by asking McKinney point-blank if she planned to vote for NAFTA. To the president's surprise, Cynthia said no. She gave her reasons. NAFTA was one of the few national issues on which her black and white constituents stood equally opposed. McKinney felt obligated to find common ground in her racially divided district. She also opposed the free-trade agreement because in her district small farmers and small textile industries relied on cheap labor. If NAFTA passed, these businesses, she feared, would abandon Georgia for Mexico. She did offer one concession on NAFTA, however: she would vote late, and she wouldn't speak on the floor against the bill.

Then, without a pause, full of Billy McKinney bravado, Cynthia launched into her own agenda—a long list of the favors she needed for her district. She needed the Justice Department to continue investigating the kaolin industry; she needed the EPA to designate Hyde Park a Superfund zone; she needed the Energy Department to clean up nuclear waste from the Savannah River site. Last of all, because a group of white constituents had just filed a lawsuit calling for the 11th District to be redrawn, claiming that its formation discriminated against white voters, McKinney needed the civil rights division of the Justice Department to defend her district.

McKinney went on and on. Gauche, blunt, she sounded as though she had been invited over to lecture the president on a wide range of issues. Clinton, for example, should not nominate John Payton to head the Justice Department's civil rights division. Although the NAACP backed Payton, he was not the right man for the job. He was not an expert on the Voting Rights Act, and he hadn't voted in several years.

The meeting had been going from bad to worse when Cynthia told the president that she was seriously considering voting for the bipartisan Penny-Kasich plan, which would trim the deficit by $103 billion over five years.

Until now, Clinton had listened patiently. He had not tried to twist her arm on NAFTA; clearly, McKinney had her reasons and her mind was made up. But Penny-Kasich was something else again. The bill was coming to the House floor in six days, and Cynthia had picked the wrong side to support. The Clinton administration had launched an all-out lobbying attack against Penny-Kasich, which it considered draconian. The president had countered Penny-Kasich with a proposal to cut the budget by $37 billion over five years.

Clinton's face turned red. He raised his voice. McKinney tried to tell the president that she felt political pressure to be fiscally conservative, but Clinton didn't seem to understand the political sensitivity the Penny-Kasich plan had in her district. He had had enough lectures for one evening's meeting on the NAFTA bill, and he began to rage: "Don't ever come back here asking for anything if you vote for that bill!"

The meeting ended abruptly. As one White House aide later described it, Cynthia had shown very bad judgment. After the meeting, Clinton simmered down, but he remained disappointed and upset. "He lost his confidence and goodwill toward Cynthia," another White House source revealed. "Her ratings were too high for her to live up to."

On November 22, Cynthia changed her mind and voted against the Penny-Kasich amendment. The vote was narrow—a margin of only five votes defeated the bill. Nonetheless, the president still felt burned by Cynthia. On January 25, 1994, when he gave his second State of the Union Address, he was a completely different Clinton from the friendly, smiling new president who had given Cynthia a bear hug. This January, Cynthia had once again saved herself the all-important center aisle seat, where she would be guaranteed exposure to the television cameras. But this year, when Clinton passed by he offered Cynthia nothing more than a brusque handshake. His eyes shifted instantly away from her. The moment—or lack of it—told the whole story. Her honeymoon with the president was over.

The next day, McKinney called everyone she knew in the White House: What could she do to make it up to the president? No one she spoke to had an answer, and most of those she called did not call back. She kept on calling. Ever since her jog with Clinton in May, Cynthia had taken up the sport for real. Again and again, she had asked Clinton's young adviser, George Stephanopoulos, to go jogging with her. It was beginning to feel a little like the eighth grade. Stephanopoulos would talk with Cynthia, but he refused to jog.

Then a few weeks later, things changed. Cynthia got the signal she had been looking for. At a Governor's Association meeting, Clinton took Georgia Governor Zell Miller aside and asked Miller to support Cynthia's district in the upcoming reverse-discrimination lawsuit. "Luckily for Cynthia," said one White House aide, "the president doesn't know how to hold a grudge."

8

$\diamond$

Harassment

Patty Murray had run for the Senate because of her out-rage at how the Judiciary Committee had treated Anita Hill. She had been sent to Washington by an electorate that, for the most part agreed with her. If she owed her Senate seat to any single issue, it was sexual harassment.

When Murray served in the Washington state senate, fe-male staffers who had been sexually harassed came to her to talk about their problems. Murray asked one secretary why she hadn't filed charges against her employer. "Are you kidding?" the woman replied. "I'll be the one who ends up really getting hurt in the process. I'll lose my job. I'll never make it."

Murray later admitted, "I was oblivious." It didn't take her long to realize how easy it was for elected officials to abuse their power. "The cards are stacked against anybody who makes a claim," she said. "When you're working for an elected official who has all of the power, who can fire you in an instant, who can make it impossible for you to get a job anywhere, you have no influence whatsoever." Sexual harassment was a power struggle that appealed to Murray because she liked to "fight for the little guy." She responded to the complaints about sexual harassment by putting regulations protecting state senate employees on the books.

When Murray went to Washington, D.C., however, she was surprised to find that congressional employees in the House and Senate had very little legal recourse when it came to filing sexual harassment claims. Conditions on the Hill became all too clear when the *Washington Post* ran a long exposé revealing that Senator Bob Packwood had made unwanted sexual overtures to ten women, several of whom had worked for him. The story was published on November 22, 1992, nineteen days after the Oregon Republican had been reelected to his fifth term.

After Murray read the account of her colleague's sexual misconduct, she called for an end to the congressional exemption to federal laws that prohibited sexual harassment. She favored creating strict rules to discipline members in cases like Packwood's. Murray also required the members of her staff to listen to a presentation on sexual harassment before starting their first day of work. "Until Anita Hill's allegations against Clarence Thomas," Murray said, "this whole issue of sexual harassment was just not a topic in the Senate. Now we need to put in a policy on sexual harassment that covers all members of Congress."

On the theory that it could not be fairly governed by the executive and judicial branches, Congress remained immune from the very laws it had passed to prevent employment discrimination. There were no unions, no job security, virtually no employee rights on the Hill: each congressional office was a little fiefdom, with staffers often doubling as servants—picking up dry cleaning, chauf-feuring, tending bar. After the Anita Hill hearings, the Senate did establish a new office on employment prac-tices. Even so, very few cases came to light, because staffers weren't convinced that the new office could maintain real independence within the power structure of the greater institution.

The history of sexual harassment of female staffers on Capitol Hill had been a long-running serial. In 1976, a blatantly sexist Capitol Hill culture was exposed when Eliz-abeth Ray revealed that she had been paid $14,000 a year to serve as mistress to Representative Wayne L. Hays, an Ohio Democrat and chairman of the House Administra-tion Committee. Ray later went to work for another con-gressman who she said compelled her to have sex with a senator in order to persuade him to support her new boss's pet project. That same congressman, Democrat John Young of Texas, also employed another woman, Colleen Gardner, to whom he gave substantial salary increases in return for having sex with him. "He did not want me to have any definite responsibility, because he wanted me to be available to him whenever he wanted," Gardner said.

Responding to what she called the "Colleen problem," Pat Schroeder tried, in 1976, to tackle gender discrimi-nation on the Hill; she was treated, one staffer remem-bered, like a "skunk at a garden party." With North Carolina Democrat Charlie Rose, Schroeder attempted to create a voluntary employee rights committee composed of three members of Congress and three staffers, who would investigate complaints of sexual discrimination. Only fifteen other members of Congress signed on to the proposal, and one congressman told Charlie Rose: "No one's gonna mess around with my slaves." On the House floor, members passed around a cartoon portraying six beautiful women and one old, ugly one. The caption said that under the Schroeder-Rose proposal, congressmen would have to hire the old crone. The proposal never passed.

By 1993, sexual discrimination on the Hill had vastly decreased but not vanished. A survey conducted by the *Washington Post* found that one out of nine female Hill staffers said that they had been sexually harassed by a congressman, and half said they were afraid to report it.

Compared with Wayne Hays and John Young, Bob Packwood was small fry. He had not been accused of forcing intercourse on a subordinate or threatening to penalize a staffer who refused his advances. Unlike some of his colleagues in the 1970s and earlier, Packwood did not hire women solely to function as his mistresses. And when it came to women's rights, Packwood had been a paragon of progress. Throughout the seventies and eighties, Packwood had been one of the few Republican senators whom pro-choice organizations could count on, not just to support their cause but to fight for it. Packwood introduced the first Senate bill to legalize abortion, in 1970, three years before the Supreme Court's *Roe v. Wade* decision. He supported the Equal Rights Amendment and the Family and Medical Leave Bill. In the 1980s, when the Reagan administration attempted to curb abortion rights, Packwood pitted himself against the White House and other Senate Republicans. He was one of only two Republicans to vote against Clarence Thomas's nomination to the Supreme Court, and he always hired women to work in key roles in his campaigns and on his Senate staff. Sixty percent of Packwood's Senate staff were women. Four of his chiefs of staff had been women.

But Packwood had made the fatal mistake of separating the personal from the political. Despite his advocacy for women's rights, Packwood fell into the old power trap. As a senator and an omnipotent employer, he regularly propositioned women who worked for him. Ultimately, twenty-six women would accuse Packwood of sexual misconduct (seventeen would give testimony to the Senate Ethics Committee). The women soon became known as the "Packwood 26," and their experiences ranged from relatively innocuous (Packwood telling a young intern dirty jokes) to physically threatening and aggressive (Packwood pushing a women repeatedly onto a couch; Packwood grabbing a staff worker's underclothes, pulling on her ponytail, and stepping on her toes while forcing his tongue into her mouth). In most cases, Packwood had been drinking, which he often did in the evenings in his office.

None of the women had reported Packwood's behavior when it occurred. None thought anyone would believe them, and they were all sure that their careers would suffer. Their only recourse was to find work elsewhere, which many of them did.

Responding to the hue and cry from women's groups and angry Oregon citizens, the Senate Ethics Committee took up what would ultimately be a three-year investigation of Bob Packwood's sexual misconduct.

Since 1969, when Packwood first went to the Senate, he had begun each morning by sitting down at 6:15 and dictating his diary into a tape recorder. The transcriptions of these personal musings eventually amounted to some 8,200 single-spaced pages. Packwood willed the entirety of this strange, Nixonian document to the Oregon Historical Society, stipulating that it remain under seal until after his death. But history would come to know Senator Packwood's chronicles under different circumstances. Soon to join the Nixon White House tapes as the smoking gun in an increasingly bizarre and self-destructive Washington drama, the Packwood diaries first came to light on October 6, 1993.

That day, during an Ethics Committee deposition, Packwood testified that his diaries contained information supporting his defense. On two separate occasions prior to the deposition, the committee had asked Packwood for all documents in his possession that related in any way to the allegations that the committee was investigating. Packwood had refused to produce his diaries. Now, for the first time, Packwood agreed to unveil them. After extensive negotiations, Packwood permitted the committee to review all twenty-five years of his diary except for sections pertaining to attorney-client privilege, patient-doctor privilege, and private family matters.

A week passed. The Ethics Committee examined twenty years of the diaries. Then, abruptly, the senator stopped cooperating. Having realized that the committee could find evidence of possible criminal misconduct totally unrelated to the sexual harassment charges, Packwood cut off access to the diaries. On October 21, 1993, after two weeks of sparring with Packwood, the Ethics Committee, comprising three Democrat and three Republican senators, voted unanimously to go to court to enforce a subpoena. There was one hitch. The full Senate had to vote to authorize the enforcement of the subpoena in federal court.

The next day, Packwood's attorneys released a statement claiming that the committee had demanded to see particular sections of the diary because they contained information about the sex lives of other senators. The senator's legal team hoped to imply that Packwood was resisting the subpoena not only to protect his own privacy but, more honorably, to protect the privacy of his colleagues as well.

On the Senate floor, Monday, October 25, Packwood attempted to reemphasize this point. His diary, he said, contained information about "an extended affair that one senator had with a member of his staff," and "an affair that a staffer had with a member of the current congressional Democratic leadership." Packwood took pains to announce that he had no intention of "ever using this for blackmail, graymail, or anything else." But it was too late. Not only did Packwood's threat sound like blackmail, it also put senators in the impossible position of appearing to be protecting themselves if they voted against the subpoena. Senate staffers would later reveal that until that moment, Packwood had had many supporters among his colleagues. By threatening to expose them, he had now "tied their hands."

At the time of Packwood's incendiary floor speech, Patty Murray happened to be presiding over the Senate. When Packwood mentioned diary entries about other senators' sex lives, Murray literally "hoist[ed] an eyebrow," the *New York Times* reported the next day. She wasn't aware of it at the time, but anyone watching the Senate proceedings on C-Span could see Senator Murray's disapproving reaction to Senator Packwood's revelation.

Murray's first thought was not about the Senate at all. She had worked as a secretary for eight years, and the secretarial pool was in her blood—she still took notes in shorthand. She could remember all too well what it was like to be a woman in her twenties: a young, blond college graduate taking dictation for high-powered men who didn't think twice about making an embarrassing comment about her legs. Murray had only been a senator for ten months, and the former secretary found herself thinking about Bob Packwood's secretary.

Her name was Cathy Wagner Cormack. Morning after morning for twenty-five years, Cormack had faithfully transcribed everything Bob Packwood had given her, including the private contents of his diaries. It made Patty Murray's blood boil. "I was thinking about how awful it would be to be his secretary, to be typing out such personal information," she said later. "You're not a machine doing this. You're listening to what's coming out."

As the drama unfolded over the next forty-eight hours, Murray did not agree with her colleagues that Packwood's diary should be protected by his Fourth Amendment right to privacy. She believed that Packwood had already made his diaries public. Murray concluded that the diaries should be considered public property, as the senator had had his diary transcribed by another person, who also happened to be a Senate employee. Besides, Packwood had already given his diaries to the Ethics Committee, which had agreed not to look at his personal family information. Hadn't he, in that case, already forfeited any wish for privacy?

But after talking to her male colleagues about the Packwood subpoena, Murray found that no one shared her concerns. In a Democratic senators' lunch on Tuesday, October 26, Murray realized that the male senators had no interest in proving to the public that the Senate could police itself. Instead, they focused on privacy—Packwood's privacy, and more important, *their* privacy. The senators worried that turning Packwood's diaries over to the Ethics Committee would jeopardize the privacy of their own personal papers. "They were saying, 'Do we want to set a precedent like this?' " recalled Murray. " 'Can't we strike a deal so this doesn't come to the floor? How do we avoid making this a public debate?' "

After listening to these arguments, Murray found herself "getting angrier and angrier." Murray had gone into the meeting expecting everyone in the room to have "understood the message of the last election." But when lunch ended, she left saying to herself, "Oh, my gosh, they didn't get it."

Early in the week, Democrats on the Finance Committee—Bob Kerrey and Daniel Patrick Moynihan—were considering voting for Packwood, an ally of theirs on the committee. Packwood, who was the ranking Republican on Finance, had asked Moynihan, the committee chairman, to introduce an amendment that would restrict the Ethics Committee's access to all his diaries. Moynihan never did introduce the amendment, but he was tempted.

Then, on Thursday, October 28, the Ethics Committee explained for the first time why it had issued the subpoena. While reviewing Packwood's diaries the committee had, as Packwood had feared, come across evidence of possible criminal misconduct, which was unrelated to the sexual harassment charges. Later, it would be revealed that Packwood had urged lobbyists to give his ex-wife a job. (Although the Justice Department would ultimately decline to prosecute Packwood for this charge, the Ethics Committee would find Packwood guilty of "improper conduct" in his dealings with lobbyists.) In order to investigate further, the committee needed to see all of Packwood's diaries. Suddenly, Packwood's warnings about the Ethics Committee's interest in information about other senators' sex lives was disclosed as a smoke screen. What Packwood really wanted to hide was serious, self-incriminating evidence. With the Ethics Committee's announcement, Packwood lost more supporters.

That weekend, Murray went home irked by the feeling that Packwood might still get his way. At the very least, it looked likely that the subpoena request might be significantly amended. A debate and vote had been scheduled for Monday. Murray spent the weekend agonizing over what she should say in the debate. She had a choice—to be an insider or an outsider. Someone who maneuvered behind the scenes without making enemies, versus someone who challenged her colleagues publicly.

She later remembered, "The thing that was going through my mind was, I have worked so hard to earn the respect of these people. If I speak my mind on this, I could incur the wrath of many of [the senators] and lose their respect." The other side of the argument, which Murray tossed around in conversations with her husband, friends, and staff, was, "I came to the Senate to do this. I don't have a choice. I owe it to the women who sent me here, and the men. I owe it to myself. I wouldn't feel like I had truly come here until I had risked what I had gained to do this."

Murray knew that her colleagues were squeamish when it came to discussing sexual harassment. "It's not an issue they feel comfortable with," she said. "They would rather deal with it in the traditional Senate procedural way, where you never talk about the real issue." Murray knew that by shoving sexual harassment down the throats of her reluctant male colleagues, she would live up to all of their fears about having more women in the Senate. "They were afraid when we [women] first came here in January, we would go out on the floor and rail against the boys' club and we would tell them all how awful they were. We didn't do that." But Murray knew that she was about to.

She had a lot at stake. For the past ten months, she had worked hard to prove that she was a team player, not a bomb thrower. The senators with whom she had worked most closely agreed that Murray had succeeded in being "an outsider who had been accepted by the institution." Murray had allied herself with two powerful committee chairmen, Robert Byrd on Appropriations and Jim Sasser on Budget. Murray accommodated their political needs, and in return, they took care of hers. On the Appropriations Committee, Murray had become known for her low-key style of personal politicking. She also worked well with Republicans, joining forces with the committee's ranking Republican, Mark Hatfield of Oregon, to pass the Murray-Hatfield amendment, providing $29 million for hard-hit timber communities.

Murray never spoke publicly against her allies, proving that she could be trusted by her colleagues. "I don't think you win by demanding respect. I think you win by earning it," Murray said, "by working hard, doing the committee work, taking up the mundane tasks and doing a good job at them." She had come to see that the Senate is like a political campaign. You don't start out as campaign manager, you start out stuffing envelopes. Murray scrupulously appeared at all her committee hearings and markups. "Patty Murray is the *only* senator I know who is on time for meetings," said a senior Budget Committee staffer. "For most senators, it is a contest to see who's the latest. Leaving people waiting is an art form—the later your are, the more important you seem."

At noon on Monday, November 1, she took her place at her desk and listened to seven hours of debate on Senate Resolution 153, the Packwood subpoena. When the

CLARA BINGHAM

Ethics Committee first announced its intention to subpoena Packwood's diaries, Murray had been concerned
that the investigation would fizzle, and in a repeat performance of the Hill-Thomas hearings, the Senate would
send the wrong message to women about sexual harassment. Here was a case in which more than two dozen
women had brought charges. "Would the Senate be able
to deal with this?" Murray wondered. That morning, she
had driven to work from her house in suburban Arlington, hoping her fears would be moot. Surely the men recognized that times had changed. Sexual harassment was no
longer just a dalliance, it was illegal. Mashing female staffers
may have been the subject of cloakroom jokes in the
seventies and eighties, but no longer. Murray knew that the
entire Senate was on trial today, not just Bob Packwood.

Gender roles and gender relations in Congress had
been in a heightened state of flux since the '92 elections.
Murray understood this as well as anyone else. Her family life had been turned upside down by her job. She could
no longer be her children's primary caregiver. Murray had
found that the all-absorbing, erratic Senate work schedule
was ideal for men who had wives at home to take care of
their families. Rob Murray had quit his job to go to Washington, where he worked for the Department of Transportation and took care of the children. Patty, of course,
was seldom home when her children needed her. She was
often required to stay on the Hill late into the night when
the Senate was in session, and had to help her daughter
with homework—sometimes with the aid of her staff—via
fax. Sara would lean more than necessary on her mother
for help with homework as a way of "making her mother
pay for not being at home with her," observed one Murray staffer. Rob Murray pulled most of the car-pool and

shopping duty, and he wasn't comfortable schmoozing at official Washington functions. The Senate social culture had proved hostile to Senate husbands. The Ladies of the Senate refused to change its name, and Patty and Rob had discovered that in Washington, Senate husbands were almost universally ignored. When Rob was invited to a Senate wives' luncheon, the invitation advised: "Red Cross uniforms optional." Rob Murray declined the invitation, but not before Patty kidded him: "Do you want to wear yours?"

The increase in the number of women in Congress had left many men clubfooted in their attempt to change with the times. After House freshwoman Lynn Woolsey gave her first floor speech, a senior member of a committee on which she served told her that he had just come from a meeting where a television monitor had been tuned to her speech. He wanted to compliment her performance, because during the meeting there had been talk of the fifty-five-year-old California Democrat's bright eyes and dramatic head of hair. "We couldn't hear you," the congressman admitted. "But one of the guys in the meeting said, 'Who's that good-lookin' broad?' And I said, 'That's Lynn Woolsey. She's on my committee!' "

Some members of the 103rd Congress remained puzzled about how to address a woman. At a press conference, Congressman James Inhofe identified the fifty-one-year-old Marjorie Margolies-Mezvinsky as "the three-M girl." Senator Phil Gramm refused to believe that he sounded condescending when he called the attorney general of the United States "a very sweet lady." Freshman Martin Hoke would find himself in full *mea culpa* after an open microphone recorded him comparing notes about a female television producer with another congressman: Hoke could be heard saying, "She has be-e-e-g breasts."

To Murray's dismay, it didn't take long that morning for the Senate floor to start sounding eerily the way it had during the Anita Hill hearings. Senator Joseph Biden, the long-winded chairman of the Judiciary Committee, rose early in the debate to ask a confusing, rambling question about Senate precedent that no one quite understood. Biden seemed to luxuriate in paranoia. He worried that anyone could make any charge against any senator—in this case, a hypothetical "Senator Smedlap"—against whom someone could write a letter to the Ethics Committee that said, "I think that Senator Smedlap killed Cock Robin." Then the Ethics Committee could, in turn, subpoena an innocent senator's diaries, speeches, or "all of anything" Smedlap had written, "because it might be relevant."

Biden's concerns were eventually allayed by Barbara Boxer, Tom Daschle, and the chairman of the Ethics Committee, Richard Bryan, who explained that the investigation into Packwood's possible criminal misconduct had not begun because of an anonymous tip but because of credible evidence found in Packwood's own diary.

The next day, to make the familiar picture complete, Arlen Specter, Anita Hill's most hostile interrogator, made a last-ditch effort to bail Packwood out. Specter's amendment (which lost) was co-sponsored by Clarence Thomas's loyal sponsor, John Danforth. The icing on the cake: throughout the proceedings Senator Edward Kennedy once more remained uncharacteristically silent.

Meanwhile, Bob Packwood, the first senator in American history to refuse to comply with an Ethics Committee subpoena, showed no signs of contrition. Long-winded, arrogant, he paced restlessly behind his desk, holding the microphone in one hand while gesturing wildly with the other. He jousted with Ethics Committee members, answering their charges and accusing the chairman, Richard Bryan, of branding him a criminal. "There is not a citizen in this country that would be subject to produce papers that this subpoena is asking me to produce," Packwood complained.

Bryan, a former prosecutor and attorney general, retaliated: "Let me just say that the most analogous situation is that if a prosecutor in the review and examination of diary information came upon such an entry, as did counsel for the committee, there is no question in my mind but [that the] information would be made available to that prosecutor. So I respectfully disagree with the observation Senator Packwood made that somehow he is being held to a different standard."

Senator Bennett Johnston of Louisiana also expressed his concerns about senators being unfairly accused of crimes they didn't commit and then punished for it by being subpoenaed: "Suppose Rush Limbaugh says, 'All senators are crooks.' And they say, well, you know, senators ought to be required to prove that they are not. So we want all your personal correspondence, your credit cards, all your telephone records, everything. So you issued a subpoena for that, and I came and I said, 'Look, there is no charge pending about this. It is not relevant to anything.' "

Bryan again defended the subpoena, based on credible evidence, "Because it [came] from the hand of the senator himself."

After listening to six hours of mind-numbing legalese, after watching the members of the Ethics Committee repeat themselves over and over again, Patty Murray became distraught. The debate, she thought, was way off target, and heading further in the wrong direction. "People were making excuses for why they could vote no on this because of the privacy issue, which I thought was a real veneer," she later said. "I felt the only way to make this happen was to say what I had to say. Nobody else was going to do it."

Even as she raised her hand to speak, Murray worried about what people would say to her afterward: "Would I become a pariah? Would I lose their respect? Would I be able to work with them on other issues?"

It was 6:00 P.M. The journalists in the press galleries had already left their seats to meet their deadlines. Murray stood and faced a full floor of somber colleagues. After thanking the Ethics Committee members for their hard work and announcing that she supported the subpoena resolution, Murray explained once more why she had become a senator in the first place: "Two years ago, I sat at home in my living room, like millions of other Americans, and watched a strikingly similar debate in front of the Senate Judiciary Committee, and I remember thinking: 'Why don't they get it? Why don't they understand that throughout this country, women who have been victims of sexual misconduct are watching?' "

She expressed her astonishment regarding the Senate's reaction to the Packwood subpoena: "Many of my colleagues are worried about their personal privacy and the implications of this vote for that privacy. I find it difficult to understand those concerns, given the nature of the materials that the committee wants to subpoena from Senator Packwood and given the nature of our job as public servants." Although Murray would later be scolded by Nancy Kassebaum for changing the subject of the debate, she did, in fact, address the procedural issues of the day.

"I do not understand how journals kept and maintained in a public office at taxpayer expense can be called personal diaries. . . . Each of us gave up a great deal of privacy when we were elected to the Senate," she said. She reminded the senators that Article I of the U.S. Constitution granted the Senate the authority to discipline its members: "I believe that members of this body must demonstrate to the people of this nation that we will not abdicate our responsibility to discipline ourselves."

Murray focused next on the larger implications of the vote at hand. As Barbara Boxer later put it, Murray brought the Senate "back to reality." Murray discussed the vote's true political implications. A vote for the resolution would send a message to the American public that sexual misconduct in the Senate would be investigated to the fullest possible extent. "A vote against this resolution," Murray warned, "sends a clear message also to every woman in this country: If you are harassed, keep quiet, say nothing; the cards are stacked against your ever winning."

Murray then lowered the boom on Packwood. She was shocked that the debate had portrayed the senator from Oregon as a victim. "I remind my colleagues, more than two dozen women have brought their allegations to this body. Clearly, they see themselves as the victims in this debate." Murray ended on a dramatic note: "A vote against this resolution would be a tragedy. It is time to move on. The nation's business awaits. But let us not forget the example that we are setting for ourselves and our country."

Murray was amazed by the response to her speech. She was treated by her colleagues as a hero rather than a pariah. The next day, her office was flooded with congratulatory telegrams and telephone calls from women across the country. As one Senate aide explained, "Patty

Murray's speech spelled out the true political situation for people who still didn't understand the political impact of Anita Hill. The politics of the vote were dictated by Anita Hill and by the women senators. If two or three women senators had stood up to support Packwood, then the rest of the chamber would have gone with them. The men needed the women for cover. The men had to do what the women did."

Soon after Murray's speech, the Senate adjourned for the night. The next day, they would vote 94 to 6 to give the Ethics Committee authority to enforce the subpoena of Packwood's diaries. All of the women senators voted for the subpoena, and Murray's speech had played a significant role in turning the tide against Packwood.

After her speech, Murray did not join the flow of tired, miserable senators streaming out of the chamber. She sat at desk No. 62, alone. Underneath her desk was a mahogany drawer with two round knobs. Murray pulled out the drawer and peered inside. Eighteen names had been scratched like grade-school graffiti onto the bottom of the drawer. Some of them were scratched in pencil, some in ballpoint pen, others in fountain pen. All were senators who had made their home at desk 62, many of them long forgotten. Charles S. Thomas and Oscar Underwood, Jennings Randolph and Olin Johnson. Inscribing one's desk is a Senate tradition that Patty Murray had deliberately not yet participated in. "I felt that I had to wait to sign my desk until I had earned it." Now she unsheathed her pen. In her neat small script she wrote, "Sen. Patty Murray."

In late March of 1994, almost five months after she had stood up to Packwood, Patty Murray was on her way to the Senate floor for a vote when something strange happened.

It was 7:30 in the evening. Members of her staff often accompanied Murray to the floor to guide her through the nuts and bolts of a vote, but tonight Murray felt confident enough to go alone. She had just stepped into a "Senators Only" elevator in the Capitol building. The elevator operator was the only other person aboard when the doors opened, and after a longer-than-usual pause, the senior senator from South Carolina tottered in.

At ninety-one, Strom Thurmond was on the verge of becoming the oldest person ever to serve in Congress. Patty Murray had been four years old when Thurmond had first gone to the Senate in 1954. Spry, wiry, with a freckled face and a head of thin but shockingly orange hair, Thurmond had not let age or contemporary politics change his personal style. Into the 103rd Congress, he still had a reputation for accosting his colleagues with what had come to be known as "the Grip"—a fierce, bone-crushing handshake. Equally well known for his love of "the ladies," Thurmond had once been married to a South Carolina beauty queen who was forty-four years his junior.

Tonight, in the elevator, he turned to the "lady" beside him, and without any hint that he recognized Patty Murray or that she was a fellow senator, he put his arm around her, groping for her breast, and said in a deep Carolina drawl, "Are you married, little lady?"

Just then, the elevator door opened, and Murray exited, flustered. Minutes later, after telephoning her office to summon a staff member to the Senate floor, Patty Murray told her aide and her colleague Barbara Boxer what had just happened to her in the elevator. Murray was visibly shaken as she reported the incident. She thought Thurmond had probably had too much to drink.

Shocked by Murray's news, Barbara Boxer laughed nervously. In the first moments of hearing the story, it seemed ludicrous: Strom Thurmond prowling around the halls of the Senate, mistaking his female colleagues for prey. But then Boxer became angry. How could a member of the Senate do this to another member? she wondered in amazement and disbelief. "You've got to go public with this," Boxer told Murray. "Who knows how many more people he'll do this to?" As Boxer would later tell it, Murray was "very shaken." She was also adamant about keeping the incident quiet. "Promise me you'll never say anything about this." Murray asked her friend. "She swore me to secrecy," said Boxer.

The next morning, Murray recited the story again, this time letting her senior staff in on it. No one laughed. Everyone felt immediately sympathetic and protective. A new rule was established: Patty must always be accompanied by a staff member when leaving the office. The bigger question was what to do with this bizarre incident.

The staff was split. Some thought that going public would be a big mistake. Murray had nothing to gain from the attention. It would be a big, juicy Washington scandal, and Murray, not Thurmond, they argued, would become the story. The press would invade what little privacy she and her family had left. Thurmond, meanwhile, would be cast as little more than what he really was—a walking relic, the spirit of Congresses past. Murray, on the other hand, would go down in history as the Sexual Harassment Senator. No matter what she did, she would always be tarred by this brush. Moreover, if Murray went public, either by filing an ethics complaint or holding a press conference, she would betray implicit rules of trust among senators.

She would damage her standing with her colleagues. Hadn't she already pushed the envelope far enough with Packwood?

But other aides expressed amazement that Murray would remain silent. Didn't she owe her election to the issue of sexual harassment? Murray had always said she hadn't gone to Washington to play by the old rules. True, the Senate was like a dysfunctional family in which no one was supposed to reveal its secrets. Strom Thurmond's habit of groping women was one of those well-known secrets. If Murray took a stand, exposing Thurmond, wouldn't everyone rally behind her and say, "Finally"?

If Murray didn't expose Thurmond, and men like him, who would? Unlike lowly staffers propositioned by a boss, Murray was in a position of power and credibility. One staffer wondered aloud what better position a woman could be in to blow the whistle—president of the United States?

Murray listened to the debate with a fixed, stony face. To some it seemed as if she had already made up her mind. Murray announced that she wanted to deal with Thurmond privately. She asked her chief of staff, Michael Timmeny, to call Thurmond's chief of staff. Timmeny would point out exactly what had happened and make clear that Thurmond had overstepped the boundaries. Meanwhile, everyone else would keep the story secret.

On the phone with Thurmond's office, things worked out pretty much as expected. Thurmond's chief of staff replied that he was certain that the senator had not meant anything by his behavior. Approaching Murray on the Senate floor a few days afterward, Thurmond told her he was sorry if he had caused her any embarrassment. Murray was indeed embarrassed. Ever since the episode, she had gone out of her way to avoid Thurmond. She had been noticeably evasive on the Senate floor when Thurmond tried several times to approach her to make his apology.

Members of Murray's staff, meanwhile, were angry. They discussed Thurmond's apology ad nauseam. The more they studied it, turning the sentences one way, then another, the clearer it became. It was a non-apology apology. Murray had done herself a disservice to accept it. The episode, however, had run its course. There wasn't anything more to say until, soon afterward, a Washington State television reporter came to Murray's office for a routine on-camera interview.

The Hill had been buzzing that week with word that the Senate women were planning to block the four-star retirement of a navy admiral because of his role in the Tailhook scandal. Sexual harassment was once again an overarching congressional issue. The interview in the hallway outside her office with Seattle's KOMO reporter Les Heinz was almost over when Heinz asked Murray the big question: Had Murray, herself, ever been sexually harassed in the Senate?

Murray stood speechless, staring wide-eyed into the camera. She looked completely unnerved. After a pause she said, "I don't want to comment on that."

Puzzled by Murray's evasive answer, Heinz telephoned the office to follow up. Murray's press secretary returned his call after at an ad hoc meeting the staff had decided that they should say Murray had *not* been harassed in the Senate. And there the story rested. No version ever appeared in the news media.

Two years later, pressed more specifically about the incident in an interview for this book, Murray changed her version of the story. She insisted that Strom Thurmond had grabbed her because he was old and frail and needed to keep his balance. "He didn't accost me. I would never use that word. I think he was merely hanging on tighter than he should have been," Murray said. She agreed that Thurmond had asked her if she was married, but, hedging, she said, "I don't think I was offended. It was honestly such a non-incident to me, really. It was one of those Washington, D.C., stories that get blown out of proportion that shouldn't be."

Days after the elevator incident, Murray was presented with four books each the size of the telephone directory for a Seattle suburb: the official Tailhook reports. The issue at hand was the Senate's approval of Admiral Frank B. Kelso's four-star retirement.

It was an astonishing story. On Labor Day weekend, 1991—coincidentally, only a month before Anita Hill's charges against Clarence Thomas became public—the Tailhook Association held their annual "symposium" in Las Vegas. About five thousand active and retired Navy and Marine aviators converged on the Las Vegas Hilton for a weekend of seminars and fraternity-like parties. The Navy paid $190,000 to fly 1,500 officers stationed all over the country to an event that would ultimately cause $23,000 in damages to hotel property.

The details of what happened during the Friday and Saturday nights of Tailhook weekend read like a script of *Animal House*. To Murray, the descriptions of heavy drinking, nudity, and sexual molestation were stomach-turning. All the raunchy spectacles were topped by the "gauntlet," a third-floor hallway crowded with a gang of inebriated men who made it a tradition to fondle and grope the breasts, buttocks, and crotches of women who dared to pass through. Some women—jet-jock groupies and strippers, for example—volunteered to go down the gauntlet, submitting to an aggressive goose or two, or three. But there had been other women at Tailhook to whom the gauntlet felt like a life-threatening nightmare.

Navy Lieutenant Paula Coughlin, a thirty-year-old admiral's aide and helicopter pilot, was one of those women. As Coughlin unknowingly entered the gauntlet, one man who knew her rank shouted, "Admiral's aide! Admiral's aide!" Coughlin found herself surrounded by a gang of large, muscular men who began tearing at her clothes. She struggled to fight them off, kicking and throwing punches. The more she struggled, the more aggressively the men attacked. One man grabbed both of her breasts, another tried to pull off her underpants. Coughlin, sure that she was about to be gang-raped, sank her teeth deep into the flesh of one man's right forearm, drawing blood. Eventually, after screaming in protest, Coughlin thrust herself out of the hallway and into an open door to safety.

Paula Coughlin became the first woman to file a formal complaint. Ultimately, investigators identified eighty-three women who had been assaulted that weekend. As one pilot who participated in the gauntlet admitted, "the more the women fought the men who were attacking them, the more the males attacked."

Even more shocking to Murray, as she read the history of the Tailhook case, was the fact that thirty admirals, two generals, and three Reserve generals attended the Tailhook convention. Many of them were socializing on the Hilton's third floor Friday and Saturday nights, when some of the most egregious behavior took place. Even if the senior officials had not actually witnessed sexual molestation, they had all been warned about the problem of Tailhook's "gang" mentality ahead of time. Tailhook '91 wasn't any worse than the conventions of previous years, but it was the first time a woman blew the whistle.

Then there had been problems with the investigations. Over the course of three years, there would be four separate investigations into the conduct of the male officers at Tailhook. The first two internal Navy investigations were seriously impeded by a wall of silence erected by a brethren of aviators bent on protecting one another. After conducting some 1,500 interviews with people who attended the Tailhook weekend, Navy investigators could identify only two suspects.

After the two Navy investigations failed, Navy Secretary Lawrence Garrett asked the Pentagon to step in, and the Department of Defense's inspector general conducted another investigation. Ultimately, the three investigations would implicate 140 Navy and Marine Corps officers in assaults of 83 women. Forty-three officers were disciplined with letters of admonition, small fines, and very little chance of promotion. Six officers faced court-martial proceedings, which were eventually thrown out of court. Twenty-nine admirals and one Marine general were issued nonpunitive "letters of caution," three admirals received letters of censure, and Lawrence Garrett resigned.

Because of widespread lack of cooperation, which amounted to a virtual cover-up, no one was convicted of any crime. Because of lack of corroborating witnesses, the officer charged with assaulting Coughlin had his case dismissed. Lieutenant Paula Coughlin felt wronged. What was more, since blowing the whistle on Tailhook, Coughlin said she had been subject to covert attacks that made her life in the Navy impossible. In February of 1994, Coughlin resigned from the Navy.

The officer in charge at Tailhook was Admiral Frank B. Kelso II, Chief of Naval Operations. Kelso, a tall, stern-looking man with a high forehead and bushy black eyebrows, had, until Tailhook, boasted a stellar thirty-eight-year Navy career. At the Tailhook convention, Kelso was the second-highest-ranking officer, under then–Secretary of the Navy Lawrence Garrett. Kelso was also one of the twenty-nine admirals to whom Secretary of the Navy John Dalton issued a "letter of caution" for displaying a failure of leadership during the Tailhook weekend. In September 1993, Secretary Dalton recommended that Kelso be fired for failing to prevent the scandal. Les Aspin, the Secretary of Defense, overruled Dalton's decision.

The fourth report on Tailhook dealt Admiral Kelso the hardest blow. In the 1994 findings of a military court-martial proceeding, Navy judge Captain William T. Vest Jr. concluded that Kelso's presence at the Tailhook convention was not entirely innocent. Vest dismissed the Navy's case against three officers who had been charged with conduct unbecoming an officer during the Tailhook weekend, because according to the strict Navy chain of command, Kelso's subordinates could not be prosecuted if he himself was a guilty party.

Kelso testified under oath in Vest's Norfolk courtroom that he did not witness any lewd behavior at the Tailhook convention, but the court's findings contradicted Kelso's testimony. Vest's ruling stated that interviews with many witnesses proved that Admiral Kelso "actually observed sexually oriented misconduct on the patio and in the various squadron hospitality suites on Friday night, and on Saturday evening as well, and he failed to take action to stop such conduct." In light of the evidence at hand, Vest denounced the entire Navy chain of command. "The failure by those responsible to take strong corrective action regarding inappropriate behavior that obviously occurred at past Tailhook Symposiums is incomprehensible," wrote Vest. "As events have proven, this embarrassing failure of leadership and 'head in the sand' attitude . . . contributed to the sexually offensive conduct which later escalated to the actual sexual assaults on female attendees."

Although Admiral Kelso had a good record with women and had overseen the Navy's inclusion of women in combat duty, he had become a lightning rod for Tailhook. He made a deal with his superiors. He agreed to retire two months early in exchange for having his name cleared. On February 15, Defense Secretary William Perry issued a statement calling Kelso a man of the "highest integrity and honor."

Now, as Patty Murray began to see, the Senate in the 103rd Congress was being asked to reward dishonor with honor. All admirals in the U.S. Navy with two or more stars automatically retire with two stars. A four-star admiral like Kelso may retire with four stars only when it is recommended by the president of the United States and approved by the Senate. No four-star admiral recommended by the president, however, had ever had his four stars withheld. Admiral Kelso's retirement therefore brought the question of his pension to the floor as well. At two stars, Kelso would collect $67,422 a year, but with four stars, his annual pension would jump to $84,340.

Murray concluded that she had to protest. "I can't go home at night and live with myself if I don't make an issue out of this," she later said. Perhaps being the unwilling object of Strom Thurmond's desires helped her identify more

than ever with women like Paula Coughlin. Perhaps her re-
luctance to reprimand Thurmond publicly encouraged her
to take a stand when it came to a serious sexual-harassment
case like Tailhook.

Murray talked to Texas Republican Kay Bailey Hutchison, the only woman serving on the Senate Armed Services Committee. Like Murray, Hutchison was new to the
Senate, elected in June 1993 to the seat vacated by Lloyd
Bentsen when he became Clinton's first Secretary of the
Treasury. The two senators had never exchanged more
than a casual hello. Hutchison's politics were conservative,
and she rarely took a stand on women's issues.

Murray crossed the center aisle in the Senate chamber
and asked Hutchison how she planned to vote when
Kelso's retirement came up in the Armed Services Committee. To Murray's surprise, Hutchison said that she had
read every word of the Tailhook investigation reports and
that she could not vote to give Kelso an additional honor.
Hutchison told Murray that she believed Kelso was ultimately responsible for bungling the Tailhook investigation. "I'll probably be the only no vote on the committee,"
Hutchison predicted.

She was nearly right. On April 12, three of the country's top military officials—Defense Secretary William
Perry, Navy Secretary John Dalton, and Chairman of the
Joint Chiefs of Staff, General John Shalikashvili—came
forth to plead Kelso's case. Never before had an admiral's
retirement brought out such big guns. Two days after the
unprecedented barrage, the Senate Armed Services Committee capitulated, voting 20 to 2 to retire Admiral Kelso
with four stars. Robert Byrd and Kay Bailey Hutchison, resisting pressure from the committee chairman, Sam Nunn,
and the weight of the military establishment, voted no.

Murray now approached the other women senators. Each one had had the same initial reaction: Do we dare do this again, so soon after Packwood? When will our male colleagues begin to call us whiners? But after reviewing the material that Murray and Hutchison had read, they all came to the same conclusion: Kelso did not deserve the extra honor of retiring with four stars.

During an April 15 Senate Democratic caucus weekend retreat in Williamsburg, Virginia, the five Democratic women met and developed a strategy. Barbara Mikulski, they decided, would lead the floor debate. They asked the majority leader, George Mitchell, for a recorded vote and four hours of debate time. The odds, they all knew, were overwhelmingly against them. Chances were that no more than a handful of senators would buck the time-honored system and vote against Kelso.

Pat Schroeder's office first heard of the Kelso vote from a journalist who happened to call on April 11. Apparently, the Senate Armed Services Committee was playing the Kelso retirement so close to the vest that even the third-highest-ranking Democrat on the House Armed Services Committee had not been informed that a vote was at hand.

Schroeder had done more work for more years on sexual harassment in the military than any of the Senate women combined. Yet an admiral's retirement, like a Supreme Court Justice's nomination, came under the sole jurisdiction of the higher body. If there was no legitimate institutional way Schroeder could get involved in the Kelso issue, she could still resort to back channels.

The next day, Schroeder sent a letter to all seven of the Senate women. The letter, which enclosed the findings of

Judge Vest, stated: "If Admiral Kelso's retirement easily slips through the Senate, the entire Tailhook episode will dissipate into the vapors of history without anyone taking responsibility for crimes that took place on their watch. Above all, the safety, professionalism, and conduct of Navy personnel is the responsibility of the Chief of Naval Operations"—namely, Kelso. Schroeder urged the senators to "use this opportunity to speak for the women and men who have been denied justice these past two and a half years after Tailhook."

On Monday, April 18, one of the women senators called Schroeder to tell her that for the first time in this Congress, all the women, Democrats and Republicans alike, stood united on an issue. Schroeder by now had a plan, which she kept mum about for the moment. She would throw a press conference in the House triangle, a small plot of grass on the east side of the Capitol, known among congressional press secretaries for its photogenic red tulips. Then, in a reprise of the famous October 1991 march to the Senate during the Hill-Thomas hearings, Schroeder would lead a delegation of House women up the steps and into the U.S. Senate to protest Kelso's retirement with four stars.

One of Schroeder's House colleagues—a freshwoman—had noticed something about Schroeder. Whenever the senior woman called a press conference, she invariably called her colleagues with less than an hour to go before the cameras started rolling—sometimes only minutes in advance. To the freshwomen in the 103rd Congress, it appeared on more than one occasion that Schroeder was unable to share the limelight.

On an issue like Kelso, the junior women had good reason to feel sensitive to slights. Because the freshwomen had been elected in the heavily hyped Year of the Woman, they felt inordinate pressure to live up to high expectations. Whenever a women's issue, especially one involving sexual harassment, came to the floor of the House or Senate, the need to be seen making a stand increasingly occupied the women's attention. Since the beginning of the session, the freshwomen had met regularly in the women's lounge—the Lindy Boggs Room—to coordinate their efforts. To remain politically viable, they all knew that on women's issues they had to make a splash.

Was Schroeder jealous of the new congresswomen who had been swept into office in the Year of the Woman? On Tailhook and Kelso, it looked that way. But Pat Schroeder had a legitimate reason to want the limelight now: She deserved it. For twenty years, since she had forced her way onto the Armed Services Committee as a thirty-two-year-old peacenik, Schroeder had used her position on the committee to benefit women serving in the military and military families. She had fought for better housing and day care facilities on military bases, for medical research on women's health in military hospitals, and for abortion availability on overseas military bases. She had pushed through legislation that allowed divorced armed service wives to receive a portion of their husband's military pension. She had introduced legislation to lift the ban on gays in the military and on women in combat. Over the years, Schroeder had also spent many hours talking to Admiral Kelso about how to integrate women into the Navy.

One senior Pentagon official pointed out that the advances that Schroeder had won for women in the military were "work for which she has been vilified by the male bastion in the military." Schroeder had been scapegoated especially harshly by male aviators, whom she seemed to threaten as no other female leader in Washington had. "She is conspicuous enough for them to latch on to her," said the Pentagon official, adding that in these years of post–Cold War uncertainty, Top Gun pilots were apt to "use her as a symbol of larger things they fear and hate."

Schroeder had taken her share of abuse. An annual talent show put on in 1992 by naval aviators in San Diego— the Tomcat Follies—projected a newspaper headline onto a screen: PAT SCHROEDER HAS SEX CHANGE. Then came a picture of Richard Cheney, the then Secretary of Defense, followed by the caption: NOW SHE'S A REAL DICK. Another skit finished with the punchline "Hickory, dickory, dock! Pat Schroeder can suck my cock!"*

The same day that Pat Schroeder was planning her press conference, Kelly Sullivan, Louise Slaughter's press secretary, and Howard Wolfson, Nita Lowey's press secretary, had also been talking about how to get in on the Kelso issue. They did not yet know about Schroeder's plan. Even so, they called Schroeder's press secretary because everyone called Andrea Camp when they wanted to organize a women's media event.

The press secretaries might just as well have been solving the koan "If a tree falls in Congress, does anybody in America know it?" Sullivan and Wolfson could send out as many press releases and newsletters as they could write, but if the proverbial fallen tree wasn't covered by their local newspaper or local television station, the congress-

---

*Ultimately, more officers would be disciplined for the Tomcat Follies than for the entire Tailhook scandal. Five of the most senior officers present at the Tomcat Follies were fired, although two were later reinstated, and eighteen junior officers were disciplined.

women's efforts were moot. From one election to the next, the inexorable name of the game on Capitol Hill was, of course, publicity, and no one was better at attracting reporters and getting her quotes in print than Pat Schroeder and Andrea Camp. Starting with *Redbook* in 1973, Schroeder had learned to take an outsider's approach by using the press to gain leverage over her colleagues.

Andrea Camp had already decided that she wanted to keep the Kelso protest small. Tailhook, after all, was Pat's issue, and Pat didn't want to swamp the Senate floor with dozens of House women. The original idea had been to have the House women go to the Senate floor in small numbers during the four hours of the Kelso debate, but with the crime bill being voted on in the House, the House women couldn't get away. They had to make one quick strike onto the Senate floor.

There was another reason why the press conference had to be small: When Pat Schroeder had called Barbara Boxer and Barbara Mikulski to tell them about her plan, the senators started to panic. They warned Schroeder that by walking onto the Senate floor with dozens of House women, she would disrupt the Senate, not just steal the show. Schroeder knew that she was in a sensitive situation. "I wasn't going to be the one who said some people can't come," she later explained. So she decided to invite a total of twenty-one House women—all those who had signed a recent letter to Ron Dellums, chairman of the House Armed Services Committee, requesting a hearing on sexual harassment in the military. But Schroeder's office left only two hours to notify all twenty-one congresswomen; few faxes or phone calls followed. The next day, Schroeder would say that she didn't understand why so many women were mad. "We faxed to everyone," she told Barbara Kennelly, the highest-ranking woman in the House. "It's not like we planned this for twelve weeks. It just all kind of came and went fast."

But certain omissions rankled. Lynn Schenk, who had a hard race in November and could have used the publicity, complained that she wasn't invited in time. To those who couldn't get to the press conference, Schroeder reasoned: "You sometimes think people think, 'Oh, well, I'm not going to do this.' But when it ends up in the papers, they say, 'Why didn't I do that!' "

The press conference took place, as planned, among the red tulips at the House triangle. The spring day was bright and breezy. Pat Schroeder, Louise Slaughter, Nita Lowey, Barbara Kennelly, and Eleanor Holmes Norton all gave speeches. Each of the women acknowledged Schroeder's work on the issue.

Getting quoted had been a struggle for Louise Slaughter throughout the 103rd Congress. In myriad press conferences over the past year and half, reporters were often puzzled by Slaughter's unfocused statements and Southern phraseology, which she frequently mumbled under her breath. Slaughter could not compete with Pat Schroeder when it came to the art of "feeding the beast"— simplifying and packaging information for the press corps. Even after a press conference on women's health in September, reporters ignored Slaughter, who, after all, was the chair of the women's health task force, and flocked to Pat Schroeder afterward for more in-depth interviews. Today, Slaughter's sound bite, written by Kelly Sullivan, was snappier than usual: "We certainly didn't think that what turned out to be a slap on the hand would turn out in the Senate to be a pat on the back. . . . This was not even just an incident of boys will be boys; it was barbarism."

At the end of the press conference, Schroeder turned to her colleagues and said, "Come on, let's march!" The cameras readjusted their positions. Congresswomen Slaughter, Lowey, Kennelly, Norton, Maloney, Furse, Woolsey, and Karen Thurman of Florida followed Schroeder across the Capitol Plaza and up the white marble Senate steps. Newspaper photographers frantically ran backwards in front of the women, capturing every angle; print reporters followed from behind. CNN carried the walk live. A tree was falling in Congress.

Senators and U.S. representatives may officially frequent each other's chambers. Senators routinely go to the House floor to listen to the president's State of the Union speech. But entering the "other body's" hallowed chambers during a daily debate is rare. When Schroeder had led seven congresswomen to a Senate Democratic caucus meeting in 1991 to demand that Anita Hill's allegations be investigated, the House delegation had been turned away at the door of the private meeting room in the Capitol. But this time, the congresswomen would make their complaint known in a location where they could legally venture. Now the women walked freely onto the Senate floor.

Schroeder looked around. It was her first time on the floor of the Senate since the 1992 elections, and she was struck by the change. The Senate chamber no longer looked as much like a stodgy men's club. To her left, Carol Moseley-Braun, Dianne Feinstein, and Barbara Mikulski dotted the chamber in bright-colored suits. Maintaining order over the Senate was Patty Murray, who sat in the president's chair. To her right, on the Republican side, Schroeder could see Kay Bailey Hutchison. Nancy Kassebaum, she noted, was the only woman senator not present.

Then Schroeder noticed something else that moved her even more. As the House women walked onto the floor, the female Senate pages had apparently realized that something important was going on. The young women had dropped what they were doing and come forward to sit on the steps ringing the senate president's rostrum, listening to every word of debate. More than anything else that day, the sight of those attentive young women made Schroeder feel that there had been a reason for everything she and her colleagues were doing.

It was sheer coincidence that Patty Murray happened to be the presiding officer at the moment when the House women walked into the Senate chamber. Murray usually scheduled time at the president's desk six weeks ahead. Freshmen are expected to bear most of the brunt of sitting in for the vice president, the official president of the Senate, primarily to learn legislative procedure.

Murray had been given no warning about the House women's grand entrance. She was just as surprised to see the nine congresswomen walk onto the Senate floor as Senator Ted Stevens, the Alaska Republican and one of Kelso's strongest backers, who roared, "What are *they* doing here?" As Louise Slaughter would later recall, Stevens looked so mad he was "ready to faint."

From Stevens' point of view, it appeared as though the House women were standing behind Barbara Boxer to horn in on C-Span coverage of Boxer's speech. The congresswomen denied this charge. "We just gravitated to the other women," said Slaughter, "and Barbara Boxer started speaking." But Stevens had already stormed down to the rostrum and asked the parliamentarian if there were any rules he could use to eject the House women from the floor. He argued that they were not just bystanders, but had in fact become part of the debate merely by appearing on C-Span. The parliamentarian told Stevens that the rules were written well over a hundred years before the advent of television. Hard as Stevens tried, he could not legally oust the House members from the Senate floor.

Stevens, meanwhile, was "right there in my face," as Patty Murray later described it. Murray worried that he would take advantage of the intrusion to sidetrack the debate into one about Senate protocol instead of Admiral Kelso's retirement. From where Murray sat on the uppermost dais, the arrival of the House women did look suspiciously staged as a photo op, and if it made Patty uncomfortable, it made her press secretary mad. As Patricia Akyama later put it, "From a Senate press secretary's point of view, it was a bummer." Here the Senate women had been fighting Kelso on the front lines, and now the House women had come over to hog the cameras and take the credit. But Murray was ambivalent. Maybe the House women's presence looked like a needed show of unity. "Does this look like grandstanding, or is it we're-all-working-together?" Murray wondered.

Of one thing Murray was certain. The congresswomen's entrance made her job more difficult. "It was a very difficult hour to be in the chair, because emotions were really high and everyone wanted to be recognized," Murray later explained. No time limits restricted the debate, so the presiding officer had to recognize each speaker. At the end of each senator's speech, Murray was bombarded by a chorus of voices all asking to speak next, making it impossible to distinguish who spoke first. "I felt in a real bind, because in the chair, you have to be fair," said Murray.

"You are in a different position than if you are on the floor debating."

Schroeder and her crew's visit to the Senate floor lasted only ten minutes, but afterward everyone would remember it as if the House women had been in the Senate chamber for the better part of an hour. On their way out, the congresswomen walked across the Senate floor to Kay Bailey Hutchison. In a show of support for Hutchison's vote against Kelso in the Armed Services Committee, all nine women shook her hand, before walking out the door.

Eight Capitol Hill policemen stood outside the chamber. They formed an irregular security detail summoned, the congresswomen suspected, by Ted Stevens, who hoped to have the women ejected from the chamber. As they walked past the policemen at the chamber door, one of the eight men cocked his right arm to his forehead in a respectful salute.

All told, the debate went on for six hours. As Patty Murray listened to the rhetoric from both sides, she concluded that the arguments against giving Kelso four stars far outweighed those in favor. "In fact, the opposition had no arguments," she later suggested. Instead of discussing the Tailhook reports, Kelso's supporters talked about Kelso's stellar Navy career. They talked about how well they knew Kelso personally, and how much integrity he had. New Hampshire Republican Bob Smith even mentioned that Kelso had made some "nice remarks" at Smith's mother's funeral.

Murray thought these arguments verged on the absurd. After John Warner pleaded in favor of Kelso's wife, asserting that by stripping Kelso of two of his four stars the

Senate would be creating hardship for Mrs. Kelso, Murray thought: *What does that have to do with someone who was the head of an agency when this harassment occurred? What are we arguing here?*

Murray was struck by how "the guys who knew [Kelso] all bunched around their friend, their pal—whereas the people who didn't know him personally, but took the time to read the records and reports from an unbiased view, all felt strongly and voted the other way." To Murray's surprise, even senators who had backed Clarence Thomas, like Republicans Arlen Specter and Al D'Amato, opposed giving Kelso four stars. Washington's senior senator, Republican Slade Gorton, who rarely voted with Murray, opposed Kelso's four-star retirement, as did Bob Packwood. None of these men sat on the Armed Services Committee, and all of them, Murray realized, were keenly sensitive to the perceptions and opinions of female voters in their states.

Barbara Mikulski spoke for all seven Senate women when she commended Kelso for advancing women's positions in the Navy. But despite the gains women had made in promotions and being permitted to serve in combat, Mikulski argued, the culture of the Navy, when it came to women, had not changed. Moreover, because of the Navy's principle of command responsibility, Kelso should not be honored with a four-star retirement. Retiring with four stars, Mikulski reminded the Senate, was an "extraordinary" reward. Kelso's direct knowledge of the Tailhook improprieties was still disputed; however, Mikulski explained, "What is not disputed is the bungled investigation, the cover-ups, and the buddy system over the honor system. That is what happened on Kelso's watch, and therefore, he must take the responsibility, pay the price."

In short, Kelso had been failed by his subordinates, but because of the military chain of command, the admiral had to take the flak. "It is not only Admiral Kelso that is being judged," Mikulski reminded her colleagues, "but the entire U.S. Navy and the military. Regrettably, it falls on the shoulders of Frank Kelso."

By the time a vote was called at 8:30 P.M., Murray knew that her side could not win, although, secretly, Murray had set her heart on winning. When the clerk announced the finally "yeas" and "nays," Murray was watching the tally with Barbara Mikulski. By a vote of 54 to 43, the Senate recommended that Admiral Kelso retire with four stars. Crushed, Murray turned to Mikulski, who surprised her:

"We really did well," she said.

9

Health Care

The Democrats of the House Budget Committee—twenty-two congressmen and Louise Slaughter—sat around a large conference table. Their aides sat quietly behind them. The scene was something Slaughter had grown accustomed to. When she first came to Congress in 1987, after unseating an incumbent Republican, she had been given a leadership position, House majority whip at large. Slaughter caught the eye of the Democratic leadership both because she had proved herself on the campaign trail and because her Kentucky roots allowed her to build coalitions between Northern and Southern Democrats on the Hill. In her second term, Speaker Tom Foley appointed Slaughter to the powerful Rules Committee. Slaughter's penchant for knowing how to play the inside game often placed her at tables where she was the only woman.

It was 1992, and the Democrats on the Budget Committee were discussing what the budget increase should be for the National Institutes of Health (the federal government's biomedical research arm). After the usual long-winded ramblings, the members agreed that an $800 million increase would be appropriate. Then Slaughter spoke. She suggested that perhaps some of the money—maybe $500 million of it—should be allocated specifically for women's health research. Funding for research on breast cancer and ovarian cancer had been neglected. A few weeks earlier, Elaine Ryan, Slaughter's administrative assistant, had arrived at the $500 million number by calculating that it was the equivalent of half of one percent of the total NIH budget.

Sitting behind Slaughter, Ryan noticed that the twenty-two men in the room were far from enthusiastic about Slaughter's suggestion. Richard Durbin of Illinois objected. He wanted to increase the NIH budget for general research without strings. Slaughter looked into blank faces and pressed on. She addressed her appeal to the then chairman of the committee, Leon Panetta: "Leon, I want you to know that every year, we lose a Vietnam Wall to breast cancer." The number of women diagnosed with breast cancer every year is approximately 183,000. The number who die annually from breast cancer—46,000—comes close to the number of names engraved on the Vietnam Veterans Memorial. Incidence of the disease had increased by 2 percent a year since 1980. One in every eight American women can expect to be diagnosed with the disease in her lifetime.

"Think about your mothers, your sisters, your daughters," Slaughter said. "It would be a disgrace if we did anything else."

When Slaughter finished, there was silence. Then, to her surprise, the committee staff members, most of whom were women, started clapping. Breaking the taboo against speaking in meetings, one of Leon Panetta's economists cheered, "Go get 'em, Lou!"

Jim Oberstar of Minnesota spoke up next, agreeing with Slaughter that breast cancer research funding should be increased. Oberstar then described his wife's death from breast cancer. Soon after Slaughter's and Oberstar's emotional remarks, the men found themselves in agreement with Slaughter: $500 million would be the right amount to reserve for women's health research. Remarkably, the $500 million survived a vote in the full committee and on the House floor, eventually becoming law. Never before had there been a line item for women's health research in the budget resolution. As Leon Panetta later admitted, "It's important to have people like Louise on the committee, to kick your pants and bring up your conscience on issues like these."

Louise Slaughter and Pat Schroeder had been monitoring the National Institutes of Health since the highly touted aspirin study in 1988, when Harvard Medical School researchers announced the results of a five-year, government-funded study on the effects of aspirin in preventing heart attacks on 22,071 male physicians. Although equivalent numbers of women die from coronary disease at older ages, women had been excluded from the study.

When news of the aspirin study hit Congress, the women on the Hill were angry. "We were told that an aspirin a day can help men prevent stroke and heart attack," Slaughter recalled. "And we said, 'Wonderful, every man we know is going to do that. Now, how much do *we* take?' And we got a blank stare."

The aspirin study became a highly charged symbol of the government's failure to invest its money and expertise in women's health research. Concerned that women were being left out of other clinical trials, Pat Schroeder, Olympia Snowe, and Henry Waxman called for an investigation by the General Accounting Office—the federal government's internal auditor—into the inclusion of women in clinical studies at NIH. Two other studies had also raised questions. A $115 million Multiple Risk Factor Intervention Trail—nicknamed "Mr. Fit"—of heart disease factors had just been conducted on 13,000 men. Also, the National Institute of Aging's largest study on aging, launched in 1958, excluded women for its first twenty years; its final report contained no research findings on women. Louise Slaughter noted, "We're told that even female rats are seldom used in laboratory studies. . . . How low can they go?"

On June 18, 1990, Mark V. Nadel of the GAO delivered the bad news: Women were still being systematically excluded from NIH-sponsored clinical trials. In response to the GAO report, the women in Congress put the NIH on trial, and the advocacy issue for equity in women's-health research was born.

The NIH responded swiftly to the embarrassing news and made several changes at once. Following the lead of legislation that the women's caucus had just introduced, the NIH began requiring researchers to include women in clinical trials in the proportion that women were affected by the disease being studied. The NIH also established an Office of Research on Women's Health to oversee the new policy. In September, Bernadine Healy, the director of a Cleveland heart clinic, was nominated to become the first-ever female director of the NIH. On

Dr. Healy's first visit to Capitol Hill, she announced plans for a study that she called the equivalent of a "moonwalk for women." The Women's Health Initiative would cost $625 million and take fourteen years to complete. It would include 150,000 women and attempt to discover how to prevent breast cancer, osteoporosis, and heart disease in older women.

On June 10, 1993, President Clinton signed the three-year, $6.2 billion NIH reauthorization—a bill that President Bush had vetoed in 1992 because it contained fetal-tissue research provisions. Clinton's signing brought to fruition a three-year effort to improve women's-health research. The NIH bill gave statutory authority to the Office of Research on Women's Health and to the policy of including women in clinical trials. An act of Congress would now be required to change either of these two provisions. The bill also increased funding for breast cancer research and detection by $325 million (a 160 percent increase over the previous year); it authorized $75 million for research on ovarian cancer (which in 1989 had been funded at only $7.5 million); and $30 million in contraception and infertility research (which in the 1980s had been funded at about $8 million a year). As Clinton's secretary of Health and Human Services, Donna Shalala, said, "women's health would not be an issue if it weren't for the women in Congress."

Overall, the NIH bill marked a 450 percent boost in breast cancer research funding over the past five years, an increase far outreaching that of any other cancer. The pressure from a newly energized grassroots breast cancer lobby, which had taken its cue from the AIDS lobby, and persuasive efforts by women in Congress helped even the score for women's health. "Since the women are a majority of this country, and since the majority of the women work, and since all of those women pay taxes, the very least we can demand is that half of that tax money be spent on us," Slaughter said.

At the time of the passage of the NIH bill, the political climate was at its peak for women's health equity. One cancer lobbyist observed, "the men are afraid to vote against money for breast cancer. It has become such a powerful issue that to vote against breast cancer research is to vote against women."

President Clinton's health care reform plan would be heralded as the most important governmental initiative since the New Deal, a sweeping government-regulated plan affecting the life of every American. Ultimately, it would become the administration's greatest failure, a political debacle of grand proportions. Although months of behind-the-scenes work came to naught, the arduous health care reform process taught the women on the Hill to form an alliance that could not be ignored by committee chairmen and the congressional leadership.

At first the news looked good. The fact that the First Lady had been appointed to head the initiative gave the women in Congress hope that for the first time in over a decade, women's medical interests would not be ignored by the White House. Soon after her appointment, Hillary Rodham Clinton formed a twelve-member task force made up of cabinet secretaries, health care experts, and senior administration officials. Not one member of Congress sat on the task force—not John Dingell, or Dan Rostenkowski, or Daniel Patrick Moynihan, the committee chairmen who were to write health reform into law. Most of the work was performed by congressional, White House, and Health and Human Services staffers, whose numbers ballooned to five hundred. They split up into fifteen cluster groups and studied issues like cost controls, benefits, and long-term care. From February to September of 1993, the task force worked in secrecy.

During this time, like many other interest groups, the women on the Hill waged a lobbying campaign behind the scenes. In February, the caucus met with Hillary Clinton and Health and Human Services Secretary Donna Shalala to discuss health care reform. In March, they met with President Clinton. Coverage for mammograms, pap smears, and abortions was at the top of the list of priorities for the women's caucus. The Democratic women senators also met as a group separately with both Hillary and Bill Clinton, trying to ensure that women's health provisions and abortion would not be overlooked or avoided.

They had three arguments for including abortion in a comprehensive benefits package. First, abortion coverage was already provided in most private health insurance plans, and excluding it from the new comprehensive benefits package would revoke benefits already available to most American women. The exclusion of abortion services would also have a widespread impact on the future of abortion availability, pushing it even farther into the outskirts of the medical profession. Including abortion in the health care plan's benefits package would not be the equivalent of the federal government's directly paying for abortions, the women argued. The government would only be subsidizing the premium for low-income women so that they could buy private health insurance.

The congresswomen also used back-channel approaches. Louise Slaughter had Donna Shalala to dinner at her Capitol Hill town house. Nita Lowey sent a letter to President Clinton, signed by thirty-seven members of the women's caucus, which called for the inclusion of a comprehensive reproductive health care benefits for women, including family planning and abortion. Barbara Boxer telephoned White House aides, one of whom said that Boxer "went nuts" over abortion. "She threw a fit. It was the only thing she talked about for months." The White House had to remind her that they were all on the same side.

On September 22, President Clinton unveiled an outline of his long-awaited Health Security Act. The president's plan would require all Americans to buy the same insurance package. The draft deftly avoided any detail on abortion. But when pressed, Clinton admitted that abortion would be insured in the new plan, under the category of "pregnancy-related services." The congresswomen's lobbying campaign had worked. "The administration probably would have included abortion coverage without the women's urging," Donna Shalala said later, "but the women in congress sealed the deal."

In the end, it wouldn't be the Clinton administration that pro-choice advocates had to worry about, it would be Congress. Abortion coverage in the health care plan, experts predicted, would meet the same fate as federal funding for Medicaid abortions in the Hyde Amendment. The women knew that they faced an uphill battle. "Most members *will not* vote for abortion funding, no matter what," said a senior White House aide. "It just isn't a political reality—regardless of the arguments that private insurers include it." Another White House official said, "Everyone knows that it will be ripped out of the bill on the Hill."

Members of the women's caucus were relieved that abortion had been included in the health care plan, but they remained dissatisfied with the plan's mammogram coverage. The early draft of the plan only covered mammograms for women over fifty, every two years. On September 23, the women's caucus sent off a letter signed by thirty-seven members to President Clinton asking for better mammogram coverage: "We have some specific concerns about the limitations your proposal places on mammograms, pap smears, and pelvic examinations." When Hillary and Bill Clinton introduced the final draft of the Health Security Act, on October 27, free mammogram coverage had been expanded to include women of all ages who were considered to be "at risk" for breast cancer, and partially funded mammograms would be granted to women of any age whose doctor decided the screening was medically appropriate. Behind the Clinton plan's evasive language on mammograms was a cost concern: if all women in their forties had an annual mammogram, it would cost $2.7 billion a year. Although an improvement over the first draft, these expanded mammogram guidelines still did not satisfy Louise Slaughter and the women's health task force. The vast majority of women with breast cancer have no risk factors, and the task force was not comfortable with women having to rely on doctors as gatekeepers.

By January 1994, the impenetrable 1,342-page Health Security Act had been surrendered to three House committees and two Senate committees for a Congressional makeover—Ways and Means, Energy and Commerce, and Education and Labor in the House, and Finance and Labor and Human Resources in the Senate. The fate of health alliances, employer mandates, premium caps, and coverage of women's health in the benefits packages would consume the second half of the 103rd congressional session.

Complicating the future of mammography coverage in health care reform were the National Cancer Institute's new mammogram screening guidelines, which had been issued in December. Retracting its earlier recommendation that women between the ages of forty and fifty should have mammograms every other year, the NCI stated that there was no proof that mammograms provided a "statistically significant reduction in mortality" for women under fifty. Therefore, the NCI made "no recommendation" for women under fifty. Each year, approximately 40,000 women under fifty are diagnosed with breast cancer—20 percent of all breast cancer mortalities occur among women between the ages of forty and fifty.

Louise Slaughter understood the science behind the NCI's new guidelines. A friend of Slaughter's from Rochester had just died of breast cancer at the age of forty-three. A few weeks after Michelle Kaplan had been told that her mammogram showed no signs of a tumor, she discovered a lump in her breast. Kaplan's tumor did not show up on the mammogram because in women under fifty dense breast tissue makes it harder for mammograms to detect tumors. Although the technology had its limitations and didn't detect Kaplan's tumor, mammograms were still the only diagnostic tool women had to detect breast tumors, and they did work in some cases. The tragedy of Kaplan's early death helped Slaughter resolve her stand on mammograms: "I've decided that I'm going to fight for mammograms at fifty and under."

During the January recess, staffers of the women's caucus met with representatives of ten breast cancer organizations in an attempt to arrive at an educated solution to the mammography controversy. After listening to experts from organizations like the American Cancer Society, NCI, the Campaign for Women's Health, and the American Medical Women's Association, the staffers concluded that the caucus should demand that mammograms be covered for women between the ages of forty and forty-nine with 10 percent co-payments. On February 23, Slaughter presented a women's caucus executive meeting with a statement declaring the caucus's new position on mammograms. Everyone in the meeting agreed.

Slaughter convened a press conference on March 8 to announce the caucus's push for broader coverage of mammogram screening. Three weeks later, the women's caucus sent out a letter signed by thirty-three congresswomen to all eight chairmen involved in health care reform. The letter called for coverage of mammograms for women over forty with co-payments, abortion services, and pap smears.

Slaughter devoted the spring of 1994 to pushing the mammogram cause with committee chairmen who were marking up their own versions of health care reform. Her position on the Rules Committee served her well, because every committee chairman had to go through Rules before they could bring their bills to a vote on the House floor. The Rules Committee, not the committee chairmen, made the final decision on which amendments went to the floor. Slaughter was therefore in a position to swap favors with committee chairmen. Her sense of humor and good political instincts helped her forge friendships with the men in charge of health care reform.

Slaughter's workload often pulled her away from her family. When Louise first came to Congress in 1987, her husband, Bob Slaughter, tried visiting her in Washington. It was the Fourth of July, and although Bob and Louise had made plans to watch the fireworks on the Mall together, Bob found himself on the Mall watching the fireworks alone. At the last minute, Louise had had to fly back to Rochester. The best way to see Louise when she was in Washington, Bob soon learned, was to tune in to C-Span.

Bob had often thought that if Louise had served in Congress when they were younger, the marriage might not have survived. He lived with Louise's schedule without complaint. But, he said of the congressional life, "it's sort of a Chinese torture, or like taking arsenic a little bit every day."

At sixty-two, Bob Slaughter had sharp blue eyes, white hair, and dark quill-like eyebrows that poked up over a pair of thick square eyeglasses. Even though Bob and Louise were grandparents, they did not lead the life of a typical couple in their sixties—no cruises, no golf. The last vacation the Slaughters took had been eleven years ago, to celebrate their twenty-fifth wedding anniversary.

By Louise's eighth year in office, Bob, retired from Kodak, had grown accustomed to the fact that he had to share his wife with 580,000 constituents. The job of congressperson, observed Bob, "takes all the time there is and more." While Louise put in sixteen-hour days in Washington, Bob went on living in their split-level house in Fairport, New York, a suburb of Rochester. The Slaughters' three daughters had by now grown up and moved away. During the week, Bob lived alone. He spent his days in his basement workshop, building furniture. He gardened. He did the marketing. When Louise came home on week-ends, Bob drove her to evening events: speeches, funeral visits, workshops at the local community college.

The upkeep of the houses in Fairport and in Washington fell to Bob. One week, in the middle of the 103rd Congress, Bob had a project to complete in Washington: painting the trim on the Slaughters' small red-brick town house on North Carolina Avenue, three blocks from the Capitol. He put on a pair of white cotton painter's pants and a pale-blue workshirt and went to work on the mustard-colored shutters of his house.

Two nights earlier, he had been decked out in black tie, escorting his wife in through the North Portico of the White House to attend a state dinner. That night, Louise sat next to President Clinton. Bob sat at another table, next to someone's wife. The White House did not stir him that night, nor did the state dinner. "It's just another piece of social small talk," he later said. "It isn't like you have a legitimate reason to be with the president. It's just what goes with being a congressional spouse."

On the same day that Slaughter and the women's caucus held their health care press conference, Patty Murray spoke passionately about ovarian cancer on the other side of the Capitol building. Murray took ten minutes during "morning business" to humanize another disease that kills women. She talked about her friends, Washington State Senator Don Charnley and his botanist wife Melinda Denton—both of whom were Murray's mentors. Over the Christmas holidays, Melinda had undergone surgery for ovarian cancer. But a few weeks later, she was back in the hospital for more tests, chemotherapy, Taxol treatments, and surgery. "A week ago," said Murray, her voice cracking, "I talked to Melinda and she told me the fight was over. Early this Saturday morning, Melinda died. The shock of her death holds me hostage. How could a vibrant woman in her forties, a mother, close to my own age, be gone so swiftly?"

Murray did some research and discovered that there is no effective screening tool for ovarian cancer. In 1993, there were 17,000 new cases of ovarian cancer, and 12,000 women died of the disease. Two out of three women diagnosed with ovarian cancer will die. "Melinda left behind my friend Don and an eight-year-old son. But Melinda's story is not unique. My colleague from the Highline School Board, Mary Louise Cline, forty-eight years old, died last week as well. The names are endless: my aunt Mary; my friend Kennie's sister, Carol Tyler; my friend Kate's mother, Ruth Cudlipp. It is too late for Melinda and the many others, but it is not too late for my daughter."

Murray's speech on ovarian cancer was covered widely by the national press. She concluded with a plea for more research funding for women's health. She asked for "strong language" in the health care reform bill to address the needs of millions of women. "It is the very least we can do." Murray used her seat on the Appropriations Committee to help increase funding for women's health research at NIH. She also joined a twenty-senator working group on health care reform, where she became a convincing voice for the middle class and pushed for health care coverage for women and children.

In May and June, the three House committees considering health care reform were in the midst of final votes and markups. Wrangling over employer mandates, cigarette taxes, and small-business exemptions had reached a fever pitch.

On May 12, the Subcommittee on Labor and Management Relations voted on chairman Pat Williams' modified version of the Clintons' health reform plan, which included "pregnancy-related services" in its basic benefits package. Ron Klink, a salt-and-pepper-haired former Pittsburgh television reporter, introduced an amendment that would exclude health insurance from covering abortion in the plan. Three days earlier, the Alan Guttmacher Institute had released a study showing that two-thirds of private health insurance plans routinely cover abortion. The pro-choice forces used the study to illustrate their point that leaving abortion coverage out of health care reform would unfairly remove an existing benefit.

The subcommittee vote was the first on the abortion issue, and Pat Schroeder anticipated that it would be an important bellwether. Schroeder's press secretary, Andrea Camp, called a handful of key women in the caucus and suggested that they all sit in the audience for the markup and "go eyeball to eyeball with these guys." Pat Schroeder, Cynthia McKinney, Nita Lowey, Maxine Waters, and Barbara Kennelly looked forceful and intimidating in the front row of the small spectators' section of the Cannon 302 hearing room. When Klink's amendment came up, the three Democratic women on the subcommittee spoke out against it. Lynn Woolsey of California said that it represented a "major step backward." Patsy Mink of Hawaii said that the amendment went "far beyond anything the Congress had ever done" because it would cut back coverage most people have in private health plans.

Jolene Unsoeld, a third-term Democrat from Washington State, elevated the skirmish into a full-scale gender war. "Reproductive health is at the very core of a woman's existence in its importance," said Unsoeld. "If you want to be brutally frank, what it compares [with] is if you had health care plans that did not cover any illness related to male testicles." Then Unsoeld took the argument one step further: "I think the women of this country are being tolerant enough to allow you men to vote on this, because you obviously don't understand."

Ron Klink exploded. "Just don't make me or anyone else pay for something that we don't believe in," the Pennsylvania Democrat shot back. "Just because I'm not a woman doesn't mean that I don't understand the issue. If I heard the woman correctly, that is one of the most sexist comments that I've ever heard, and to hear it in the United States Congress is appalling." Before the vote, Klink made one last argument in favor of his amendment. "The American people do not want to pay for this. Even those who believe in a woman's right to choose don't necessarily want to fund abortion. This is a direct subsidy."

Klink's amendment was defeated by a vote of 16 to 11. All four women on the committee, including Republican Marge Roukema, voted against Klink's amendment.

Next, Richard Armey of Texas, the third-highest-ranking Republican in the leadership, introduced another anti-abortion amendment. He wanted to protect state restrictions on abortion from being overridden by the health care plan. During the debate over his amendment, Armey stared at Nita Lowey, who sat in the audience. Red-faced, he shouted, "Are we going to be so *fem-centric* that we're going to condone the self-indulgent conduct of the body of a woman who has already demonstrated in most cases they were damned careless with it in the first place?"

The audience, comprising mostly pro-choice lobbyists and staffers, first gasped, then hissed. George Miller, a Democratic congressman on the panel, asked that he be dissociated from Armey's outrageous comments.

Armey's amendment was defeated by a vote of 14 to 11. This time, Roukema voted with Armey.

Pat Schroeder and Olympia Snowe followed up on Armey's remarks with a letter. "As cochairs of the congressional caucus for women's issues, we want to take a strong exception to your remarks at the health care reform markup on May 12. The remark was offensive. It demonstrated a disrespect for women and an insensitivity to their health care needs that has no place in this important debate."

Two months earlier, on March 21, Schroeder and Snowe had sent a similar letter to Pete Stark, a California Democrat, and chairman of the Ways and Means Health Subcommittee. In a health care hearing, Stark had become angered by Nancy Johnson's criticism of his health reform proposal, and he retaliated with a sexist insult "The gentlelady got her medical degree through pillow talk," said Stark, referring to the fact that the Republican congresswoman's husband was a doctor. An irate Johnson responded: "I got my knowledge from endless hours as a representative in this Congress, from endless hours in hospitals and physicians' offices talking to patients." At the end of the hearing, Stark apologized to Johnson.

Even though she had not been present at the hearing, Deborah Pryce was the first to come to Johnson's defense. Pryce had heard about Stark's comment in Newt Gingrich's office. Gingrich, campaigning for minority leader at the time, was holding a meeting with a group of Republican women. He had asked Pryce to be his liaison with the women, to whom he was trying to show more sensitivity. Relishing the fact that a male Democrat had insulted a female Republican, instead of the other way around, Ed Gillespie, the policy and communications director of the House Republican Conference, helped Pryce's staff compose a letter from her to Stark. "You denigrate us all," the letter read. "We demand that you offer a public apology to Representative Johnson at the earliest opportunity to remove the intimidating cloud of sexism that darkens your control over the subcommittee markup." Gillespie's involvement proved that Pryce was now in the pocket of the right wing of the House Republicans. Gillespie's boss was none other than Dick Armey of *fem-centric* fame.

Although they were unaware of the fact that Dick Armey's staff had helped write Pryce's letter, none of the Democratic women signed the letter. Pryce had only circulated the letter to a few Democratic freshwomen who had suspected that the letter had partisan origins. None of the senior Democratic women were shown that letter before it was sent to Stark, but fearing that they would look like hypocrites, Schroeder sent her own, less strident rendition to Stark a few days later.

By July, the women had succeeded. All of the major congressional committees had agreed that abortion should be paid for by the health care plan. Mammograms, meanwhile, were slated to be covered every two years for women between forty and fifty and annually for women over fifty. The final fight on abortion would take place on the House and Senate floors in August. In the House, the Rules Committee would select the amendments to be allowed on the floor, which put Louise Slaughter, the only woman on the Rules Committee and the committee's torchbearer on abortion rights, in an extremely influential position.

The battle lines had been drawn. Pro-life and pro-choice forces within the Democratic party had staked out their territories. Both sides had become so entrenched that it looked as though abortion alone could sink health care reform. In order for health care reform to pass, the votes of 218 out of the 256 Democrats were needed, and abortion looked as though it could divide Democratic members seriously enough to jeopardize finding those 218 votes.

To make matters worse, the National Conference of Catholic Bishops threatened to drop its support for health reform if abortion remained in the plan. The 390 male Catholic bishops were represented by an articulate thirty-four-year-old woman named Helen Alvare. Alvare couched the bishops' argument as a women's issue. In a press conference on July 13, Alvare produced a poll showing that 59 percent of the women they polled were against including abortion in the health care benefits package. "It's always been the case that women have been more pro-life than men across the board," said Alvare—a statistic pro-choice groups ardently disputed. "If you actually go to the women [constituents] and let them speak for themselves, that's where they stand," said Alvare, making a not-so-subtle reference to the congresswomen who had been driving the pro-choice public policy debate.

Also in July, thirty-five Democrats (only one of whom was a woman) signed a letter to Speaker Tom Foley vowing to vote against health care reform if it included abortion. The letter, drafted by Harold Volkmer a Democrat from Missouri, and dated June 23, declared, "We are unable to support any reform legislation that does not explicitly exclude elective abortion from the scope of any government-defined, government-mandated, or government-funded health benefits package." Seventy-six Democrats retaliated with a more mildly worded letter drafted by pro-choice Oregonian Peter DeFazio and Pat Schroeder claiming that they would not vote for a reform bill that did *not* include abortion. As one staffer on the pro-choice side put it, "this is a game of chicken," and neither the pro-choice nor the pro-life side wanted to be the first ones to blink.

The signers of the anti-abortion Volkmer letter, most of whom were conservative Democrats, were less likely to blink first, because they rejected the health care reform package on grounds other than just abortion. Many of the pro-choice signatures, on the other hand, were empty threats. Although DeFazio told the press that fifty of the seventy-two people who signed his and Pat Schroeder's letter to Foley would certainly not vote for the bill if it did not include abortion funding, the true count was closer to five. The bill included too many other provisions that, when push came to shove, liberal members would not sacrifice for abortion.

As a member of the Rules Committee, Louise Slaughter did not have the political freedom to make a protest statement on abortion. She had also lobbied for an exemption for Rochester from certain parts of the health care plan that would harm the city's model health care system. When Daniel Patrick Moynihan and Richard Gephardt both agreed to help Slaughter with the Rochester exemption, her hands were tied on abortion.

Cynthia McKinney had two goals: universal health care coverage and aligning herself with Majority Leader Richard Gephardt. Universal coverage would improve health care delivery for thousands of her poor constituents; loyalty to Gephardt would give her embattled district the powerful Democratic party leadership's blessing. If it came down to losing the whole bill over abortion, McKinney would balk. Pat Schroeder, on the other hand, never one known for her loyalty to the party leadership, would have fallen on her sword for abortion.

By early August, the leadership's health care reform prochoice task force, chaired by Nita Lowey and Don Edwards, began strategy sessions every three days on how to find a compromise. A group of staffers had worked out a way to build a "fire wall" between public funds and private premiums that would prevent federal tax money from paying for abortions. Nita Lowey presented the compromise to Gephardt, and she approached Marcy Kaptur, a conservative Democrat from Ohio. Kaptur claimed, curiously, to be neither pro-choice nor pro-life, but she was against including abortion funding in the basic benefits package. During a long August 11 meeting between the two congresswomen, Nita Lowey asked Kaptur, "Why can't the women work this out?" Kaptur was receptive to Lowey's "fire wall" compromise, and it looked as though she might be able to bring some other middle-of-the-road Democrats along with her.

Unfortunately, the delicate alliance forged between Lowey and Kaptur had no future. The Senate started debating health care reform on August ninth, only to be stalled from voting on any serious legislation for two weeks by Republican filibuster threats. In the House, the Democratic leadership's health care plan, brokered by Majority Leader Richard Gephardt, never garnered enough votes to pass. To avoid the embarrassment of a sure loss, the leadership delayed voting on the plan, concentrating instead on the crime bill.

In the end, employer mandates and new taxes proved to be larger, more fundamental stumbling blocks for health care reform than abortion. After thousands of hours of meetings, hearings, markups, and press conferences; after nineteen months of political posturing and behind-the-scenes deal making, health care reform died. Only one Republican, Senator James Jeffords of Vermont, backed President Clinton's bill. More than $50 million had been spent by scores of lobbying groups on advertisements opposing health care reform. On August 25, the House and the Senate both recessed without ever voting on one major proposal. The 103rd Congress's health care fight had fizzled.

The congresswomen had mixed feelings about the loss—and their staff members perhaps even more so. More than a year of their work had been squandered. For women like Slaughter, Schroeder, and Lowey, health care reform had consumed time and passion. Now their efforts to shape the legislation would never be realized. At the same time, the women were also relieved. They knew that they had been spared voting on a complex, controversial, expensive government program that was not popular in their home districts.

But despite the failure of health care reform, the congresswomen's struggle had not been wasted effort. Their agenda—coverage of women's health issues and abortion—had been heard and successfully acted upon. Before health care reform sank, the congresswomen had won virtually every vote on abortion coverage in the committees considering the bill. They had also convinced the relevant committees to provide full coverage for mammograms and pap smears. In short, the women's health agenda had become a political force to be reckoned with. The aspirin-study days were history.

10

⊷◈⊶

Winner's Guilt

As the 103rd Congress headed into its final lap, the women on the Hill won a series of hard-earned legislative victories.

On May 26, President Clinton signed the Freedom of Access to Clinic Entrances Act (FACE) into law, marking a major victory for pro-choice forces. The bill sought to protect women seeking abortions and doctors who had been victims of abortion clinic violence by making it a federal crime to obstruct access to the clinics. The new law also imposed criminal and civil penalties on people who physically blocked women from trying to obtain an abortion. Over the past twelve years there had been 123 arson cases, 37 bombings, and 1,500 cases of stalking, assault, and sabotage against abortion clinics in 33 states. In 1993, militant anti-abortion activists had murdered two abortion doctors, David Gunn and Wayne Patterson.

A dramatic series of floor fights erupted over the clinic-violence bill each time it came up for a vote in the House.

Pat Schroeder was responsible for getting the bill through the Judiciary conference committee, and she assumed the critical role as the bill's floor manager. Louise Slaughter pushed FACE through an unwilling Rules Committee. A bipartisan spirit among the congresswomen prevailed: 75 percent of the Republican women supported the bill, while only 20 percent of Republican men did. The debates on FACE recalled the Hyde Amendment floor fight, but with a new twist. The women were no longer novices. They had worked together earlier in the session to provide abortion coverage for poor women in Washington, D.C., federal employees, and female federal prisoners. This time the pro-choice women worked closely with the parliamentarians and the Democratic leadership. This time they won.

Also in the spring of 1994, in the midst of election primaries, the women as a group took on the National Rifle Association, making gun control a woman's issue. The assault-weapons ban, which had originally been introduced in the Senate by Dianne Feinstein, would abolish the sale of nineteen kinds of semi-automatic weapons over ten years. The ban's chances of becoming law had been considered unlikely: in 1991, the House had defeated a similar bill by 70 votes. But in 1994, with the Democratic leadership divided over the legislation, Chuck Schumer, chief sponsor of the House bill, set up his own whip organization. Women dominated the whip meetings, constituting eleven of the fifteen members in the group. Louise Slaughter, Cynthia McKinney, Pat Schroeder, Nancy Pelosi, and Rosa DeLauro provided most of the arm twisting that pushed the bill over the top. "We couldn't have passed the assault-weapons ban without the women members of Congress," admitted Schumer. "Women feel the issue. They are victims. They don't have any of this macho baloney." In the end, the House narrowly passed the ban by a vote of 216 to 214, with women's votes providing the margin of victory. Eighty-three percent of the women in the House voted for the ban, compared with only 46 percent of the congressmen.

Gun control was a highly emotional issue that ignited gender skirmishes across the country. For Patty Murray, advocating gun control was a high-stakes gamble. Murray had received death threats in the mail that extended to her husband and children as early as the summer of 1993 after she introduced her first piece of legislation—the Firearm Victims Prevention Act, which would levy a 25 percent sales tax on guns and ammunition.

Gun advocates in Washington state retaliated against the bill by writing letters and calling Murray's office. After Murray voted for the Brady bill and the assault-weapons ban, the tone of the letters grew angrier, and Murray for the first time considered getting personal security. Another senator, then Democrat Ben Nighthorse Campbell of Colorado, had cast the deciding vote in the Senate on the assault-weapons ban and had received so many death threats he hired bodyguards.

Public anger reached a climax in the summer of 1994, when Hillary Rodham Clinton went to Seattle for the kick-off of her health care reform bus tour. Murray met Clinton in a suite at a downtown hotel. Just before the two women were scheduled to go on stage in an outdoor square, the Secret Service told Murray that two men in the crowd had been arrested. One was carrying a loaded gun, the other a knife. Taking Murray to a room at the top of the hotel where she could see the crowd below, the Secret Service asked her if she wanted to cancel the rally.

They wanted Murray to see exactly what she was up against—the size of the crowd, the inherent difficulty of guaranteeing her safety. Murray said she would speak as scheduled: "We can't let these people intimidate us."

The rally was a disaster. The crowd heckled Murray and Clinton throughout their speeches. Looking out over the sea of people, Murray unwittingly attached the angry faces in the crowd to the threatening letters and phone calls that had poured into her office over the past year. For the first time, she realized that she was exposing herself to serious danger. "Standing in front of that crowd made me feel completely vulnerable," she later revealed. "It was really frightening." She sensed that the anger was coming from irrate men, incited by talk-radio hosts' scapegoating of Hillary Clinton. To these men, the sight of Patty Murray and Hillary Clinton on stage together represented everything they hated: powerful, liberal "feminazis" who wanted to take their guns away.

After the rally, Murray rode in the limousine with Clinton back to the Westin Hotel. As the motorcade drove into the hotel, all of Murray's fears were confirmed when she heard a man on the street corner shout, "Kill the bitch!"

As five House and Senate committees inched forward on health care reform, the 1,100-page, $33.5 billion, omnibus Crime Bill had deadlocked the other half of Congress's summer agenda. While conferees wrangled over death-penalty provisions and the assault-weapons ban, the bill's sleeper proved to be the Violence Against Women Act.

House and Senate conferees (all of whom were men) agreed to every provision in the $1.8 billion landmark bill, which would provide grants to reduce the rising tide of domestic violence and sexual-assault crimes. The lavish funding would be used to create a national domestic-violence hotline, more shelters for battered women, and stricter federal penalties for repeat sex offenders. The bill's most controversial provision would create a civil rights violation allowing victims of gender-based crimes to sue for damages in federal court. Although Republicans were looking for crime-prevention provisions in the crime bill to cut, VAWA proved untouchable. "The Republicans *never* tried to cut the Violence Against Women Act," said Melanie T. Sloan, a House Judiciary subcommittee staffer. "There was no way that they were going to say 'I'm against money for domestic violence.' "

Joe Biden, the chairman of the Senate Judiciary Committee, was the bill's chief sponsor and most powerful advocate. Biden first authored and introduced the Violence Against Women Act in June of 1990. Barbara Boxer had co-sponsored VAWA on the House side, but neither Biden nor Boxer had been able to attract attention to the bill until 1992. Anita Hill and the Year of the Woman changed that. The influx of new women in Congress added visibility and political prestige to the issue.

In the overheated partisan politics of that July and August, the fate of the assault-weapons ban and the Violence Against Women Act were both tied to the crime bill, the passage of which looked precarious. Crime had become the number-one issue in the upcoming election. Polls showed that public fear of crime had eclipsed concern over health care. Every politician on the Hill wanted to look tough on crime. Therefore, weeks of posturing followed, and not until August 25 did the crime bill pass both houses. After the dust settled, the *New York Times* pronounced the women the "quiet winners" of the crime-bill war.

The legislative victories of the women on the Hill did not come without personal sacrifices. By the spring of 1994, Cynthia McKinney was depressed and burned-out. A year earlier, in May, she had suffered an exhaustion breakdown; her doctor had ordered her to take a week of vacation. As the anniversary of her breakdown arrived, McKinney's staff worried that their boss might be overdoing it again. On a typical day in May, McKinney started off with an 8:00 A.M. French class, preparing for her Ph.D. oral exams. She then met groups of constituents, one after another, followed by an interview with a reporter about an international arms-sales bill she had introduced in February. Next she testified in front of the Labor and HHS Appropriations Subcommittee on budget line items for children, then fulfilled her Democratic whip assignment for the assault-weapons ban on the House floor, followed by a television interview on the situation in Haiti. All the while, she worked the phones, talking to legal experts about the suit challenging the constitutionality of her district, which was about to go to trial in Savannah.

Late in the evening, Cynthia went home to an apartment in which two borrowed armchairs stood alone in an empty living room. For a while, until the neighbors complained, McKinney had tacked up pink bed sheets for curtains. She had yet to make a meal that involved the oven. Yet when her nine-year-old son Coy came to visit, as he did four or five times in the year, Cynthia somehow had to make this two-bedroom flat in a cinder-block complex near the Potomac River feel like home.

During the week, Coy lived with his grandparents in Atlanta. When Cynthia returned for the weekend, Coy moved home to a house Cynthia had bought in a brand-new suburban Atlanta subdivision. When she was home, her work schedule remained crowded with political events. Sometimes Cynthia would forget to ask Coy if he had done his homework. Sometimes she would lose track of his soccer and baseball game schedules, occasionally forgetting to clean his uniform in time for each game. Coy had met President Clinton and Vice President Gore; he had attended the White House Christmas Party, as well as dozens of church services and political meetings in McKinney's district. For all that, Coy would happily trade the fast lane for a stay-at-home mother. "He doesn't like me in this job," said Cynthia. "He would rather have a regular, average, ordinary mother."

By early spring of 1994, with the first primaries of the election season on the horizon, McKinney met with her staff to review her schedule for early summer. In June, her staff informed her, Cynthia would be spending every weekend campaigning across the country for House colleagues facing close reelection races. The fact that she had been recruited was a high compliment. Cynthia was now seen as a national figure, capable of influencing tight races in Arizona and Ohio and Virginia. But in the middle of the discussion, Cynthia's mood inexplicably dropped. In a low, tight voice, she said, "I feel like Coy doesn't have a mother." Everyone in the room fell silent.

At two o'clock in the afternoon on October 7, the House floor was full of bleary-eyed members who had been up until 3:00 A.M. that morning, voting on the California desert bill. The cloakroom was crowded with suitcases. This would be the last day that the 103rd Congress met before the November 8 elections.

Pat Schroeder took the podium. This was the same woman who on an official mission to China had taken to the Great Wall in a bunny costume to celebrate Easter. After all this time in Congress, Schroeder still signed her signature with a smiley face inside the "P." She still left Easter baskets for her interns, still let herself be the goofy, sometimes annoying, sometimes charming first-grade teacher that, in fact, her mother, Bernice Scott, had been throughout Pat's childhood. This morning, she had more good news to deliver, news so good that, in classic Schroeder lingo, it gave her "goosebumps."

The Congressional Caucus on Women's Issues had just tallied all the bills in the 103rd that would now, as law, benefit the lives of women and families. The total: an astounding sixty-six. "On women's issues, this has been the most historic Congress I've ever seen," Schroeder said. "While the number of measures passed in this Congress is historic and impressive, the other story is the one behind the numbers: the cooperation between congresswomen, their persistence in working to bring legislation important to women to the House and Senate floors, and their political savvy in making this a record-setting Congress." The number of bills enacted in the 103rd Congress equaled the total amount of women's legislation passed in the previous six years. When it came to women's rights, the 103rd Congress had made a greater impact for women and by women than any previous Congress—despite the Hyde Amendment loss, the failure of health care reform, and Admiral Kelso's four-star retirement.

Schroeder listed some of the caucus's advances: family leave, over $500 million in breast cancer research funding, the Violence Against Women Act, Gender Equity in Education, the Freedom of Access to Clinic Entrances Act, women's health in the defense industry and for veterans. The list was so long that she only had time to mention a few. The women of the 103rd had lived up to the Year of the Woman's mandate: women's interests were finally being represented on the Hill, because more women had been elected to Congress.

"We got a lot of these things passed because of strong bipartisan support from women," said Schroeder. "I just hope someone will cover it!" The next day, as it turned out, Schroeder had to settle for a few low-profile wire stories. On the Hill, good news was still no news.

The speech would be Pat Schroeder's swan song as co-chair of the women's caucus. In December, elections for the caucus's new leadership would put Nita Lowey and Connie Morella in Schroeder's and Snowe's places as co-chairs.

Meanwhile, outside the halls of Congress, beyond the Beltway, the political climate was changing. Although the women on the Hill had won many battles, they were about to lose one phase of the war.

By 9:00 P.M. the House was still in session. As the bells rang for the last roll call, a crowd of freshwomen gathered, primarily because Nita Lowey was donating her own money, in $1,000 checks, to colleagues who faced tough races in November. Many of the women had been targeted by the Christian Coalition and the NRA. Some would not be returning. Marjorie Margolies-Mezvinsky was trailing in the polls behind Jon Fox in her Republican-leaning suburban Philadelphia district. As Lowey handed her a check, Margolies-Mezvinsky realized how much she had come to depend on the other congresswomen, and how much was about to change. "We knew there was a nasty atmosphere out there," she recalled later. Pat Schroeder had been spat upon in an airport, Karan English had been called a "feminazi" on a radio talk show, and Elizabeth Furse had all but been accused of being a lesbian because she supported gay rights. "We had had each other to rely on for emotional support, but now we had to go out there and fight the war," said Margolies-Mezvinsky.

In two years, the congresswomen had created their own neighborhood within the larger community of Congress. Between votes, they had taken naps side by side on couches in the Lindy Boggs Room. They had chatted in the bathroom, shared meals, stayed overnight at one another's apartments, exchanged stories about their children. They had shared the spotlight in press conferences and the confusion that came with learning the ropes in Congress. They knew that the special circumstances that had brought them all to Congress at the same time might never happen again. The women crowded together on the floor of the House and wept as they hugged each other goodbye.

The signs had been visible for months. Clinton's rock-bottom popularity ratings. The demise of health care reform. The failure of Congress to pass campaign finance reform laws or to cut its own bloated committees. The Christian Coalition's swelling war chest and snowballing anger over Clinton's stand on gays in the military, sex education, and abortion. The NRA's fury over the passage of the Brady Bill and the assault-weapons ban. Voter anger over the 1993 tax increase.

The political climate had changed dramatically since 1992. Crime had become the number-one issue of concern among voters, and being "tough on crime" had always been harder for female candidates. Voters were angry that the "change" they had demanded in the 1992 elections had not taken place fast enough in Washington, and they wanted to punish incumbents for not producing. Political consultants had begun to think that an increasingly impatient electorate would now hold women to a higher standard on change than men.

In 1994, women faced a new barrier to getting elected: the high expectations created in 1992. As far as voters were concerned, little had changed in Washington, and the women were getting blamed. When a freshman congresswoman like Marjorie Margolies-Mezvinsky cut a deal with the president on the budget vote, playing the same game everyone else did, she was held to a higher standard, accused of hypocrisy. "If a guy had done the same thing, that would just be politics," one strategist observed.

Patty Murray would not have to run for reelection until 1998. Cynthia McKinney and Pat Schroeder faced relatively easy races. Louise Slaughter, however, was on the front lines. She represented a district with a dangerously slim Democratic majority. New York's 28th Congressional District, with its 111,220 registered Republicans and 106,561 registered Democrats, had always been the Republicans' for the taking. As the nation leaned toward the Republican party, so too would Slaughter's district.

Slaughter found herself facing, of all challengers, a woman: Renee Forgensi Davison, a thirty-six-year-old Republican county legislator, who was anti–gun control, anti-choice, and anti-taxes. By nominating Davison, Republicans hoped to cripple Slaughter's support among Republican women. Renee Davison wasn't the only conservative Republican woman running against a female Democratic incumbent. A total of eight incumbent Democratic congresswomen were facing challenges by Republican women, most of whom were pro-life antifeminists who wouldn't have been caught dead marching to the Senate to protest the Tailhook scandal. The right wing of the Republican party had plans to elect *their* women to Congress in what one feminist activist viewed as a divide-and-conquer strategy.

Early in the 103rd Congress, the national Republican party targeted Slaughter's district and backed Davison to the hilt, dispatching political heavies such as Dick Cheney, Bob Dole, Phil Gramm, and Lamar Alexander to Rochester. The Republican National Committee ran television ads in Rochester criticizing Louise for voting to raise taxes in Clinton's budget. Republicans took Louise to task for hurting Rochester's export-dependent business community when she voted against NAFTA. Radio talk-show host Rush Limbaugh lampooned Louise for co-sponsoring the Clinton health plan while at the same time seeking exemptions from the legislation for Rochester. By the summer of 1994, political analysts had put Slaughter's reelection chances in the toss-up category.

Slaughter had won her reelection in 1992 by a relatively slim 9-point margin, and the campaign had been nasty. Her opponent, William Polito, ran a barrage of negative advertisements, to which Slaughter had wanted to respond, but her political consultants argued her out of it, maintaining that the polls showed that she was safe. In the last week of the campaign, Slaughter's support collapsed dramatically. Then and there she vowed never to play political softball again. "These days," she had come to realize, "in order to beat people, you have to destroy them." Slaughter's goal in 1994 was to "win big enough so they will leave me alone and stop running after me like a dog in heat."

The stress of facing another grueling reelection campaign weighed heavily on Slaughter. She was known for her spunk and wit, but she also had a reputation as a hothead. At times, Slaughter had been unable to cope with the anxiety she felt about her reelection, and she passed it on to her aides. In late January, nine months before election day, Slaughter got furious at her staff for not working hard enough. Her staff had actually been working to the point of exhaustion. Even so, it was not enough for Louise. After the election, she went on to her fifth administrative assistant in two years.

In 1994, Slaughter hired Joe Trippi. His firm, Trippi, McMahon & Squire, based in Washington, D.C., had a reputation for ruthlessness. In 1992, as Jerry Brown's media consultant, Trippi had created a devastating attack ad showing Bill Clinton in a golf cart: "While Bill Clinton plays golf at a restricted all-white club," the narrator droned, "Arkansas remains one of the only two states with no civil rights act."

"I'm hiring you guys," Louise Slaughter told Trippi in 1994, "because I'm not going to relive 1992."

"She hired us," Trippi agreed, "because we had a reputation that we took no prisoners."

During the campaign, Slaughter met every Saturday with a kitchen cabinet of advisers. Two Saturdays before the September 13 primary, they screened the first three TV spots Joe Trippi had prepared. Each of the spots reinforced the message that Slaughter "listens" and "works hard for you." Polls had shown that voters believed that Slaughter listened. What was more, Slaughter polled one of the highest numbers that Trippi had ever seen for any candidate he had worked for: "Even the people who didn't like her said she listened."

On all other questions, though, Slaughter polarized her constituents. The polls consistently split 55 percent for Slaughter and 45 percent against her. "Everything in the damned poll was 55–45," said Trippi. "No matter what we said good about her in the poll, she didn't go above 55. If you were not for Louise Slaughter, there didn't appear to be a damned thing you could do to get them to vote for her."

Trippi analyzed the first poll and found that about 75 percent of the undecideds were leaning against voting for Slaughter. Meanwhile, 25 to 30 percent of the people who supported her were soft. If Slaughter started with 46 to 55 percent and then lost 9 points from the soft votes, while picking up only 25 to 30 percent of the undecideds, Slaughter would win with a very small margin of 51 or 52 percent. If Slaughter didn't do anything to depolarize the voters, Trippi warned in a memo, she would have to settle for winning by the skin of her teeth, which would make her an easy target in 1996.

Hoping to "depolarize" some of the voters and give Slaughter a safer margin of victory than 51 percent, Trippi devised a strategy to soften the opposition by emphasizing the qualities that encouraged voters to support Slaughter. Trippi wanted to start the positive ads early, two weeks before the September 13 primary. Three "warm and fuzzy" ads were born.

Slaughter hated them. The kitchen cabinet hated them. But they didn't tell Trippi until two days before the campaign was scheduled to air the first spot. The money had already been sent to the TV stations to pay for the airtime. Trippi got a call from a Slaughter staffer on Friday. Slaughter and the kitchen cabinet had decided against using the ads. The ads were too soft. They didn't have the hard edge Slaughter needed. Slaughter and her cabinet saw Renee Davison as a much more formidable opponent than Polito had been. Davison was articulate, she was a woman, and the Republican party machinery was behind her. Davison was running a stronger campaign operation than Polito. They didn't think this was the kind of campaign where Slaughter could afford to look soft.

Trippi flew to Rochester to face the music. Slaughter asked how this mean, mad-dog firm could have come up with such soft spots. "I thought I hired you exactly because you weren't going to fall into the same trap," she complained. Trippi explained his strategy, which was to increase Slaughter's positives. "For three weeks," he insisted, "I wanted this campaign to try to depolarize. Then, we'll go fight." He promised Slaughter that he wasn't going to allow her to look vulnerable. "Look," he warned, "the day this woman coughs, the day she touches a hair on your head I'm going to shove her into the gutter, and put my foot on her head until she drowns." He added, "I'm not even going to wait for her to cough before I do it."

Convinced that Trippi would come through in a pinch, the kitchen cabinet voted almost unanimously to go with the ads, though one adviser still insisted that Trippi's plan was the dumbest thing she had ever heard of.

The ads went on the air. Three weeks later, polls showed that 69 percent now believed that Slaughter "listened"— an increase of 20 points. "I had *never* seen movement like that," said Trippi. "It burst the polarized bubble. When we punched 60 percent and came close to 70 percent, it was done. It was three weeks out, and it was done."

Then Slaughter's opponent made a fateful move. She ran a spot saying that taxes were too high and the government was spending too much. Trippi seized on the ad and twisted it beyond recognition. He took the four-second sound bite "taxes are too high" from Davison's ad and repeated it three times in an ad that pointed out that Davison had voted to raise the sales tax in Monroe County, with the kicker, "She raises your taxes and tells you taxes are too high."

The ad was devastating. Davison hardly had a chance to introduce herself to Monroe County before she was attacked on the very issue on which she had hoped to attack Slaughter: taxes. By mid-October, Slaughter was polling 20 points ahead of Davison, and by the end of October, she was leading by 32 points. Davison's anti-abortion views and nonexistent record on women's issues kept her far from Slaughter's strong, 60 percent lead among women in the district. Just being a woman candidate was not enough to convince women in Rochester to vote for Davison. Slaughter had raised four times more money than Davison, and she had successfully neutralized the tax, jobs, and incumbent issue. Davison, who never got to touch a hair on Slaughter's head, was spared Joe Trippi's brass knuckles. "We never pulled the trigger on her," Trippi said afterward, with regret.

It's nice to see you! . . . Good to *see* ya! . . . Hello!" said Louise Slaughter, as she greeted the workers outside a large, low-slung factory. It was 3:00 P.M. on November 7, the hour when the morning shift trades with the evening shift. "Hi! How are you?" Louise said in her folksy Southern accent, extending her hand to the slightly quizzical automotive electrical-systems workers.

Wearing a bright-red overcoat and flanked by her placard-carrying daughter and husband, Slaughter looked homey and accessible. On this eve of election day, she preached to the converted—the Local 509 International Union of Electrical Workers, her core constituency. Slaughter's 97 percent pro-labor voting record, topped by her vote against NAFTA, made her one of Congress's staunchest union supporters. In return for her loyalty, Slaughter had become one of the top ten recipients of labor union campaign donations in the House of Representatives. Nearly $200,000 of the $700,000 Slaughter raised for her re-election came from labor unions.

Most of the workers walking in and out of the factory willingly shook Slaughter's hand, which was callused from a month of straight retail campaigning. Slaughter had spent October calling Bingo games for senior citizens, singing in inner-city churches, warming crowds at Democratic party rallies, and debating her opponents.

By four o'clock, the sun began to dip over the factory's roof. November days in Rochester are cold and short. "Appreciate your vote tomorrow," said Slaughter, while her staff thrust blue "Times are tough but we have Louise Slaughter on our side" pamphlets into unsuspecting hands. The fliers told of Louise's ability to "get it done" in Washington and bring jobs to Rochester: $6 million for a high-tech business incubator that would create 550 jobs a year, $4 million for a wave surge barrier on Lake Ontario that would allow development for Rochester's harbor, and a $50 million Defense Department contract for AT&T and Xerox that would bolster those local companies' payrolls. Using her clout in Congress to bring federal money and jobs to Rochester had been the mainstay of Slaughter's reelection campaign message.

As the crowd entering and exiting the plant thinned and the sunlight faded, Slaughter and her entourage reluctantly folded up shop. The last day of campaigning was over. There was nothing they could do but wait.

That night, Slaughter watched the returns at home with her family. The early reports were ominous. Exit polls showed that Democratic senators Harris Wofford of Pennsylvania and Jim Sasser of Tennessee would surely lose. The Senate would have a Republican majority. Slaughter had expected the Senate to lose its slim Democratic majority, but she still held out hope for House Democrats. At 8:45 P.M., CNN announced that four-term Democrat Jill Long had lost. Long's loss in her Republican-leaning Indiana district was considered a bellwether.

By 9:30, Slaughter couldn't believe what she was hearing. Big-name Democratic institutions were falling right and left. A seismic change in the congressional landscape had begun. Dan Rostenkowski, Congress's most stalwart, powerful Chicago pol, was a goner. Dan Glickman, the eighteen-year incumbent from Kansas City and chairman of the Select Intelligence Committee, had lost. Jack Brooks, the crusty, tough-guy chairman of the Judiciary Committee, looked like he was going down in Texas after forty-two years in the House. Neal Smith, the eighteen-termer from Iowa and one of the Cardinals—the chairman

of the Labor and HHS Appropriations Subcommittee—
had lost. Louise's closest friend among the freshmen
women, Leslie Byrne of Virginia, had gone, as had Marjorie Margolies-Mezvinsky.

At 10:50, Slaughter and her family climbed out of their
wood-paneled Ford Taurus station wagon and walked into
the eerily quiet lobby of a modern office building in downtown Rochester. They took the elevator to the "Top of the
Plaza" on the sixteenth floor, where the Monroe County
Democratic party was hosting its victory party. When the
elevator doors parted, the floodlights of five television
cameras blinded the Slaughters. Louise was the winner:
the 28th Congressional District had returned Louise
Slaughter to Congress with a solid 57 percent of the vote.
Renee Davison had picked up only 40 percent.

New York's Governor Mario Cuomo, meanwhile, had
lost to Republican George Pataki. Tom Foley, the Speaker
of the House, was down in polls against an unknown,
George Nethercutt. In a few hours, Foley would become
the first speaker to lose his reelection since 1862. But
somehow, in Rochester's Republican-leaning 28th Congressional District, Louise Slaughter had managed to win.
Voters in her district had split their tickets, voting for
Slaughter and Republican George Pataki. Slaughter
received twice as many votes in Monroe County as her
former boss, Mario Cuomo. Surviving the Democratic
carnage gave her a profound case of winner's guilt.

After celebrating her victory and basking in the limelight, Slaughter went back to her campaign headquarters
to find out if what she had been seeing on TV was really
true. She called her friends Jack Brooks, Leslie Byrne, Jolene Unsoeld, and Nita Lowey. Everyone but Lowey had
lost. Slaughter was in shock. She went to bed knowing that

the Democrats, for the first time in forty years, had lost their majority in the House of Representatives.

In the morning, the implications were hard to absorb. All told, Democrats had lost fifty-two seats in the House and seven in the Senate. With the Republicans in the majority, Slaughter knew that her entire congressional career would unravel. She would lose her seat on the Rules Committee. She would be stripped of the power she had worked so hard to gain over the past eight years. Ironically, Slaughter had won reelection partly *because* of her power as an insider in Congress. Now the historic Republican landslide would render her all but powerless.

When the dust settled, it became clear that Slaughter was one of the lucky ones. The Democratic women on the Hill had been held hostage to the fate of all Democrats across the country. Even though they had run well-financed campaigns, they had suffered serious setbacks. Six women in the celebrated class of '92 lost their reelections: Margolies-Mezvinsky (Pennsylvania), Leslie Byrne (Virginia), Lynn Schenk (California), Karen Shepherd (Utah), Karan English (Arizona), and Maria Cantwell (Washington State). Oldtimers Jill Long and Jolene Unsoeld had also lost. All but two of the eight women came from districts that were "marginally" Republican in 1992 but by 1994 had turned overwhelmingly Republican.

Eleven new women were also elected in 1994, the second-highest number in history. Six of the new congresswomen were Republicans. The number of women in the House had remained unchanged, at forty-eight, and the number of women in the Senate had increased by one. What *had* changed was the ratio of the congresswomen's party affiliation. In the 103rd, Democratic women outnumbered Republican women by thirty-six to twelve. In the 104th Congress, there would be thirty-one Democratic and seventeen Republican women.

If 1992 had been the Year of the Woman, 1994 would be dubbed the Year of the Angry Man. In 1992, both men and women went to the polls to vote for women candidates; women, it was believed, were in touch with the problems of average Americans. But in 1994, because of the prevailing anti-Clinton sentiment and the Democratic Congress's failure to reform itself, Democratic incumbents in general were perceived as being out of touch with average voters, and Democratic women were caught in the fray of partisan politics. "People paid a lot more attention to gender in '92 than they did in '94," said Democratic pollster Geoff Garin. Although women candidates still did well with woman voters, especially college-educated, working women, "electing women was less of a priority in '94," according to Garin, who worked on Dianne Feinstein's hard-fought reelection campaign.

In 1992, electing women had taken on a life of its own. "Women self-consciously said, 'We'd be better off if we elected women to office,' " said Garin. "True to form, after '92 was over, voters said, 'We've done that; let's go on to the next thing.' " In fact, fewer women voted in 1994 than in 1992—the percentage of voters who were women dropped from 54 to 51 percent. Voter turnout was low. Only 38 percent of all eligible voters went to the polls in 1994.

Voters are always more likely to go to the polls to vote out of a sense of anger than out of satisfaction. The gains made by women in the 103rd Congress did not drive voters to the polls to vote for more women in 1994. "All of the triumphs that women made in the 103rd Congress—

FACE, the Violence Against Women Act, Family Leave, increasing Head Start funding—all those things weren't players. They were nonentities," complained Eleanor Smeal, president of the Feminist Majority Foundation. If anything, the women's gains drove conservatives to the polls in the form of a backlash.

In 1994, Democrats alienated male voters more than female voters. The women voters who made up the core of the Democratic party constituency—working, college-educated young women—were happier with Clinton's domestic agenda than male voters were. According to Democratic pollster Celinda Lake, men as a whole vote more often for Republicans, showing a stronger affinity for smaller government, less spending on social programs, and a bias against taxation. As a result, the 11-point gender gap in 1994 between men and women voters was the largest ever recorded. White men, angry with Bill Clinton, constituted the bulk of the Republican Revolution in 1994. Fifty-three percent of men voted for the GOP, while only 42 percent of women did. The gender gap confirmed a trend that had begun in the early 1980s: "Men have become more conservative and more Republican, and women have stayed as tied to the Democratic party as they were going into the eighties," said Susan Carroll, a senior research associate at the Rutgers University Center for the American Woman and Politics.

The victors of the 1994 Republican Revolution were seventy-three House freshmen—most of them conservative white men from the South, West, and Midwest. In the Senate, for the first time in history, all eleven freshmen were Republicans, and all but one, Olympia Snowe, were pro-life men.

The conservative male freshmen were joined by an entirely new breed of congresswomen: archconservative, pro-life Republicans. The new crop of six right-wing Republican women—Helen Chenoweth (Idaho), Barbara Cubin (Wyoming), Andrea Seastrand (California), Sue Myrick (North Carolina), Linda Smith (Washington State), and Enid Greene Waldholtz (Utah)—would denounce feminism and the women's-caucus agenda that prevailed in the 103rd Congress. Gloating over its gains, the National Right to Life Committee called 1992 the "Year of the Pro-Abortion Woman" and 1994 the "Year of the Pro-Life Woman."

Pat Schroeder and Cynthia McKinney both won their reelection races, but with narrower margins than in 1992. Schroeder beat Republican William Eggert with 60 percent of the vote, a significant drop from her 69 percent win in 1992. McKinney beat the same Republican opponent she ran against in '92, retired former Woodrow Lovett. McKinney's campaign goal had been to gain up to 75 percent in '94, but unable to attract white voters, she came away with 65 percent, 8 points below her '92 victory.

The 1994 Republican sweep showed itself most dramatically in the South, where Democrats lost nineteen seats. Conservative Southerners objected to President Clinton's liberal social policies, especially on gun control. In Georgia, Republicans won seven out of eleven House seats. Only one white Democrat, Nathan Deal, survived the unprecedented slaughter, and Deal would switch over to the Republican party early in the 104th Congress. Before the 1992 election, nine of Georgia's ten congressional seats had been occupied by Democrats. The Democrats' losses in Georgia were partly attributed to the "bleaching" of their districts caused by concentrating black voters into McKinney's 11th District.

The vote in McKinney's district split very closely along racial lines. Her attempts to reach out to her rural white constituents had been repeatedly rejected. Racial suspicions escalated into open hostility in Wilkinson County, where a band of hostile locals drove by the house of a McKinney campaign volunteer one night, stuffed his mailbox with stolen McKinney signs, and fired gunshots over his roof. When 1,500 farmers in the district received invitations from McKinney to talk with Congressman Charlie Rose, a white agriculture expert from North Carolina, about the 1995 Farm Bill, only eighteen farmers came to the meeting. McKinney lost to Lovett in every rural, white-majority county in her district.

Shocked by the election results, McKinney fell ill. The next day she was in bed with a high fever. "I was hurt for my own race, I was hurt for all of my friends, I was hurt for what I thought was going to happen. If I thought it was ugly last year, it's really going to be ugly next year," she said.

Before the election, McKinney had planned to travel to Africa with the Foreign Affairs Committee from November 11 to 22. Now, deflated by election results, she wondered about her priorities. Maybe, for a change, Cynthia should let the world solve its own problems while she stayed home. She asked her son Coy if he wanted her to go to Africa "to try to help the people there" or if he wanted her at home. Coy voted to have his mother at home. McKinney canceled the committee trip. "I was a mommy. I packed his lunch every day. It was very healthy."

In late November, *Time* magazine included McKinney in a roster of the nation's most promising leaders age forty and under. Twenty years earlier, Pat Schroeder and Bill Clinton had been featured on *Time's* 1974 list. This year the newsweekly picked fifty leaders with the "vision and community spirit to help guide us in the new millennium." McKinney, the only Democratic member of Congress on the list, received recognition for battling to improve the lives of the poor, fighting for a tax cut for working families, and an EPA investigation into an impoverished Georgia community. "Whenever you see a good fight, get in it," she told *Time*.

When McKinney returned to Washington on November 30 to vote in a lame-duck session on the General Agreement on Tariffs and Trade, the luster of the *Time* article had faded. The white marble halls of the House office buildings were quiet, the mood dark and low—as if there had been a death in the family. Two years earlier, McKinney had come to Washington as the embodiment of the new change in Congress. She had been on top of the world. Now, uncharacteristically dour, reserved, she returned to an office where the phones had fallen silent.

In the corridors on the Hill, large orange trash Dumpsters stood outside the office doors of members who had lost. In Longworth, on the fifth floor, Jill Long and Marjorie Margolies-Mezvinsky's offices were both marked by the ominous orange Dumpsters. Inside Margolies-Mezvinsky's office, the walls stood bare. The photographs of Margolies-Mezvinsky with the Clintons and with the other women on the Hill had been taken down. Piles of flat cardboard boxes crowded the foyer. In Cannon, Lynn Schenk's Dumpster was so full of papers that it looked as if every filing cabinet in her office had been emptied. A five-high pile of brown file boxes marked "Thomas S. Foley" sat on dollies in the basement, waiting for a library that would accept them.

On the fourth floor of the Rayburn Building, the windowless office of the women's caucus would, within weeks, be full of boxes to be sent to the National Archives. They were stacked four high and three deep, sandbagging the front of the receptionist's desk. The caucus had once employed a former welfare mother to take calls; there was no receptionist now. The funding mechanism for the women's caucus, and all the other caucuses on the Hill, was about to be obliterated by the new Republican leadership in a sham budget-cutting maneuver designed to quiet voices of opposition. No staff could be hired, no office space would be provided. Nita Lowey and Connie Morella would be left to pick up the pieces.

Meanwhile, Lesley Primmer, the executive director of the caucus, was debating how long the caucus files should be sealed before the public could have access to them. She worried that a right-wing journalist or right-wing interest group might lay hands on the papers and use them against the women on the Hill. The files would reveal, for example, the details of their internal squabble over the Freedom of Choice Act, as well as their strategy for luring reluctant Democrats into including abortion in health care reform legislation. The files would show that when the caucus women needed to meet with President Clinton to discuss abortion in the health care bill, in January 1994, the White House, reluctant to discuss the unpopular issue, had failed repeatedly to return telephone calls. Frustrated, a caucus staffer had finally asked Pat Schroeder to lobby the White House herself. Below the memo, in thick black felt pen, Schroeder answered, "I called. Hopefully, it's taken care of." The note was signed with a large letter "P" illustrated with a smiley face. In ten or twenty years someone might also find that when called upon to campaign in Maine against Olympia Snowe, Schroeder had refused out of a sense of sisterhood.

Here were the memos, the minutes of meetings, the offers and refusals, all the successes and failures of the women on the Hill. They demonstrated how far and fast women had come in the 103rd Congress. Even two years earlier, the presence of women and women's issues had seemed infinitesimal, a minor fact of legislative life. Now, as the caucus passed into history, its influence on the larger institution would be revealed. For as the world would see when the Republicans took over in January, the Congress they had been elected to control was no longer the same place it had been just two years earlier. Anita Hill's class of congresswomen and senators had made their mark on the institution. In the words of Tennessee's outgoing senator, Democrat Jim Sasser, "the women have changed the culture of the congress."

Afterword

After three years of trying to do it all, Patty Murray recognized her efforts hadn't been entirely successful. She could not fulfill her promise as a United States senator and at the same time keep her family happy in Washington, D.C. The Murrays had never felt at home in their new surroundings. Sara and Randy, students at the public high school in Arlington, remained homesick for Seattle. For Rob, a specialist in the computer systems that run industrial ports, the landlocked nation's capital failed to provide job opportunities. Rob had worked for the Department of Transportation, and as a part-time consultant for a private firm, but he never found permanent employment.

In December 1995, after three years of enduring his family's relocation and supporting his wife's career, Rob Murray returned home to the security of his old job. Randy Murray had graduated from high school that June, and joined his father in Seattle. Six months later, Sara Murray also moved home, leaving Patty in D.C., alone and with a long weekend commute.

By 1996, practically everyone who had worked with Murray since she first arrived on the Hill agreed that she had changed. No one knew why. One staffer thought that it was because of the hormonal changes she suffered after she had a hysterectomy. Another supposed that she had come under the spell of a controlling new chief of staff. Perhaps it was the pain of seeing her family return home without her. One episode seemed to sum up the change.

In June 1995, a week before Pam Norick, Murray's national security adviser, gave birth to her second child, Patricia Akiyama, the new chief of staff in Murray's office, presented Norick with a fait accompli: Within four months of returning from maternity leave, Norick would have to work five days a week in the office or find a new job. This was a big change. When Murray hired Norick in 1993, she was Murray's model for a family-friendly work schedule.

Despite the fact that Pam Norick was a Seattle native, she just didn't fit in with the new regime in Murray's office—a "new management team" with closer political connections to Washington State than to Capitol Hill. In one year, Murray's office had seen a turnover of some twenty staffers. Norick would have to go. But instead of coming clean with Norick, Murray now maintained that Norick's four-day work week wasn't fair to the other employees. She claimed that she had always intended it to be a temporary arrangement. According to Murray, Norick had pushed her luck by having children only two years apart. No other senator, Murray insisted, would give an employee two maternity leaves in under three years. Sounding very much like the boss who had fired her when she became pregnant with Randy eighteen years earlier, Murray told Norick, "You have to choose."

In December 1995, Pam Norick left the Murray staff.

On June 29, 1995, the Supreme Court dealt Cynthia McKinney's congressional career a stunning blow. In *Miller v. Johnson,* the court held that Georgia's 11th Congressional District—Cynthia's district—was unconstitutional because its lines had been drawn primarily for racial reasons. By a vote of five to four, the Supreme Court accepted the 1994 Georgia federal court's finding that McKinney's district violated the equal protection rights of its white constituents. The Supreme Court's decision crippled the Voting Rights Act and weakened the Justice Department's role in ensuring districts that maximize black and minority representation.

A new map of Georgia's congressional districts was drawn by a three-judge panel in Georgia, and only one out of three black-majority districts survived—John Lewis's 5th District in Atlanta. Cynthia found herself back at square one. After learning how to be an inside player in Congress, she would have to reverse direction and take to the barricades. On the House floor, she proudly compared herself to Billy McKinney, calling herself a civil rights warrior, and reminding her colleagues, "I am really just a chip off the old block." Cynthia would continue to challenge what she called her "oppressors," the powerful interests in Georgia who she believed had worked to undermine her district—the state Democratic party and the kaolin industry.

In 1996, Cynthia ran for reelection in Georgia's newly drawn 4th Congressional District, a small bundle of suburban counties surrounding Atlanta. Only 32.8 percent of the voting-age population was black, or, in other words, likely to vote for McKinney. Political experts in Georgia predicted that McKinney would lose in the primary, but in a racially charged campaign, she defeated two prominent white male Democrats with 67 percent of the vote. Then McKinney faced off against moderate Republican lawyer John Mitnick, who tried to turn white voters against her by accusing McKinney of supporting Louis Farrakhan's views because she had refused to vote against a 1994 House resolution condemning an anti-Semitic speech made by one of Farrakhan's top aides. Once again, Billy McKinney could not control himself. Defending Cynthia, who had cast her vote on first amendment grounds, Billy took the campaign further into the gutter, calling Mitnick a "racist Jew."

The incident became national news. With the final weeks of the campaign underway, McKinney looked doomed. *Roll Call* placed her on its 25 Most Vulnerable list. Mitnick demanded an apology. Cynthia denounced her father's statement (a week after it was made) and fired him from her campaign. But Billy's defense of his daughter would ultimately motivate black voters to sympathize with Cynthia and turn out for her in record numbers. She won with a resounding 58 percent. McKinney's strategy of targeting white women voters also helped her transcend racial lines and reach a comfortable majority. Ironically, after five years of fighting for majority black districts in Georgia, McKinney made history by becoming the first African American woman ever to win a seat in Congress from a mostly white district in the South.

Louise Slaughter turned sixty-seven at the close of the 104th Congress. To an old hand like Slaughter, the 104th and its backlash against women's issues was a nightmare come true. "I feel demeaned and angry," Slaughter said. "I want to run up and down the street and shout, '*Wake up!'* "Slaughter worked closely with the Democratic leadership and became an effective voice of protest. No longer in a position to pass bills, she blocked the opposition's bills from passing. She concentrated on retaining funding for women's health research, and for the most part, she succeeded.

By November 1996, Gingrich's popularity had plummeted, his revolution rejected by an electorate uncomfortable with radical change. Slaughter took advantage of this sea change by tying her Republican opponent, millionaire businessman Geoffrey Rosenberger, to Gingrich and "extremists in Congress" who had gone too far in trying to cut funding for education and Medicare. The strategy worked for both Slaughter (who gained 57 percent of the vote) and President Clinton, who easily won a second term.

One morning in the fall of 1995, Pat Schroeder walked into her office on the Hill, looked around, and realized that her life was going by. She had toilet-trained her children in this job. She had gone through menopause here. She had never planned on being a congressional "lifer." She hadn't even thought she would get elected the first time she ran. But here she still was, at fifty-five, with twenty-four years of service in twelve congresses, and time was running out. "If I'm going to do anything else with my life," she told herself, "I'd better get on with it."

On November 29, 1995, to the shock of everyone on Capitol Hill, and to the dismay of the women's movement, Schroeder announced that the 104th Congress would be her last. Tributes and testimonials to "America's Congresswoman" immediately followed on evening news programs. Rumors circulated in Washington that Schroeder had quit because she had cancer. But as far as Schroeder knew, she was in perfect health. "Everyone wants me to be sick," she said. "I'm sick of *the place.*" The partisan rancor and antigovernment fervor that characterized the 1994 class of freshmen was largely responsible for pushing Schroeder into the private sector. "They think you should be road kill," Schroeder said about her new Republican colleagues.

One afternoon during her last spring on the Hill, Schroeder found herself saying something she had said many times before: "I can't get into the meetings where the decisions are made." Being in the minority for the first time in her congressional career had placed Schroeder farther outside the power structure than she had ever been, and she began to feel more helpless than rebellious. "My being here is like parsley on a potato. I can be a voice, but it's a voice in the wilderness."

It was the wilderness of 1972 all over again, only worse. Being snubbed by the likes of Edward Hebert, former chairman of the House Armed Services Committee, had been less demeaning, because expectations in the early 1970s had been so low. By 1996, Schroeder had hoped for more. "It's twenty times more painful to watch everything you've built come under attack and watch sexist attitudes loom," she said. "It's a lot more painful because I thought we had moved beyond that, and in fact you only realize how far we still have to go."

On women's issues, the 104th Congress had been a throwback. The women's caucus, shunned by nearly every Republican congresswoman, its meetings underattended by Democrats, stripped of its staff, no longer functioned as a bipartisan legislative service organization. Republican women were well represented in the party's leadership, "but they're not leading for women," Schroeder noted. Even pro-choice Republican women like Susan Molinari and Deborah Pryce, under pressure from Newt Gingrich, often voted with the Republican leadership on some abortion issues. Eleven anti-abortion bills were passed in the House, rolling back virtually every abortion-rights gain Schroeder and the bipartisan women's caucus had made in the 103rd Congress. The House cut funding for Medicaid, Medicare, welfare, child-nutrition programs, education, the Violence Against Women Act, and the Earned-Income Tax Credit, all of which would disproportionately hurt women.

In the end, Schroeder realized she would feel freer to speak her mind and defend her causes outside Congress. Within a year, Schroeder would be teaching at Princeton University's Woodrow Wilson School of Government, although she was not yet sure how she was going to tell a roomful of graduate students what raw power really meant. For the moment, as she reflected on the gains and losses of twenty-four years on the Hill, Schroeder consoled herself with a parting thought: "As a historian, I know that women's advances are always followed by a retreat." Schroeder also knew that it would not be long before the pendulum would swing back. In 1996, after all, 236 women were running for Congress, and Shroeder herself hadn't shut the door on her political future. Schroeder also knew that it would not be long before the pendulum would swing back. In 1996, after all, twelve new women were elected to Congress, the Republican majority was reduced in the House, and President Clinton, who made women's issues a top campaign priority, was reelected with the widest (10-point) gender gap in presidential history.

NOTES ON SOURCES

The principal research for *Women on the Hill* consisted of some 300 confidential and on-the-record interviews I conducted between December 1992 and May 1996. At the conclusion of the 103rd Congress, I was granted access to archival material, including internal memoranda and records of meetings, from the Congressional Caucus on Women's Issues. I also drew on coverage of the 103rd Congress from *Congressional Quarterly, Roll Call,* C-Span, the *Washington Post,* and the *New York Times.*

INTRODUCTION

For the history of women in Congress, I relied primarily on two books: *Running as a Woman: Gender and Power in American Politics,* by Linda Witt, Karen M. Paget, and Glenna Matthews (Free Press, 1994); and *Congressional Women: Their Recruitment, Treatment, and Behavior,* by Irwin N. Gertzog (Praeger, 1984), which chronicles the history of the women's caucus.

I also referred to Glenna Matthews, *The Rise of Public Woman: Women's Power and Women's Place in the United States 1630–1970* (Oxford University Press, 1992); J. McIver Weatherford, *Tribes on the Hill: An Investigation into the Rituals and Realities of an En-*

dangered American Tribe—The Congress of the United States (Rawson, Wade, 1981); William Chafe, The Paradox of Change: American Women in the 20th Century (Oxford University Press, 1991); Hannah Josephson's biography, Jeannette Rankin, First Lady in Congress (Bobbs-Merrill, 1974); Kevin S. Giles, Flight of the Dove: The Story of Jeannette Rankin (Touchstone, 1980); Remarks by Joan Hoff-Wilson, Executive Secretary of the Organization of American Historians, presented at the Dedication of the Statue of Jeannette Rankin, United States Government Printing Office, 1987; Senator John F. Kennedy's article, "Three Women of Courage," McCall's, January 1958; coverage of Jeannette Rankin in the New York Times, April 6, 1917; David Brinkley, Washington Goes to War (Alfred A. Knopf, 1988); Wilfrid Sheed, Clare Boothe Luce (Dutton, 1982); Women in Congress, 1917–1990, by the Office of the Historian, U.S. House of Representatives (U.S. Government Printing Office, 1991); Frank Graham, Jr., Margaret Chase Smith, Woman of Courage (John Day, 1964); Newsweek, June 12, 1950, p. 24; Emily George, Martha W. Griffiths (University Press of America, 1982); Ethel Klein, Gender Politics (Harvard University Press, 1984); Betty Friedan, The Feminine Mystique (W. W. Norton & Company, 1963); Ruth Mandel, Running as a Woman (Ticknor & Fields, 1981); Don Reigle with Trevor Armbrister, O Congress (Doubleday, 1972); Shirley Chisholm, Unbought and Unbossed (Houghton Mifflin, 1970); Shirley Chisholm in McCall's, "A Visiting Feminine Eye," August 1970; Bella Abzug, Bella! (Saturday Review Press, 1972); Pat Schroeder, Champion of the Great American Family (Random House, 1989); Janann Sherman, "Margaret Chase Smith and the Impact of Gender Affinity," published in Gender and Policymaking: Studies of Women in Office, (Center for the American Woman and Politics at Rutgers, 1991).

CHAPTER 1

Peter Hereford, Brock Adams' spokesman, was quoted by Jim Simonin in a Seattle Times story, December 5, 1991; "I'm real" declaration was found in Mindy Cameron's December 29, 1991, *Seattle Times* story. The April Times-Mirror Center poll results were found in a *Time* May 4, 1992, cover story, "Politics: The Feminist Machine," by Jill Smolowe. Murray's "all the men in dark suits" quote was in the *Seattle Times*, September 4, 1992; Murray's "I might not fit the standard" statement was quoted in Witt, Paget, and Matthews, *Running as a Woman*, p. 235; Coverage of the Bonker-Murray debate and the Murray-Chandler debate was provided by Mark Matassa in the *Seattle Times*, on June 19, 1992, and October 15, 1992. The telephone poll conducted the weekend before the primary was published in the *Seattle Times*, the story written by Susan Gilmore, September 16, 1992. Murray's "I've watched women come into politics" quote was in a *New York Times* story by Timothy Egan, September 17, 1992. Voter Research & Surveys provided the exit polls for the Washington Senate race in 1992. Murray's victory speech was quoted by Guy Gugliotta in the *Washington Post*, November 4, 1992. Anita Hill's phone call to Murray was chronicled in the *Seattle Times* by Mark Matassa, November 5, 1992.

CHAPTER 2

Billy McKinney's statements after Cynthia's state assembly election victory were found in a *South Fulton Extra* story by Bernadette Burden, December 29, 1988; Cynthia's "We're friends" was in *Jet* magazine, March 12, 1990, p. 26; "I have a different constituency" was quoted by Rhonda Cook in the *Atlanta Journal Constitution*, April 23, 1991. On the history of voting rights in the South, I am indebted to *Quiet Revolution in the South: The Impact of the Voting Rights Act 1965–1990*, Chandler Davidson and Bernard Grofman, editors—chapter three, by Laughlin McDonald, Michael Binford, and Ken Johnson, is specifically about Georgia. Columnist Frederick Benjamin called McKinney "a good ol' boy's worst nightmare," in the *Atlanta Focus*, November 20, 1991; Cynthia McKinney's "It's good ol' boy politics as usual" was in a story by Rhonda Cook in the *Atlanta Journal Constitution*,

August 10, 1991. Billy McKinney's "Can you believe we won" statement was quoted by Steve Harvey in the *Atlanta Journal Constitution*, August 13, 1992. Another Steve Harvey story in the *Constitution* on October 11, 1992, called Cynthia McKinney the "darling of the party establishment."

CHAPTER 3

The total number of women running for office in 1990 and 1992 was tabulated by the Center for the American Woman and Politics (CAWP), National Information Bank on Women in Public Office, Eagleton Institute of Politics, Rutgers, and issued in the center's August 10, 1994, fact sheet. The amount of money raised by women's political action committees was published in CAWP's "News and Notes," Winter 1993, in a paper entitled "Women's PACs Dramatically Increase Their Support in 1992: An Overview," by Lucy Baruch and Katheryne McCormick. On the women's vote in 1992, see Witt, Paget, and Matthews, *Running as a Woman*, p. 154.

Information on Pat Schroeder's background can be found in her own *Champion of the Great American Family*, as well as in "The Prime of Pat Schroeder," by Susan Ferraro, *The New York Times Magazine*, July 1, 1990; "Congresswoman Pat Schroeder: The Woman Who Has a Bear by the Tail," by Judith Viorst, *Redbook*, November 1973. Schroeder's "After I was elected I realized . . ." quote was in "Congresswoman Pat Schroeder," by Ilene Barth, *Ms.*, June 1976; "They don't care if anyone does it," was quoted by Danielle Herbuin, "Women Still Outside 'Boy's Club' Congress," in *States News Service*, July 1, 1991; Ronald D. Elving's book on the family-leave bill, *Conflict and Compromise: How Congress Makes the Law* (Simon & Schuster, 1995), tells the story of Schroeder's vote against the plant-closing amendment in 1985, pp. 50–52.

The *Washington Post* story on the women's caucus's first meeting with Hillary Rodham Clinton was written by Lloyd Grove, and published on February 24, 1993. Leonor Sullivan's view of the differences between male and female was quoted by Margaret Scherf in an Associated Press story, published in the *Washington Post,* November 18, 1971. The clash between Sullivan and Abzug is detailed in Gertzog's *Congressional Women,* pp. 164–66.

Jane Danowitz, executive director of the Women's Campaign Fund, described Louise Slaughter as a "combination of Southern charm and backroom politics" in a *Washington Post Sunday Magazine* story by David Finkel, "Women on the Verge of a Power Breakthrough," May 10, 1992.

CHAPTER 4

For the history of blacks in Congress, I referred to *Black Americans in Congress, 1870–1980,* by Bruce A. Ragsdale and Joel D. Treese, Office of the Historian, U.S. House of Representatives (U.S. Government Printing Office, 1990), and William Clay's *Just Permanent Interests: Black Americans in Congress 1870–1991* (Amistad Press, 1992). Maureen Dowd's description of Cynthia McKinney was published on March 5, 1993, in the *New York Times;* Clara Germani wrote the March 8, 1993, profile of McKinney in the *Christian Science Monitor.*

CHAPTER 5

Sources on the history of the family- and medical-leave bill included literature provided by the Women's Legal Defense Fund, articles in *Congressional Quarterly,* Heidi I. Hartman and Roberta M. Spalter-Roth's "Family and Medical Leave: Who Pays for the Lack of It?" (The Women's Research and Education Institute, 1989), and Ronald Elving's *Conflict and Compromise.*

Murray's "I wasn't elected to be a senator" was reported by Marla Williams in the *Seattle Times,* special report, July/August 1993. Pat Schroeder's "Even if you have to vote no" quote was in Ronald Elving's *Conflict and Compromise.*

CHAPTER 6

The description of the Hyde Amendment floor fight as a high school dance and Carrie Meek's "Just let me at him" come from

Marjorie Margolies-Mezvinsky with Barbara Feinman, *A Woman's Place: The Freshmen Women Who Changed the Face of Congress* (Crown, 1994). Henry Hyde's "It is intimidating" statement was quoted by the *Washington Post*'s Kevin Merida, July 1, 1993; Merida also provides some of the quotes for the women's post-mortem press conference in the *Washington Post,* July 2, 1993; Lynn Schenk's "I was shocked to learn" comment was quoted by Richard E. Cohen in the *National Journal,* July 31, 1993; Adam Clymer's *New York Times* story of July 3, 1993, said the congresswomen looked "naive, unprepared and inept."

CHAPTER 7

Carol Moseley-Braun told Jacob Weisberg that FOCA was an "unacceptable compromise" in an interview for the *Los Angeles Times,* October 31, 1993; Lynn Schenk's "I am at an age" remark about jogging with Clinton was published in the *New York Times* on June 26, 1993.

CHAPTER 8

Murray's "Until Anita Hill's allegations" was in Timothy Egan's *New York Times* story, November 23, 1992; Colleen Gardner's revelation "He did not want me to have any definite responsibility" was quoted by John M. Crewdson in the *New York Times,* June 11, 1976; the Elizabeth Ray–Colleen Gardner saga and Pat Schroeder's attempt to rectify it is chronicled by Myra McPherson in the *Washington Post,* August 1, 1976; the present-day *Washington Post* survey on female Hill aides was published on February 21, 1993, in a story by Richard Moran. John Lancaster and Eric Schmitt's coverage of the Tailhook scandal for the *Washington Post* and *New York Times* was particularly helpful to me, as was Jean Zimmerman's book, *Tailspin: Women at War in the Wake of Tailhook* (Doubleday, 1995).

CHAPTER 9

Leon Panetta told the *Washington Post Sunday Magazine*'s David Finkel, "It's important to have people like Louise on the committee," October 10, 1992. The history of women's-health research at the NIH is outlined in an article written by Pat Schroeder and Olympia Snowe entitled "The Politics of Women's Health," published in *The American Woman, 1994–95: Where We Stand*, edited by Cynthia Costello and Anne J. Stone for the Women's Research and Education Institute, 1994. *Congressional Quarterly Almanac*, 1993, carried the "the men are afraid to vote against money for breast cancer" quote from health care lobbyist Stacy Beckhardt, of the American Society of Clinical Oncology. Michael Kinsley's TRB "From Washington" column, "Screen Test," in the April 11, 1994 *New Republic*, makes the point that annual mammograms for women in their forties would cost $2.7 billion a year. The Associated Press's coverage of the May 12, 1995, Education and Labor Subcommittee meeting's abortion vote provided a helpful record.

CHAPTER 10

Statistics on abortion-related violence were found in the *Washington Post*, in a story by Laurie Goodstein and Pierre Thomas published on January 17, 1995. The breakdown of Republican votes by gender on the Freedom of Access to Clinic Entrances Act (FACE) was provided by *Voices, Views, Votes: The Impact of Women in the 103rd Congress*, by Dodson, Carroll, Mandel, Kleeman, Schreiber, and Liebowitz, Center for the American Woman and Politics, Eaglton Institute of Politics, Rutgers, 1995. The breakdown of votes by gender on the assault-weapons ban was provided by Lesley Primmer, executive director of the Congressional Caucus for Women's Issues. Catherine S. Manegold wrote the August 25, 1994, *New York Times* story "Quiet Winners in House Fight on Crime: Women." Slurs and insults aimed at Pat Schroeder, Karan English, and Elizabeth Furse were published in *Newsweek*'s "The Year of the Smear," by Eleanor Clift, July 11, 1994. The mid-October poll showing Louise Slaughter 20 points ahead of Davison was published in the Rochester *Democrat and Chronicle* on November 1, 1994, in a story by Blair Clafin. Common Cause, in December 1993, reported that Slaughter received $712,447 from labor unions between 1983 and 1993.

ACKNOWLEDGMENTS

In the summer of 1992, while covering the presidential campaign for *Newsweek,* I received a letter from Times Books associate editor Ken Gellman. Would I be interested, he asked, in writing a book about women in Congress? I jumped at the chance. Here was an opportunity to write about people who had always fascinated me: women in politics. I am grateful to Ken for the idea.

My first challenge when I started work, in January 1993, was to find congresswomen who would cooperate with me. Several turned me down. To Cynthia McKinney, Louise Slaughter, Patty Murray, and Pat Schroeder, I owe an enormous debt of gratitude for granting me what amounted to dozens of hours of interviews during the two years of the 103rd Congress. I am also indebted to their press secretaries: Susie Rodriguez, Kelly Sullivan, Patricia Akyama, and Andrea Camp, all of whom kept me in close touch with events in their offices, helped arrange interviews, and provided crucial support for my project. I also want to thank Gary Cox and Tom Bantle in McKinney's and Slaughter's offices for guiding me through their bosses' political and legislative lives.

Lesley Primmer and Susan Wood, the senior staff at the now defunct Congressional Caucus for Women's Issues, spent hours explaining the intricacies of women's issues legislation to me. I am grateful to them both. Their expert knowledge and dedication to women's causes were invaluable to the research of this book.

Many of my most helpful sources on the Hill were staffers who did not want their names made known. To all of them, my thanks for their time, trust, and guidance.

In my first months on the Hill, I counted on a handful of friends to show me around and introduce me to people I needed to know. James Pratt and Lawrence O'Donnell were wise and generous guides on whom I depended frequently. Missi Tessier, Michael Meehan, Virginia Moseley, Thomas Nides, Andrew Plepler, Richard Jerome, Jean Christensen, and Smith Bagley opened many doors. I also want to single out Cary McCall, Tandy Levine, Jennifer Maguire, and my *Newsweek* colleagues George Hackett and Mark Miller for their constant encouragement of my work on this project.

I am grateful to Melissa Hardin for scouring the Library of Congress with enthusiasm and creativity. The manuscript benefited greatly from Laura Leedy Gansler's sharp and critical eye, and I owe her a debt of gratitude. Many thanks also to Michael Michaelis, who was an indispensable computer consultant.

My father, Worth Bingham, covered the Hill as a reporter in the early 1960s; my mother, Joan Bingham, and my brother, Rob, helped me realize that I wanted to carry on in my father's line of work. My grandmother Mary Bingham died before I could show her this book; her passion for politics and love of the English language are on every page.

The esteemed Esther Newberg, herself a former woman on the Hill, protected and promoted this project from the start. I could not have been blessed with a wiser agent.

From the moment I met Steve Wasserman of Times Books, I knew I could rely on him. With patience and great skill, he brought new life to *Women on the Hill.* I will always be thankful to him for believing in this project. Beth Thomas of Times Books ably saw the work through numerous drafts. I am grateful to the staff at Times Books, to Toni Rachiele, my copy editor, and especially to Steve and Beth for their hard work and support.

Three weeks before the manuscript's final deadline, I gave birth to my son Jamie. His arrival, two weeks early, was a joyous surprise that has made life forever worth living. Finally, I want to thank my husband, David Michaelis, for his love, generosity, and most of all, his talent as a writer and editor. David read every draft and tirelessly guided me through to better efforts. This book is largely the result of a team effort that I am honored to have been a part of.

Washington, D.C.
July 14, 1996

INDEX

abortion, 5, 7, 166; and class of
'92, 73, 132–33; and Clinton
administration, 88, 125–26,
133; and court decisions
about, 88, 133; and Democratic party, 221–22; and elections of 1994, 233, 236, 240,
246, 247; executive orders
about, 125–26; and FACE,
225–26, 233, 245–46; and
health care, 209, 210, 217,
218–19, 220–22, 224, 250–51;
men's role in fight about, 132,
137, 138; and "Mexico City"
policy, 126; and parental notification, 89–90, 146; as parliamentary issue, 126–32, 140–41;
press conferences about, 221,
140–42; and pro-choice factions, 133, 144, 146–47; and
pro-choice task force, 126–27,
129, 133, 142; and race, 125,
128, 134, 135, 138, 143, 146;
and rape and incest, 128, 140;

and Republican party, 4, 88,
109, 138, 139–40, 258; and
Women's Caucus, 82, 87–93,
217, 250–51. *See also* Freedom
of Choice Act; Hyde Amendment; *Roe v. Wade; specific person*

Abzug, Bella, 23–24, 25, 75,
83–84
Adams, Brock, 35–36, 37
Agriculture Committee (U.S.
House), 21–22, 102
Akiyama, Patricia, 198, 253
Alvare, Helen, 221
American Civil Liberties Union
(ACLU), 58
Appropriations Committee (U.S.
House), 101, 104, 130, 131
Appropriations Committee (U.S.
Senate), 26, 173, 216
Armed Services Committee (U.S.
House), 24–26, 193–94
Armed Services Committee (U.S.
Senate), 190, 191, 200

Armey, Richard "Dick," 218–19, 220
Aspin, Les, 188
assault-weapons ban, 227, 228, 229, 230, 234
AuCoin, Les, 89, 132, 133
Augusta, Georgia: toxic waste dump in, 153–54, 159, 160

Biden, Joseph, 176, 229
Bishop, Sanford, 151, 152
blacks, 95–97, 137, 155–58. *See also* race; *specific person*
Boggs, Lindy, 23, 87–88; room named after, 120, 193, 233
Bond, Julian, 55
Bonker, Don, 39, 41–42
Boxer, Barbara, 117, 181–82, 210, 229; and Kelso case, 195, 198; and Packwood case, 4, 176, 179; and VAWA, 92, 94
Brady bill, 227, 234
breast cancer research, 82, 93, 204–5, 207, 208, 212–13, 233
Brooks, Jack, 242, 243
Bryan, Richard, 176, 177
Budget Committee (U.S. House), 203–4
Budget-Reconciliation Act, 153, 158
Bush (George) administration, 81, 88, 108, 109, 110, 111, 123, 207
Byrd, Robert, 173, 190
Byrne, Leslie, 72, 80, 118, 243, 244

Camp, Andrea, 92, 93, 194, 195, 217
campaign financing, 69–70, 233. *See also specific candidate*
Campaign for Women's Health, 213

Campbell, Ben Nighthorse, 227
Caraway, Hattie, 12
Carroll, Susan, 246
Caucus on Women's Issues: and abortion issue, 87–93, 126–27, 129, 133, 142, 145–46, 210, 211, 217, 250–51; children's task force of, 147; and class of '92, 71–74; and Elders' nomination, 147–48; and elections of 1994, 247; and FOCA, 88–93, 145–46, 250; formation of, 83, 84; and health care, 206, 209, 210, 211, 213, 217, 219, 250–51; and Hyde Amendment, 126–27, 129, 133, 142; impact of, 232–33; leadership of, 79–81, 233; pro-choice task force of, 90–93, 126–27, 129, 133, 142, 145–46; and race issues, 81, 137; records of, 250–51; and Republican party, 81–82, 250–51. *See also specific person*
Celler, Emmanual, 18, 20–21
Chafe, William, 8–9
Chandler, Rod, 42, 43–46
Chapman, Mario, 159
Charnley, Don, 215, 216
Cheney, Richard "Dick," 194, 236
Chisholm, Shirley, 7–8, 21–22, 23
civil rights, 5, 15, 49, 96, 100, 229
Civil Rights Act (1964), 17–19, 20, 26
class of '92: and abortion, 73, 132–33; committee assignments of, 80; and elections of 1994, 244; and Family and Medical Leave Act, 73; and